Contents

Introduction	v	
Examination Section	vii	
		Revised
1: Nutrition	1	☐
2: Diet and Health	31	☐
3: Food Commodities	51	☐
4: Food Preparation and Cooking Processes	88	☐
5: Food Additives and Food Legislation	110	☐
6: Microbes and Food Spoilage	117	☐
7: Food Preservation	134	☐
8: Food Safety and Hygiene	146	☐
9: Family Resource Management	153	☐
10: Household Technology and Home Management	169	☐
11: Textiles in the Home	179	☐
12: Consumer Studies	186	☐
13: Social Studies	200	☐
14: Elective 1 – Home Design and Management	223	☐
15: Elective 3 – Social Studies	265	☐
Study Plan	289	

For information on the Textiles, Fashion and Design elective, visit www.edco.ie/tfd

Key Points Logo
This logo indicates the key points you need to know.

Points to Note Logo
This logo indicates important information.

Exam Hints Logo
This logo indicates important examination information.

Higher Level
This line indicates the Higher Level syllabus.

Introduction

This revision book covers all the core areas and two of the elective areas for your Leaving Certificate exam in Home Economics.

What do you have to study?

All of the core area.
This consists of:
- Food Studies (Chapters 1–8)
- Resource Management and Consumer Studies (Chapters 9–12)
- Social Studies (Chapter 13)

Elective area

The elective area consists of three topics. You must study **one** topic only.
1. Home Design and Management (Chapter 14)
2. Textiles, Fashion and Design (Textiles, Fashion and Design students will also have to produce a practical garment for their exam – this is worth 10%)
3. Social Studies (Chapter 15)

How can this book help you?

- The language used throughout this book is straightforward and to the point.
- **Exam questions** and references to exam questions are included for each topic.
- **Tables and bullet points** facilitate effective revision.
- **Learning Objectives** at the start of each chapter and **Key Points** at the end of each chapter help reinforce learning.
- **Exam Hints** and **Points to Note** further highlight important information.

Exam Hints

- Nutrition will be examined in Section A (short questions) and Section B, question 1, on your exam paper.

Points to Note

Freezer burn discolours (through oxidation), toughens and dries out foodstuffs, e.g. meat, which is exposed in the freezer.

Before starting your revision, read the Examination Section on page *vii*. It contains advice on:
- The format of the paper.
- How to approach your exam.
- How to gain full marks when answering questions.

Remember to keep your written questions organised in a copybook or a folder so you can use them for revision towards the end of the year. It is a good idea to put all Section B questions 1 together and questions 2 together and so on.

Check with your teacher to ensure that you are revising the correct elective or check your notes from class.

The **Study Plan** on page 289 helps you plan your revision.

For information on the Textiles, Fashion and Design elective, visit www.edco.ie/tfd

Good luck!

Examination Section

How is home economics assessed?

Students who choose Elective 1 (Home Design and Management) or Elective 3 (Social Studies):
Written examination = 80% (June 6th year)
Food Studies Coursework = 20% (November 6th year)

Students who choose Elective 2 ('Textiles, Fashion and Design):
Written examination = 70%
Food Studies Coursework = 20%
Textiles, Fashion and Design Practical Work= 10%

Structure of Paper – Higher and Ordinary Level (320)

- Study old exam papers to familiarise yourself with the instructions.
- Spend 10 minutes reading the exam paper and deciding on questions.
- Write a brief answer plan for each long question to help you later.

Section	Type of question	Number of questions	Marks per question	Total marks	Time allocation
A	Short	10/12	6	60	25 minutes
B	Long	3 questions – Q1 compulsory + 2 others	Q1 = 80 marks Others = 50 marks	180	Q1 = 35 minutes Others = 20 minutes each
C (Electives 1 + 3)	Long	Part A and B or C	80 marks	80	35 minutes
C (Elective 2)	Long	Part A and B or C	40 marks	40	35 minutes

Allow 5 minutes at the end to read over your answers and highlight keywords or diagrams.

Section A
Topics covered are:
- Food Studies
- Resource Management and Consumer Studies
- Social Studies

Section B
Topics covered are:
- Food Studies
- Resource Management and Consumer Studies
- Social Studies

Long questions: 3 questions from this section
- Question 1 is compulsory (80 marks)
- Spend about 35 minutes on question 1
- Choose two questions from questions 2, 3, 4 and 5; each question is worth 50 marks
- Spend about 20 minutes on these questions

Section C
- Elective 1: Home Design and Management and Elective 3: Social Studies
- Spend 35 minutes on this question
- It is worth 80 marks
- Part A is compulsory
- A choice from part B and C

Elective 2: Textiles, Fashion and Design
- Spend 35 minutes on this question
- It is worth 40 marks
- Part A is compulsory
- A choice from part B and C

Exam Guidelines

How to approach your exam

1. Read the questions carefully and highlight the important words.
2. Time: Higher Level = 2 hours 30 minutes
           Ordinary Level = 2 hours 30 minutes
3. Leave 5 minutes to read over the paper at the end and highlight the important keywords.
4. Remember marks are only given for information asked in the question so answer questions accurately.
5. Answer all of the short questions.
6. Remember to attempt each part of the question, otherwise valuable marks will be lost.

7 Address all parts of questions, e.g. if dietetic and nutritive values are asked for, subdivide your answer into the two areas, otherwise you could lose marks.
8 Answer in point form and answer each new question on a new page.
9 Do not go over your allocated time otherwise you will have to rush at the end or may lose a whole question.
10 Think before you answer the question.
11 Remember to put menus in a box.
   - A day's menu = breakfast, lunch and dinner
   - A three-course meal = starter, main course and dessert
12 Label all diagrams clearly.
13 Do not leave until the exam is finished.
14 For Elective 1, ensure that you can draw and interpret floor plans for a whole house and individual rooms, e.g. a sitting room.

Understanding terms

- **Characteristics:** List the qualities.
- **Classify:** Group the items into categories.
- **Define:** Write down the precise meaning of a word or phrase; in some cases it may be necessary to give an example or a very brief description.
- **Describe:** Give a written description in point form. Use a diagram to back up your answer, if possible.
- **Dietetic value:** Covers information on the value the particular food has in the diet.
- **Discuss or give an account of:** Requires a very detailed description of what is being asked. Remember to structure your answer in point form. Provide at least six points in your answer.
- **Enumerate, list, state:** List the points, no elaboration is necessary.
- **Evaluate:** Make an assessment of the worth of something. Refer to negative and positive uses.
- **Explain:** Give a detailed account. Back up your answer with a specific example and include a diagram if applicable.
- **Illustrate:** Make something clear by the use of concrete examples (diagrams) to explain or clarify a point.
- **Informative paragraph:** Provide at least five points in your answer and structure it in point form.
- **Name, select, suggest:** State the answer in one or two words. There is no need for detail.
- **Outline:** Write one or two sentences on each point, i.e. give a brief description.
- **Principle:** Give a reason for or a description of a working method.
- **Properties:** List the features of a substance, e.g. fat-soluble.

Answering Questions

To gain full marks:
- Read the question carefully.
- Write a brief plan of the question.
- Note the specific requirements of each question, e.g. nutritive value of fish, the functions of the family.

- Each question will show the amount of marks allocated, e.g.
  - Outline the protection provided to the consumer by the Hire Purchase Act 1960. (8)
  - State one property of water. (2)

How marks will be awarded

To gain full marks = accurate and detailed information
To gain ¾ marks = limited detail but generally accurate
To gain ½ marks = lacking detail, basic information
Less ½ marks = inaccurate or irrelevant information

- Avoid writing irrelevant information.
- Use the appropriate vocabulary, e.g. sociology, scientific terms.

An A standard answer

Explain what deamination and denaturation are. (16)

Deamination
Deamination occurs when excess protein in the body is broken down by the liver.

The NH_2 (amino group) is broken down into ammonia, which is then converted to urea, and urine in the kidneys, where it is excreted.

The COOH (carboxyl group) is oxidised and stored as heat and energy in the body until needed.

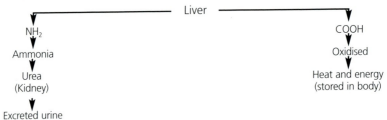

Comment: Accurate, detailed information, keywords are mentioned, e.g. liver, NH_2 ammonia, urea, kidney, urine, oxidised, heat and energy. (8/8 marks)

Denaturation

Denaturation is the untwisting of a protein molecule in which the structure and shape are changed or altered during food preparation or cooking.

This occurs due to the following:
1. Heat - this causes the protein to coagulate, e.g. boiled eggs.
2. Agitation - this is due to physical action, e.g. whipping a protein food such as egg white can cause it to change as partial coagulation occurs during the whipping process and causes the egg white to form foam, e.g. meringues.
3. Chemicals - acids, alkalis and enzymes cause a change in the protein structure, e.g. lemon juice (acid) added to albumin (eggs) causes it to curdle; enzyme rennin coagulates milk protein casein in the stomach.

Comment: Explanation is detailed and accurate; examples are used and three areas of denaturation are mentioned. (8/8 marks)

Exam Paper Analysis

The following section shows an analysis of the previous Leaving Certificate papers Section B and Section C and also provides space to fill in other years.

Exam Topic	2004	2005	2006	2007	2008	
Higher Level Section B						
Protein			*			
Fats (Lipids)					*	
Carbohydrates		*		*		
Vitamins A, D, E, K	*					
Vitamins B group/folic acid/C				*		
Minerals – Calcium			*			
Special Diets	*		*	*	*	
Food Labelling		*				
Food Poisoning and Safety	*				*	
Food Preservation			*		*	
Food Additives			*	*		
Profile Processed Food			*	*		
Convenience Foods			*			
Fish	*					
Yoghurt			*			
Dairy Spreads					*	
Fruit & Vegetables					*	
Sensory Analysis				*		
Microwave			*			
Refrigeration Appliance				*		
Appliance Heating Element	*					
Family Resource Management			*			
Consumer Studies	*	*	*			
Housing & Mortgage					*	
Budgeting	*					
The Family	*	*	*		*	
Roles & Conflict					*	
Older People	*					
Divorce			*			
Special Needs				*		
Higher Level Section C						
Elective 1: Home Design and Management						
Housing	*					
Housing Provision			*		*	

EXAMINATION SECTION

Exam Topic	2004	2005	2006	2007	2008
Energy Use	*			*	
Electricity					*
Materials Used in the Home		*			
Heating/System				*	*
Ventilation	*				
House Design	*		*		*
Interior Design		*		*	*
Lighting				*	
Elective 3: Social Studies					
Poverty				*	*
Population Settlement				*	
Education	*	*	*		*
Childcare	*				*
Work			*		*
Employment/Unemployment			*		
Women in the Workplace	*				
Leisure	*			*	

Exam Topic	2004	2005	2006	2007	2008
Ordinary Level Section B					
Protein					
Fats (Lipids)		*			
Carbohydrates				*	
Vitamins A, D, E, K					
Vitamins B, C					
Minerals Calcium/Iron	*				*
Healthy Eating				*	
Special Diets	*	*	*	*	*
Meat		*			
Fruit and Vegetables	*				
Fish				*	
Food Safety & Spoilage			*		*
Food Preservation				*	
Meal/Menu Planning				*	*
Food Packaging			*		
Refrigerator		*			
Microwave				*	
Food Additives	*	*			
Consumer Studies	*	*	*	*	*
Insurance	*				

LEAVING CERTIFICATE HOME ECONOMICS – HIGHER AND ORDINARY LEVEL

Exam Topic	2004	2005	2006	2007	2008
Budgeting		*	*		
Savings		*			*
Housing	*		*		*
Environment	*				
Textile Studies					*
Children/Adolescence	*			*	
Communication and Conflict	*			*	
Marriage		*			*
Family (Roles)			*		
Older People			*		
Making a Will			*		
Ordinary Level Section C					
Elective 1: Home Design and Management					
House Design		*	*		
Kitchen Design					*
Flooring		*			
Wall Finishes			*		
Cold Water System	*				
Central Heating				*	
Energy: Electricity/Gas			*		*
Lighting	*				
Housing	*	*			
Interior Design				*	*
Ventilation				*	
Elective 3: Social Studies					
Settlement Patterns	*				
Family				*	
Poverty	*			*	
Childcare			*		
Work/Voluntary	*			*	*
Women in the Workforce			*		*
Un/Employment			*	*	
Education				*	*
Leisure		*			*

Remember to use the **Study Plan** on page 289.

1: Nutrition

●●●Learning Objectives

In this chapter you will learn about:
1 Food Choices
2 Nutrients
3 Protein
4 Carbohydrates
5 Lipids
6 Vitamins
7 Minerals
8 Water

Food Choices

A number of factors influence why we eat certain foods. Some factors are within our control, while others are not, and some will influence us more than others.

Exam Hints

- Nutrition will be examined in Section A (short questions) and Section B, question 1, on your exam paper.
- Exam questions have been included at the end of the chapter.

Main influences

Table 1.1 Factors influencing food choices	
1 Culture	Family, country or religion can determine the type of food that is eaten
2 Availability	Consumers can eat only a choice of food which is readily available to them
3 Personal preferences	Each person will have likes and dislikes
4 Sensory aspects	Consumers are attracted by food's taste, colour, texture and aroma
5 Economic	The amount of money a person has to spend on food
6 Nutritional value	Consumers are more aware and informed about the benefits of a balanced diet
7 Marketing and advertising	Creates a need or a want for a particular food product

Nutrients

Each food that we eat contains some or all of the following:

Macronutrients (g)	Protein Lipids (Fat) Carbohydrate
Micronutrients	Vitamins (fat-soluble or water-soluble) Minerals

Points to Note
Water, while not a nutrient, is essential to living. We need large quantities of water to stay healthy.

Table 1.2 Key words used to describe nutrients	
Key words	**Explanations**
Elemental composition	Each nutrient is made up of a combination of the elements carbon (C), hydrogen (H) and oxygen (O_2) (Nitrogen, sulfur, phosphorus and iron are also present in protein)
Chemical formula	Each macronutrient has a chemical formula or equation which explains how it is formed This basic structure can be shown in a diagram
Classification	Most nutrients can be placed in categories according to shape, chemical structures, etc. These categories are called classifications
Properties	Properties are characteristics which are unique to each nutrient
Culinary uses	The way in which properties of the nutrient are used in food preparation
Biological functions	Why the nutrient is needed in the body
Deficiency diseases	Diseases that are the result of a lack of nutrients in the body
RDA	The recommended daily allowance (RDA) states how much of the nutrient is required daily
Effect of heat	The application of heat results in specific changes to the nutrient
Digestion	The breakdown of nutrients in the digestive system
Absorption	The way in which nutrients are taken into the bloodstream
Utilisation	The way in which the body uses the digested nutrients

Protein

Elemental composition

Points to Note
Some proteins also contain small quantities of sulfur (S), iron (Fe) and phosphorus (P).

The following elements are required to make protein:

- Carbon (C)
- Oxygen (O)
- Hydrogen (H)
- Nitrogen (N) – for growth and repair of body cells

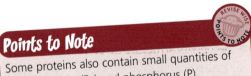

Chemical structure

- Each amino acid is made up of C, H, COOH, NH$_2$ and a variable, which changes with each amino acid (see fig 1.1).
- Proteins are large molecules made up of a number of amino acids.
- Amino acids are linked together by peptide links to form long chains of protein.

The chemical structure of a basic amino acid:
C = Carbon
H = Hydrogen
NH$_2$ = Amino group (alkali)
COOH = Carboxyl group (acidic)
R = Variable, which is different in each amino acid
When R is hydrogen = Glycine is the amino acid

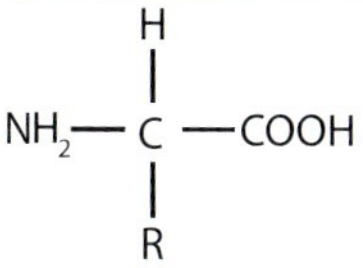

C = Carbon
H = Hydrogen
NH$_2$ = Amino group (alkaline)
COOH = Carboxyl group (acidic)
When R is hydrogen = Glycine

Fig 1.1 Amino acid

Peptide links

A peptide link is formed when two amino acids join together. The acidic group of one amino acid (COOH) reacts with the alkali group (NH$_2$) of the other, with the elimination of a water molecule. This process is called condensation. The reverse of this process, which occurs during digestion, is called **hydrolysis** (addition of a water molecule). This results in the peptide link being broken. The new molecule is called a dipeptide.

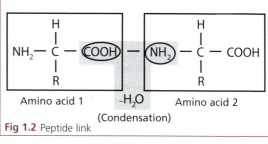

Fig 1.2 Peptide link

Protein structure classification

The protein structure is classified as follows:

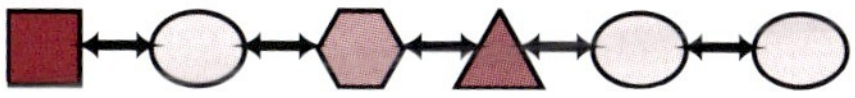

Fig 1.3 Primary structure

1 **Primary structure**
- Amino acids are joined together by peptide links.
- This arrangement of amino acids along the protein chain is the primary structure.

2 **Secondary structure**
- Secondary structure involves the folding of the primary structure.
- This causes the chain to coil and form a spiral shape.
- It gives the protein definite shape and structure; these structures are called cross-links.
- Links which occur between polypeptide chains can be disulphide links when two sulfur molecules join together, e.g. cysteine contains a SH group.

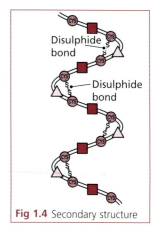

Fig 1.4 Secondary structure

3

3 Tertiary structure
- Tertiary structure is the pattern of folding polypeptide chains into a three-dimensional organisation.
- The protein chains cross-link to form a fibrous or globular structure.
- Fibrous structures are coiled, zigzag or straight, e.g. gluten (wheat), keratin (hair).
- Globular structures are spherical, e.g. myoglobin (meat), haemoglobin (blood).

Fig 1.5 Tertiary structure

Classification of protein

- Simple: Contain only amino acids in their structure.
- Conjugated: Contain a protein and a non-protein part.

Table 1.3 Simple protein		
Group	Examples	Sources
Animal		
Fibrous	• Collagen • Elastin	• Connective tissue in meat
Globular	• Lactoalbumin • Ovalbumin	• Milk • Eggs
Plant		
Glutenins	• Glutenin	• Wheat • Rice
Prolamins	• Gliadin • Zein	• Wheat • Corn

Table 1.4 Conjungated protein		
Group	Examples	Sources
Lipoproteins	• Casein • Lecithin	• Milk • Eggs
Nucleoproteins	• Chromosomes	• Cell nuclei (DNA)
Chromoproteins	• Haemoglobin • Myoglobin	• Blood • Meat
Phosphoproteins	• Casein • Lecithin	• Milk

Essential and non-essential amino acids

- There are 20 common amino acids.
- Eight of these are termed essential amino acids (EAA): isoleucine, leucine, lysine, methionine, threonine, phenylalanine, tryptophan and valine.

> Children need the same eight amino acids plus two more to help growth: arginine and histidine.

- They cannot be manufactured by the body so they must be taken from the food we eat.
- The body can manufacture non-essential amino acids, e.g. alanine, aspartic acid, cysteine, glutamine, glycine, proline and serine.

Points to Note
Essential amino acids cannot be made in the body. Adults require eight amino acids.

Biological value (BV) of protein

- The biological value of protein is a measure of the protein quality in a food and is shown in percentage.
- It is determined by the number of essential amino acids a food contains in proportion to the body's requirements.

There are two types of proteins:
1. **High biological value protein (HBV):** Contains all the essential amino acids required and is also called a complete protein. It comes mostly from animal foods.
2. **Low biological value protein (LBV):** Lacks one or more of the essential amino acids and is therefore also called an incomplete protein and is found mostly in plant food.

Table 1.5 Sources and biological value of protein

Source	Food	HBV	LBV	Proteins present
Animal	Eggs	100%		• Ovalbumin • Vitelin • Livetin
	Milk	95%		• Casein • Lactoalbumin • Lactoglobulin
	Meat	80–90%		• Elastin • Gelatine • Collagen • Myosin
				• Actin • Myosin • Collagen
	Gelatine		0%	• Gelatine
	Fish	80–90%		
Vegetable	Soya bean	74%		• Glycinin
	Rice		67%	• Oryzenin
	Wheat		53%	• Gluten
	Maize		40%	• Zein

Supplementary role of protein

When foods that lack certain amino acids are eaten together, they provide a full complement of essential amino acids. The deficiency of amino acids in one food can be made up by the amino acids in the other food, e.g. beans on toast provide a complete protein. This complementary role of proteins allows vegans and vegetarians to receive their full complement of essential amino acids from plant sources.

> **Exam Hints**
> Nutrients can also be asked in a question with a food commodity or methods of food processing.

Table 1.6 Properties of protein	
1 Solubility	Most proteins are insoluble in water, except albumin in egg white and collagen in hot water
2 Elasticity	Gluten, a fibrous protein in wheat, is quite elastic, which allows bread to rise when heat is applied
3 Denaturation	Denaturation is a change in the nature of the protein chain. It causes the protein chain to unfold which leads to an irreversible loss of structure, e.g. a boiled egg Denaturation is caused by heat, agitation and chemicals • **Heat:** causes the protein to coagulate (harden) and set • **Agitation** (mechanical action): whipping a protein food can cause partial coagulation, e.g. whipping an egg white turns it into foam • **Chemicals:** acids, alkalis and enzymes also cause a change in the protein structure, e.g. lemon juice, an acid, added to albumin which is present in eggs causes it to curdle
4 Maillard reaction	The non-enzymic browning of protein foods: an amino acid reacts with sugar, a carbohydrate, under dry heat conditions, e.g. roast potatoes
5 Moist heat (stewing, boiling, steaming)	These methods cause the connective tissue of meat to change to gelatine, which makes it more digestible
6 Gel formation	• A gel is a semi-solid viscous solution with a three-dimensional network in which water molecules can become trapped • Gelatine is made from the protein collagen; it can absorb large amounts of water to form a gel. If this is heated it forms a sol and liquefies • The sol cools and sets, becomes solid and this process is called gel formation • This setting power is used in the preparation of cheesecakes, jellies and soufflés
7 Foam formation	• When egg white is whisked, the protein structure unfolds and air bubbles form around it • The air bubbles entrap air, thus creating foam • The whisking also produces a small amount of heat which sets the egg white slightly. However, it will collapse after a time unless heat is applied, e.g. meringues

Table 1.7 Biological functions of protein

Type	Function	Result of deficiency
Structural protein	• Growth and repair • Production of cells, muscle and skin	• Retarded growth • Delayed healing of wounds
Physiologically active protein	• Production of enzymes, hormones, antibodies, blood proteins and nucleoproteins	• Malfunctioning of body organs and systems • Susceptibility to illness and infection
Nutritive proteins	• Excess protein provides energy • Provide the body with essential amino acids	• Lack of energy • In severe cases leads to kwashiorkor and marasmus

RDA: the recommended daily allowance

An adult needs approximately **1g protein per kilogram of body weight**. However, at certain periods of their lives, people need more protein.

Table 1.8 The RDA

Children	30–50g/day
Teenagers	60–80g/day
Adults	50–75g/day
Pregnant/lactating women	70–85g/day

Points to Note

Energy value of protein: 1g of protein provides 4kcal/17kJ of energy.

Digestion of protein

- During digestion the protein chains are hydrolysed, i.e. for each peptide link, one water molecule is added and broken down into amino acids with the help of protein-splitting enzymes.

There are two enzymes in the stomach: **rennin** and **pepsin**.

- **Rennin** acts on caesinogen to produce casein, whereas **pepsin** acts on protein to produce peptones.
- In the duodenum **trypsin**, a pancreatic enzyme, changes the remaining protein to peptones.
- In the small intestine **erypsin** breaks down the peptones into amino acids.

Absorption of amino acids
Amino acids are small molecules which can diffuse into the blood capillaries via the villi of the small intestine. They are carried in the bloodstream through the portal vein to the liver.

Utilisation
The amino acids in the liver are used:
- To maintain and replace liver cells.
- To pass into the bloodstream and body tissues to help form new cells, hormones, enzymes and antibodies.
- To be deaminated.

Deamination
The excess protein is deaminated (broken down) by the liver:
- The NH_2 portion of the amino acid is converted to ammonia and urea and then excreted by the kidneys as a waste product in urine.
- The COOH portion of the amino acid is oxidised and used to produce heat and energy.

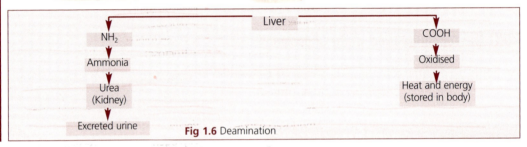

Fig 1.6 Deamination

Carbohydrates (CHO)

Photosynthesis

- Carbohydrates are produced in plants through photosynthesis.
- Green plants use energy from the sun to make food.
- They contain chlorophyll (a green pigment), which converts sunlight to energy.
- The sunlight reacts with water from the roots and carbon dioxide from the air to produce glucose, which is stored in the plant, and oxygen, which is released into the air.

Elemental composition
Carbohydrates (CHO) contain the following elements in the ratio 1:2:1:
- Carbon (C)
- Hydrogen (H)
- Oxygen (O)

Classification of carbohydrates

Carbohydrates are classified as:
- Monosaccharides: Simple sugars (mono = one)
- Disaccharides: Double sugars (di = two)
- Polysaccharides: Complex non-sugars (poly = many)

Exam Hints
Practise drawing the chemical structures and writing an explanation of each one.

Table 1.9 Carbohydrates

Class	Chemical formula	Properties	Example	Source
Monosaccharides	$C_6H_{12}O_6$	• Simple sugars • Hexagonal ring structure	• Fructose • Glucose • Galactose	• Honey • Fruit • Digested milk
Disaccharides	$C_{12}H_{22}O_{11}$	• Two simple sugars joined together with loss of an H_2O molecule	• Lactose (glucose + galactose) • Maltose (glucose + glucose) • Sucrose (glucose + fructose)	• Milk • Barley • Table sugar • Jam
Polysaccharides	$(C_6H_{10}O_5)n$	• Long chains of sugar; 'n' refers to the number of monosaccharides linked together	• Starch • Cellulose • Pectin • Glycogen	• Cereals • Fruit and vegetable skins • Fruit • Meat
Non-starch polysaccharides (NSP) (dietary fibre)		• Indigestible	• Pectin • Cellulose • Gums	• Fruit skins • Seaweed • Plant seeds

Chemical structure

The chemical structure of all carbohydrates is based on a monosaccharide unit which has a hexagonal ring structure.

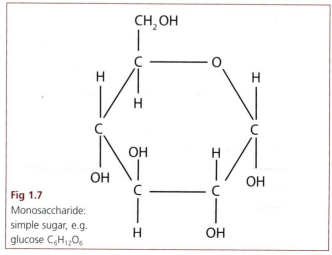

Fig 1.7 Monosaccharide: simple sugar, e.g. glucose $C_6H_{12}O_6$

- **Disaccharide:** Formed when two monosaccharides are joined together with the elimination of a water molecule (condensation).

- **Polysaccharide:** Consists of long chains of monosaccharides joined together with the elimination of a water molecule (condensation).

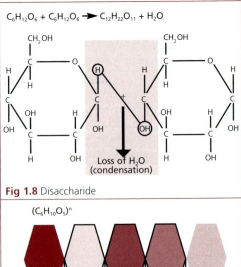

Fig 1.8 Disaccharide

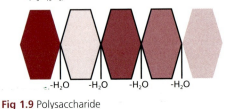

Fig 1.9 Polysaccharide

Properties of carbohydrates NB

Sugar
1. A sweet, white crystalline solid, soluble in water.
2. **Moist heat** dissolves sugar.
3. Dry heat causes **caramelisation** and further heating causes **carbonisation** (burning).
4. **Maillard reaction** causes browning.
5. **Hydrolysis:** Disaccharides react with water and are broken down into monosaccharides. Disaccharide + water = 2 monosaccharides, maltose + water = Glucose + glucose
6. **Inversion of sugar:** When sucrose (disaccharide) reacts with water in the presence of an acid or an enzyme (invertase/sucrase) it produces two monosaccharides, glucose and fructose, e.g. used in jam-making and the manufacture of sweets.
Sucrose + water + acid or enzyme (invertase) = Glucose + fructose
7. **Crystallisation** occurs when a liquid has dissolved as much sugar as it can and the solution is saturated. If more sugar is added, crystals form when the mixture cools down.
8. **Reducing sugar:** Sugar is a reducing agent and can remove oxygen from other substances. It is referred to as a reducing sugar, e.g. glucose, fructose, maltose.

65% sugar - preserve jam / prevent growth of organisms

Starch
1. Insoluble in cold water.
2. Uncooked starch is **indigestible** by the human body.
3. **Hygroscopic:** Can absorb moisture from the air, e.g. biscuits go soft if exposed to air.
4. **Dextrinisation:** Short chains of polysaccharides called dextrins change starch foods to brown when heated, e.g. toast.
5. **Gelatinisation:** When starch is combined with water and heated it swells, bursts and absorbs moisture which causes the mixture to thicken, e.g. used for sauces and soups. A temperature in excess of 85°C creates a sol.
6. **Dry heat:** Causes starch grains to burst and absorb the fat present, e.g. popcorn.
7. **Gel formation:** Pectin contains long chains of polysaccharides which form a three-dimensional arrangement when heated, which entraps water. When the mixture cools a gel is formed, e.g. in jam-making.

8 **Pectin extraction:** The pectin in under-ripe fruit is called protopectin. It cannot absorb water and therefore cannot form a gel. Addition of an acid produces pectin, e.g. jam-making.

$$\text{Protopectin} + \text{acid} = \text{Pectin} \longrightarrow \text{Ability to form a gel}$$

Non-starch polysaccharides (NSP), cellulose, gums, pectin
1 **Gel formation:** Gums can absorb large quantities of water to form gels.
2 Cellulose, pectin and gums cannot be digested and therefore add bulk to the diet. Cellulose is **insoluble** in water.
3 Pectin forms a gel in the presence of acids, such as lemon juice and sugar, e.g. in jam-making.

Table 1.10 Culinary uses of carbohydrates		
Sugar	**Starch**	**Non-starch polysaccharides**
1 **Sweetener:** For sweetening beverages, cakes, desserts	1 **Thickener:** Used in sauces, gravy, soups	1 **Gel forming:** Pectin forms a gel with acid and sugar during jam-making
2 **Preservative:** Prevents microbial growth, e.g. in jams	2 **Hygroscopic:** Ability to absorb moisture from the air which increases the shelflife of cakes etc.	2 **Cellulose:** Absorbs water and gives a feeling of fullness
3 **Caramelisation:** Dry heat causes the sugar to caramelise, e.g. used for desserts	3 **Dextrinisation:** The browning of food under heat, e.g. fried potatoes, toast	
4 **Fermentation:** Sugar stimulates yeast in breadmaking		
5 **Gel formation:** Sugar combines with pectin to form a gel, e.g. used in jam-making		
6 **Colour:** A sugar solution prevents discolouration of cut fruit		

Table 1.11 Biological functions of carbohydrates	
Sugar and starch	Provide heat and energy in the body
Sugar	Stored as an energy reserve in the liver. Insulates the body by converting excess sugar into fat and storing it as adipose tissue
NSP	Cellulose helps prevent bowel disorders by stimulating the movement of food through the intestines. Absorbs water and gives a feeling of fullness

RDA: the recommended daily allowance

There is no precise RDA for carbohydrate intake as deficiency is rare.

Table 1.12 Good carbohydrates and those to avoid	
Increasing the cellulose (NSP) intake	**Carbohydrate foods to avoid**
Wholemeal or brown bread, rice, pasta	White bread, rice, pasta
Wholemeal flour	White flour
Skins of fruit and vegetables	
Whole oranges	
High-fibre breakfast cereals	High sugar breakfast cereals
Add wheat germ to dishes	High sugar biscuits
Wholegrain biscuits and crackers	

Digestion of carbohydrates

Energy value of carbohydrate
1g of carbohydrate provides 4kcal/17kJ of energy.

Disaccharides and polysaccharides are hydrolysed (broken down) into monosaccharides.

1. The salivary glands in the mouth produce salivary **amylase** which breaks down starch into maltose.
2. The pancreas produces **amylase** which acts on starch and produces maltose.
3. The intestinal juice contains three enzymes: **maltase**, **sucrase** and **lactase**.
   - Maltase breaks down maltose into glucose (monosaccharide).
   - Sucrase breaks down sucrose into glucose and fructose (monosaccharides).
   - Lactase breaks down lactose into glucose and galactose (monosaccharides).

Points to Note

Remember the enzyme ends in 'ase', e.g. maltase, while the product ends in 'ose'.

Absorption of monosaccharides

Monosaccharides are small units which diffuse easily into the bloodstream via the villi of the small intestines. The portal vein transports them to the liver.

Utilisation

1. Glucose is converted into glycogen and stored in the liver and muscles as an energy reserve.
2. It is oxidised and used to produce heat and energy.
3. Excess monosaccharides are converted into fat and stored as adipose tissue, providing insulation.

Inter-relationship between carbohydrates and B group vitamins

The following B group vitamins are needed for the metabolism (breakdown) of carbohydrates: B_1 (thiamine), B_2 (riboflavin), niacin and pyridoxine.

Lipids

Elemental composition of fats consists of carbon (C), hydrogen (H) and oxygen (O).

Chemical structure

- Lipids are made up of a triglyceride.
- A triglyceride contains three fatty acid molecules and one glycerol molecule.
- The formula R-COOH represents a fatty acid.
- R symbolises the hydrocarbon chain.
- Glycerol is a trihydric alcohol.
- A trihydric alcohol molecule contains 3OH (hydroxyl) groups.
- During the formation of a triglyceride each OH group combines with an H molecule (hydrogen) from the fatty acid with the loss of a water molecule (H_2O). This is known as condensation.

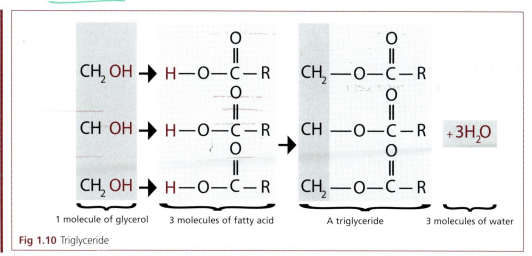

Fig 1.10 Triglyceride

Fatty acids

- R-COOH is the chemical formula used to represent fatty acids.
- Fatty acids are organic compounds.
- They consist of a chain of carbon atoms which can vary in length.
- Each fatty acid carbon chain has a hydrogen atom attached with a carboxyl group at the end.
- The number of carbon atoms is an even number between 4 and 24.

Table 1.13 Classification of fatty acids according to degree of saturation

Class	Structure	Properties	Sources	Examples
Saturated	Each carbon molecule has its full complement of hydrogen; there are no double bonds. It is saturated between the carbon atoms $$HO-\overset{O}{\overset{\|\|}{C}}-\overset{H}{\underset{H}{\overset{\|}{\underset{\|}{C}}}}-\overset{H}{\underset{H}{\overset{\|}{\underset{\|}{C}}}}-\overset{H}{\underset{H}{\overset{\|}{\underset{\|}{C}}}}-\overset{H}{\underset{H}{\overset{\|}{\underset{\|}{C}}}}-H$$	• Solid at room temperature • Higher melting point • Increase blood cholesterol levels	• Meat • Butter • Cheese • Cream • Milk • Lard	• Stearic acid • Butyric acid • Coconut oil
Unsaturated	The carbon chain is not saturated with hydrogen, so double bonds can be found between the carbon atoms 1 Monounsaturated 2 Polyunsaturated	• Liquid at room temperature • Lower melting point • Help lower blood cholesterol		
1 Monounsaturated	Contain one double bond $$HO-\overset{O}{\overset{\|\|}{C}}-\overset{H}{\underset{H}{\overset{\|}{\underset{\|}{C}}}}-\overset{H}{\overset{\|}{C}}=\overset{H}{\overset{\|}{C}}-\overset{H}{\underset{H}{\overset{\|}{\underset{\|}{C}}}}-H$$	• Liquid at room temperature • Lower melting point • Help lower blood cholesterol	• Plants	• Olive oil • Oleic acid
2 Polyunsaturated fatty acid (PUFA)	Contain more than one double bond between the carbon atoms $$HO-\overset{O}{\overset{\|\|}{C}}-\overset{H}{\underset{H}{\overset{\|}{\underset{\|}{C}}}}-\overset{H}{\overset{\|}{C}}=\overset{H}{\overset{\|}{C}}=\overset{H}{\overset{\|}{C}}-H$$	• Soft or liquid at room temperature • Lower melting point • Help reduce blood cholesterol	• Corn oil • Vegetable oils • Most nuts • Margarines	• Linolenic acid (two double bonds) • Linolenic acid (three double bonds) • Arachidonic acid (four double bonds)

Cis- and trans-fatty acids

In polyunsaturated fatty acids, the hydrogen atoms can be arranged in two ways.
1 **Cis**: Two hydrogen atoms are on the same side of the double bond. Found in all foods that contain some fat or oil.
2 **Trans**: Two hydrogen atoms are on opposite side of the double bond. Found in dairy products and meat.

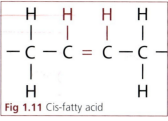
Fig 1.11 Cis-fatty acid

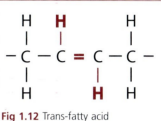
Fig 1.12 Trans-fatty acid

Essential fatty acids
Essential fatty acids (EFA) must be obtained from food as our body cannot manufacture them. They are needed for normal body functioning. EFA are:
- Linoleic acid
- Alpha linolenic acid

Omega-3 fatty acids
Omega-3 fatty acids are needed to prevent coronary heart disease, stroke and to lower blood pressure.

> **Points to Note**
> Polyunsaturated fatty acids (PUFA), linolenic acid and arachidonic acid are not referred to as essential fatty acids because they can be made in limited amounts in the body from linoleic acid.

Table 1.14 Sources of omega-3 fatty acids

Animal	Vegetable	Marine
Meat	Margarine	Fish oils, e.g. cod liver oil
Butter	Vegetable oils	Oily fish, e.g. salmon
Cream	Nuts	

Properties of lipids

1 Lipids are insoluble in water.
2 Soluble in organic solvents such as ether or benzene.
3 Absorb flavours quickly.
4 Effect of heat on lipids:
   - At 100°C any water present evaporates.
   - **Melting point**: Fats melt when heat is applied. The melting point varies depending on the type of fat. Most melt between 30°C and 40°C, while oils melt just below room temperature.
   - **Smoke point**: When fats are heated to 200°C and oils to 250°C, they decompose (break down) into their component parts, glycerol and fatty acids. The glycerol converts into acrolein, which creates a blue haze and an acrid (choking) smell.

- **Flash point:** When fats reach 310°C and oils reach 325°C, the vapour produced spontaneously ignites (bursts into flames).
5. **Rancidity** refers to the spoilage of lipids and can occur in two ways:
   - **Oxidative rancidity** occurs when oxygen in the air reacts with the carbon atoms of a double bond in an unsaturated carbon chain. Antioxidants such as vitamin C and vitamin E prevent rancidity by reacting with the oxygen in the air and thus making it unavailable.
   - **Hydrolytic rancidity** is caused by the reaction of enzymes or micro-organisms with the lipid.
6. **Hydrogenation:** Used in the manufacture of margarine and cooking fats. Using nickel as a catalyst, hydrogen (H_2) is added to the unsaturated fatty acid. This converts the unsaturated fat into solid saturated fat. The double bonds are broken and the hydrogen attaches itself to the carbon atoms.
7. **Plasticity:** Lipids can have properties of both a solid (saturated) and a liquid (unsaturated) fat, e.g. margarines have shape and structure but they are also soft and spreadable.
8. **Emulsions:** If oil and water are mixed together, the oil forms a separate layer above the water. Oil and water do not dissolve in each other. They are immiscible (cannot be mixed).
   - If the oil and water are shaken vigorously, the oil disperses in the water for a short period of time before separating again due to its instability. This is known as a temporary emulsion.
   - To create a permanent emulsion, a third substance is required. This is called an emulsifier or an emulsifying agent.

How the emulsifier works:
- It lowers the surface tension between the oil and the water.
- It contains a hydrophilic (water loving) head and hydrophobic (water hating) tail.
- The hydrophilic end attaches to the water.
- The hydrophobic tail attaches to the oil.
- This stabilises the mixture and prevents it from separating.

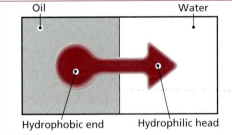

Fig 1.13 Hydrophilic (water loving) head and hydrophobic (water hating) tail. Oil and water are held together by an emulsifier

Exam Hints

Ordinary Level students need to know the formation of an emulsion. Higher Level students need to be able to identify emulsifying agents and their functions.

Stabilisers are used to improve the stability of an emulsion by increasing its viscosity, e.g. stabiliser starch, gelatine.

Biological functions of lipids
1 Lipids provide large amounts of heat and energy.
2 Excess lipids are stored as adipose tissue and provide insulation.
3 Adipose tissue protects delicate organs such as heart and kidneys.
4 Lipids provide a supply of the fat-soluble vitamins A, D, E and K.
5 Lipids provide essential fatty acids.

RDA: the recommended daily allowance
- Approximately one-third of our energy intake should be in the form of fats.
- 50 per cent should come from saturated sources and 50 per cent from unsaturated sources.
- However, due to the overconsumption of fats in Western countries obesity is reaching epidemic proportions.

Energy value of lipid
1g of lipid provides 9kcal/37kJ of energy.

Digestion of lipids

- Hydrolysis breaks the triglyceride into glycerol and three fatty acids.
- The liver produces bile salts which emulsify (break down) the lipids.
- The enzyme lipase, which, is produced in the pancreas, aids hydrolysis.
- Intestinal lipase continues the breakdown of lipids into fatty acid and glycerol.

Absorption of lipids
- As the fat molecules are larger molecules they cannot pass directly into the bloodstream.
- Lacteals which are found in the villi of the small intestine absorb the fatty acids and glycerol.
- The lacteals carry the fatty acids and glycerol to the thoracic duct which empties into the blood via the left subclavian vein.

Utilisation
- Lipids are oxidised in the liver or muscles and provide energy.
- Excess is stored as an energy reserve in the form of adipose tissue.
- The adipose tissue also provides protection for delicate organs such as the heart.

Vitamins

Classification of vitamins

Vitamins are divided into two groups: fat-soluble and water-soluble.

Fat-soluble vitamins

Vitamin A (retinol and beta-carotene)

Vitamin A is available to the body in two ways: retinol and beta-carotene.

Table 1.15 Fat-soluble and water-soluble vitamins

Fat-soluble	Water-soluble
A Retinol, beta-carotene	C Ascorbic acid
D Cholecalciferol, ergocalciferol	B_1 Thiamine
E Tocopherol	B_2 Riboflavin
K Naphthoquinones	B_6 Pyridoxine
	B_{12} Cobalamin
	Folic acid (folate)
	Niacin

Table 1.16 Retinol and beta-carotene

Retinol	Beta-carotene
Animal sources	Brightly coloured fruit and vegetables (DGLV)
Pure vitamin	Provitamin A (converted to retinol in body)
Fish, fish oils, butter, margarine, liver, milk	Carrots, tomatoes, yellow peppers, cabbage, broccoli

> **Points to Note**
> Learn both the letter and the name of each vitamin.

Table 1.17 Vitamin A (retinol and beta-carotene)

Properties	Functions	Deficiency	RDA (micrograms per day)
1 Fat-soluble alcohol 2 Insoluble in water 3 Destroyed by exposure to oxygen 4 Heat stable: unaffected by cooking 5 When dried there may be some vitamin loss 6 Acts as an antioxidant	• Healthy vision: produces rhodopsin • Necessary to maintain the lining membrane (epithelial cells) of the tissue in nose, mouth, oesophagus and lungs • Epithelial cells produce mucus to lubricate body interiors • General growth and repair of all body cells • Boosts immune system therefore protecting the body from infection	• Night blindness due to lack of rhodopsin • Inhibits growth • Rough, dry skin (follicular keratosis) • Lack of mucus in the eyes can cause infection as the eye dries, which eventually can lead to blindness (xerophthalmia)	• Children: 400–500μg • Teenagers: 600–700μg • Male adults: 700μg • Female adults: 600μg • Pregnant women: 700μg • Lactating women: 950μg

Vitamin D (cholecalciferol/ergocalciferol)

Vitamin D is available to the body in two forms.

1 Cholecalciferol (D_3)
- 7-dehydrocholestrol present in skin is converted to cholecalciferol (D_3) by UV light (sun)
- Food and skin
- Fish liver oils, margarine, eggs, milk, oily fish

2 Ergocalciferol (D_2)
- Ergosterol, a compound found in fungi and yeasts, produces ergocalciferol when exposed to UV light
- Plant sources
- Fungi, yeasts

Table 1.18 Vitamin D (cholecalciferol and ergocalciferol)

Properties	Functions	Deficiency	RDA (micrograms per day)
1. A fat-soluble vitamin 2. Insoluble in water 3. Heat stable 4. Unaffected by normal cooking temperature 5. Unaffected by oxygen, acids or alkalis	• Healthy bones and calcification of teeth • Aids the absorption of calcium and phosphorus • Controls the levels of calcium in the blood • Inhibits the development of bone diseases such as osteomalacia and rickets	• Dental decay • Rickets: Softening of bones in children • Osteomalacia: Softening of bones in adults • Osteoporosis: Weakening of bones in adults, especially women	• Children: 7–10µg • Teenagers: 15µg • Adults: 10µg • Pregnant or lactating women: 10µg

Hypervitaminosis

Overconsumption of vitamin D, particularly in children, can quickly lead to toxic levels due to the excess calcium in the blood, which in turn can lead to calcium deposits in the body, e.g. the kidneys. The symptoms include excessive thirst, vomiting, diarrhoea and mental confusion. In extreme cases, hypervitaminosis of vitamin D can lead to death.

> **Points to Note**
> The properties of all the vitamins are Higher Level material.

Table 1.19 Vitamin E (tocopherol)

Properties	Functions	Deficiency	RDA (micrograms per day)	Sources
1 Fat-soluble 2 Insoluble in water 3 Heat stable even in very high temperatures 4 Acts as an antioxidant 5 Stable in acid environments 6 Unstable when exposed to oxygen and light	• Acts as an antioxidant, reducing the risk of heart disease and cancer • Destroys free radicals, reducing the effects of aging • Protects red and white blood cells from damage	• Available in a wide variety of foods so deficiency is rare • In infants it can lead to eye disorders and anaemia • Increases the risk of lung cancer among smokers	• No fixed RDA	• Found in PUFA foods • Wide variety in diet • Wholegrain cereals • Nuts • Pulses • Olive oil • Fish • Eggs

Vitamin K (naphthoquinones)

There are three types of vitamin K.
1 Phylloquinone: Plant sources
2 Menaquinone: Bacteria present in intestine
3 Menadione: Synthetic or converted to phylloquinone in the body

Table 1.20 Vitamin K (naphthoquinones)

Properties	Functions	Deficiency	RDA (micrograms per day)	Sources
1 Fat-soluble vitamin 2 Insoluble in water 3 Heat stable especially during cooking 4 Destroyed by exposure to UV light	• Synthesises prothrombin necessary for blood clotting • Helps to maintain calcium levels in the bones	• Available in a wide variety of foods so deficiency is rare • Infants may need a supplement due to their restricted diet and lack of intestinal bacteria • May delay blood clotting	• No precise RDA due to its availability in a variety of foods and the manufacture of vitamin K in the intestine	• Spinach • Cabbage • Peas • Cereals • Intestine

Table 1.21 Vitamin C (ascorbic acid)				
Properties	**Functions**	**Deficiency**	**RDA (micrograms per day)**	**Sources (mg per 100g)**
1 Water-soluble vitamin	• Antioxidant: helps to prevent heart disease and cancer	• Scurvy: rare in developed countries. Symptoms include bleeding gums, joint pains, loose teeth and haemorrhages under the skin	• Children: 45mg	• Blackcurrants: 200mg
2 Sharp taste			• Teenagers: 50–60mg	• Rosehip: 175mg
3 Heat unstable			• Adults: 60mg	• Strawberries: 60mg
4 Destroyed by oxidation, which is aided by the action of the enzyme oxidase found in cell walls	• Necessary for the formation of collagen (protein), which unites all body cells, e.g. as in blood vessels		• Pregnant and lactating women: 80mg	• Oranges/lemons: 50mg
				• Cabbages: 20mg
	• Necessary for the development of bones and teeth	• Anaemia due to incomplete absorption of iron		• Tomatoes: 20mg
				• Potatoes: 6mg
5 Destroyed by exposure to UV light		• Slower healing of wounds		• Apples: 5mg
				• Pears: 3mg
6 Destroyed by iron, copper and zinc, which can be present in saucepans	• Aids white blood cells in fighting infection	• Bruising and bleeding due to the fragile structure of blood vessels and body tissues		
	• Prevents scurvy			
7 Good reducing agent	• Necessary for the assimilation of non-haem iron in the intestine			

Table 1.22 Vitamin B$_{12}$ (cobalamin)

Properties	Functions	Deficiency	RDA (micrograms per day)	Sources
1 Water-soluble vitamin 2 Relatively heat stable (100°C) 3 Generally stable in light and with acids and alkalis	• Manufacture of red blood cells, aided by folic acid and iron • Metabolism of fatty acids and folic acid • Necessary for the formation of myelin sheaths which insulate nerve fibres in the nervous system	• Pernicious anaemia (inability to absorb B$_{12}$ from diet). Symptoms include tiredness, breathlessness, poor blood clotting • Vegans need to supplement their diet as B$_{12}$ is found only in animal foods. Extreme cases can cause nerve degeneration	• Children: 0.7–1.0μg • Teenagers: 1.0–1.4μg • Adults: 1.4μg • Pregnant women: 1.6μg • Lactating women: 1.9μg	• Offal • Meat • Fish • Eggs • Milk • Dairy products

Table 1.23 Folic acid (folate)

Properties	Functions	Deficiency	RDA (micrograms per day)	Sources
1 Water-soluble vitamin 2 Stable in an acidic environment 3 Affected by exposure to light and oxygen 4 Unstable at cooking temperatures	• Essential for the manufacture of DNA and RNA • Helps B$_{12}$ form red blood cells • Essential for the development of the brain and spinal cord of the foetus, preventing neural tube defects such as spina bifida • Required for protein metabolism	• Tiredness and fatigue • In pregnant women the foetus is at risk of neural tube defects (NTDs) • Lack of folic acid can cause megaloblastic anaemia to which pregnant women are susceptible	• Children: 100–200μg • Teenagers: 300μg • Adults: 300μg • Pregnant women: 500μg • Lactating women: 400μg	• Liver • Kidney • Cabbage • Spinach • Wholegrain cereals • Fortified foods, e.g. bread and breakfast cereals

Table 1.24 Vitamin B_1 (thiamine)

Properties	Functions	Deficiency	Sources
1 Water-soluble vitamin 2 Destroyed by high temperatures and alkalis 3 Loss of up to 70% during milling 4 The most unstable vitamin	• Release of energy from carbohydrates and fats • Normal functioning of the nervous system • Growth in children and general good health	• Beriberi (heart enlargement, muscle wasting, death) • Irritability, lack of concentration, memory loss • Fatigue and muscle cramps • Retarded growth	• Milk • Eggs • Yeast extract • Meat and offal • Wholegrain cereals

Table 1.25 Vitamin B_2 (riboflavin)

Properties	Functions	Deficiency	Sources
1 Water-soluble vitamin 2 Extremely sensitive to light and alkalis 3 Unstable at high temperatures, e.g. in food processing	• Release of energy from protein, fats and carbohydrates • Healthy membranes in nose and mouth • Healthy skin • Growth of children	• Eye infection • Loss of appetite • Broken skin in lips and mouth • Enlarged red tongue	• Milk • Eggs • Yeast extract • Meat and offal • Dark green leafy vegetables, e.g. cabbage and spinach

Table 1.26 Vitamin B_6 (pyridoxine)

Properties	Functions	Deficiency	Sources
1 Water-soluble vitamin 2 Destroyed by exposure to sunlight 3 Mostly heat stable 4 Destroyed by high temperatures and exposure to oxygen	• Metabolism of protein and fats by acting as a co-enzyme • Healthy nervous system • Production of red and white blood cells • Healthy skin • Helps adjust hormone changes	• Can cause anaemia • Inflammation of the skin • Convulsions in young babies (milk fed) • Intensifies symptoms of PMT such as headache, mood swings, etc.	• Meat • Fish • Wheat germ • Dark green leafy vegetables, e.g. spinach • Oranges and bananas

Table 1.27 Niacin

Properties	Functions	Deficiency	Sources
1 Water-soluble vitamin 2 Very stable in heat and with acids and alkalis 3 Loss of 80–90% during milling	• Aids the metabolism of carbohydrates • Prevents pellagra • Healthy nervous system	• Pellagra (4 Ds: diarrhoea, dermatitis (skin condition), dementia (forgetfulness) and death	• Yeast products • Meat • Dairy products • Wholegrain cereals • Breakfast cereals • Produced in intestine from amino acid tryptophan

Minerals

Classification of minerals

Table 1.28 Major and trace minerals

Major mineral	Trace mineral
Calcium (Ca)	Iron (Fe)
Phosphorus (P)	Zinc (Zn)
Chlorine (Cl)	Copper (Cu)
Sodium (Na)	Manganese (Mn)
Potassium (K)	Fluorine (F)
Magnesium (Mg)	Cobalt (Co)
Iodine (I)	Selenium (Se)
Chromium (Cr)	

Points to Note

Osteoporosis results in a decrease in bone density and brittle bones which can cause fractures. Hormonal changes (menopause), old age, lack of activity and vitamin D intake also contribute to osteoporosis.

Calcium

Calcium works with vitamin D and phosphorus.

Table 1.29 Calcium

Functions	Deficiency	RDA	Sources
1 Required for bone and tooth formation 2 Essential for normal blood clotting 3 Required for muscle and nerve functioning 4 Necessary for enzyme activity	• Osteomalacia in adults • Rickets in children • Dental decay • Osteoporosis • Muscular spasms (cramps) • Inability of blood clotting causing haemorrhaging	• Children: 800mg • Teenagers: 1200mg • Adults: 800mg • Pregnant and lactating women: 1200mg	• Flour • Milk, cheese • Sardines • White bread • Cabbage and spinach

Absorption

Absorption of calcium into the body occurs in the lining of the small intestine.

Absorption is helped/aided by:
- Vitamin D.
- Phosphorus which combines with calcium to create calcium phosphate.
- A diet rich in amino acids.
- Lactose (milk sugar) which makes calcium more soluble and easier to absorb.
- The parathyroid gland (part of the endocrine system) which produces parathormone.
- Oestrogen.

Absorption is inhibited/prevented by:
- Phytic acid (e.g. in cereals) which prevents calcium absorption as it attaches to the calcium, making it unavailable to the small intestine.
- Oxalic acid (e.g. in rhubarb and strawberries).
- Dietary fibre which has a similar effect.
- Saturated fatty acids which make calcium unavailable by producing insoluble soap.
- Lack of oestrogen during the menopause.
- Lack of vitamin D and phosphorus.

Iron

Iron works with vitamin C.

Table 1.30 Iron			
Functions	**Deficiency**	**RDA**	**Sources**
1 Haemoglobin in the red blood cells 2 Transports oxygen around the body 3 Essential for the manufacture of haemoglobin 4 Necessary for the efficient functioning of enzymes in the body	• Anaemia: body stores of iron are exhausted and the blood levels fall below normal • A severe loss of blood from the body, e.g. heavy periods, haemorrhoids • Tiredness and lack of energy • Breathlessness	• Children: 10mg • Teenagers: 13–14mg • Male adults: 10mg • Female adults: 14mg • Pregnant or lactating women: 15mg	• Haem iron (ferrous iron) easily absorbed by the body, e.g. that found in meat, chicken and liver • Non-haem iron (ferric iron) has to be altered to ferrous iron before absorption, e.g. that found in fish, eggs and plant sources such as cereals, broccoli, cabbage

Absorption

Absorption is helped by:
- Vitamin C, which is essential to the conversion of non-haem iron into ferrous iron.
- Hydrochloric acid found in the stomach, which aids non-haem iron absorption by converting it to usable haem iron.

Absorption is inhibited by:
- Phytic acid (e.g. in cereal) which attaches to the iron, making it insoluble so the body cannot absorb it.
- Oxalic acid (e.g. in fruit and vegetables) which also binds to iron, making it unavailable to the body.
- High fibre intake.
- Tannins found in tea and coffee.

Table 1.31 Zinc, iodine, sodium and potassium

Mineral Zinc (Zn)

Sources	Functions	Deficiency	RDA (mg per day)
Meat, meat products, milk, bread, seafood	• General good health • Metabolism of protein and carbohydrates • Aids enzyme activity, especially in the lungs	• Extreme delayed mental and physical development • Slow healing of wounds • Development of skin problems	• Children: 4–7mg • Teenagers and adults: 7–10mg

Mineral Iodine (I)

Sources	Functions	Deficiency	RDA (mg per day)
Seafood, seaweed, milk, eggs, meat	• Manufacture of thyroxine in the thyroid gland • Regulates metabolism	• Lack of thyroxine which effects BMR • Goitre, a swelling of the thyroid glands, recognisable by a swollen neck • Slow mental and physical growth in children	• Children: 60–90µg • Adults: 140µg

Mineral Sodium (Na)

Sources	Functions	Deficiency	RDA (mg per day)
Marmite, salt, snack foods, smoked meat, fish	• Transmission of nerve impulses • Regulates water balance in the body • Necessary for normal muscle activity	• Rare due to high salt content of many processed foods • Low blood pressure • Tiredness	• Adults: 1.6g

Mineral Potassium (K)

Sources	Functions	Deficiency	RDA (mg per day)
Found in most foods, e.g. in meat, milk, wholegrain cereals, fish, bananas	• Protein metabolism • Nerve transmission and muscular contraction, e.g. the heart	• Rare due to the wide availability of sources • May cause muscular weakness, fatigue and cardiac arrest	• Adults: 3.5g

Water (H$_2$O)

- Water is essential for life.
- Two-thirds of our body is made up of water.
- Water is the main component of blood, lymph and digestive secretions, as well as all other liquid parts of the body.
- It is made up of hydrogen and oxygen molecules in the ratio 2:1.

Table 1.32 Water			
Properties	**Functions**	**RDA**	**Sources**
1 Colourless, odourless and tasteless liquid 2 Boils at 100°C and freezes at 0°C 3 Neutral pH of 7 4 Excellent solvent capable of dissolving a number of substances 5 Exists in three states: solid (ice), liquid (water) and gas (steam) 6 Able to absorb heat and maintain it	• Transporting nutrients, oxygen, enzymes and hormones around the body • Removal of waste products from the body, e.g. from the kidneys • Quenches thirst • Contains the minerals calcium and fluorine • Controls body temperature through perspiration • Significant in the hydrolysis of nutrients during digestion • Essential element of all body fluids and tissues	• Between 2 and 3 litres per day	• Tap/bottled water • Beverages such as tea and coffee • Fruit and vegetables • All foods contain a certain amount of water

Questions

1. Name and explain three properties of carbohydrates that are useful in food preparation. (18)
   (2005, HL, Section B, 1c)

2. Describe the chemical structure of each of the following: (a) monosaccharides, (b) disaccharides, (c) polysaccharides. And give one example of each. (24)
   (2005, HL, Section B, 1b)

3. Give an account of carbohydrates and refer to: (a) classification, (b) one example of each class, (c) functions in the body. (18)
   (2006, OL, Section B, 1)

4. Explain each of the following and give one source in each case: (a) cis-fatty acid, (b) trans-fatty acid. (6)
   (2006, HL, Section A, 1)

5. Name two proteins present in meat. (6)
   (a) Explain (i) high biological protein (ii) essential amino acid. (12)
   (b) Describe (i) the primary structure and (ii) the secondary structure of protein. (24)
   (2006, HL, Section B, 1)

6. Give one main function of potassium and list two good sources of potassium in the diet. (6)
   (2008, HL, Section A, 2)

7. State: (a) two reasons why it is important to include iron in a teenager's daily diet and (b) one ill effect of a diet deficient (lacking) in iron. (15)
   (2008, OL, Section B, 1)

8. (a) State two functions of ascorbic acid (vitamin C) in the diet. (4)
   (b) State how vitamin C assists the absorption of iron. (2)
   (2004, HL, Section A, 2)

9. Describe the structure and give one example of each of the following: saturated fatty acids, monounsaturated fatty acids and polyunsaturated fatty acids. (24)
   (2008, HL, Section B, 1)

Key Points

Food Choices
- Culture
- Eating patterns
- Availability
- Sensory aspects
- Economics
- Health status
- Nutritional awareness
- Marketing and advertising

Protein
- Elemental composition: Carbon, hydrogen, oxygen, nitrogen, sulfur, iron and phosphorus
- Chemical structure: Amino acid and the joining of two amino acids forms a peptide link
- Classification of protein: Classified according to structure and biological value
- Essential amino acids: Cannot be produced by the body, e.g valine, lysine
- Non-essential amino acids: Can be produced by the body

Key Points

- Biological value (BV) of protein: Protein foods can be high biological value or low biological value depending on the amount of essential amino acids present
- Supplementary role of protein: How foods can supplement or complement each other in relation to essential amino acids, e.g. beans on toast
- Sources of protein: Animal and vegetable sources
- Properties: Solubility, elasticity, denaturation, Maillard reaction, moist heat, gel formation, foam formation
- Biological functions: Growth and repair, production of cells, muscle and skin, production of enzymes, hormones and antibodies, blood and nucleoproteins, energy and essential amino acids
- Digestion: Enzymes used – rennin, pepsin, trypsin and peptidase
- Absorption: Villi of the small intestines
- Utilisation: Used to maintain and replace liver cells, to form new cells, hormones, enzymes and antibodies, deaminated → NH_2 → excreted
  COOH → stored

Carbohydrates
- Elemental composition: Carbon, hydrogen and oxygen in the ratio 1:2:1
- Chemical structure: Monosaccharide, disaccharide and polysaccharide
- Classification of carbohydrates: Monosaccharide, disaccharide and polysaccharide, non-starch polysaccharides (NSP)
- Properties of starch, sugar and fibre, NSP including hydrolysis, crystallisation, dextrinisation, gelatinisation, gel formation
- Culinary uses: Sweetener, preservative, fermentation, gel formation, thickener, and dextrinisation
- Biological functions: Heat and energy, stored as an energy reserve, insulates the body, prevents bowel disorders, gives a feeling of fullness
- RDA: No precise RDA as deficiency is rare
- Digestion: Mouth – salivary glands, in the intestine enzymes are released to break down maltase, sucrase and lactase
- Absorption: Into the bloodstream and transported to the liver via the portal vein
- Utilisation: Heat and energy, provide insulation

Lipids
- Elemental composition: Carbon, hydrogen and oxygen
- Chemical structure: Triglyceride = glycerol plus three fatty acids
- Classification of fatty acids = fats can be classified according to degree of saturation = saturated, unsaturated, monounsaturated and polyunsaturated
- Cis- and trans-fatty acids: Arrangement of hydrogen in polyunsaturated fatty acids
- Essential fatty acids: The body cannot manufacture these fatty acids
- Properties: Insoluble in water, effects of heat, rancidity – oxidative and hydrolytic, hydrogenation, plasticity, emulsions
- Biological functions: Provide heat and energy, provide insulation, protect delicate organs, supply fat-soluble vitamins A, D, E, K
- Digestion: Triglyceride is broken down, lipase helps the digestion of it into glycerol and fatty acids
- Absorption: Small intestine via the lacteals in the lymphatic system
- Utilisation: Provide energy, insulation, protection of delicate organs

Key Points

Vitamin A: Retinol and Beta-carotene
- Properties: Fat-soluble, insoluble in water, heat stable, antioxidant
- Functions: Healthy eyesight, epithelial cells, growth, immune system
- RDA: Children 400–500µg, teenagers 600–700µg, adults 600–700µg, pregnant women 700µg, lactating women 950µg

Vitamin D: Cholecalciferol and Ergocalciferol
- Cholecaliferol: Food and skin
- Ergocalciferol: Plant sources
- Properties: Fat-soluble, insoluble in water, heat stable, unaffected by oxygen, acid, alkalis
- Functions: Absorption of calcium and phosphorus; healthy bones and teeth
- RDA: Children 7–10µg, teenagers 15µg, adults 10µg, pregnant and lactating women 10µg

Vitamin E: Tocopherol
- Properties: Fat-soluble, insoluble in water, stable to heat and acid, unstable to oxygen and light
- Functions: Antioxidant, protection of red and white blood cells

Vitamin K: Naphthoquinones
- Properties: Fat-soluble, insoluble in water, heat stable, destroyed by UV light
- Functions: Blood clotting, calcium levels

Vitamin C: Ascorbic Acid
- Properties: Water-soluble, unstable in heat, oxygen and UV light
- Functions: Antioxidant, collagen, bones, teeth, white blood cells, prevents scurvy
- RDA: Children 45mg, teenagers 50–60mg, adults 60mg, pregnant and lactating women 80mg

Vitamin B_{12}: Cobalamin
- Properties: Water-soluble, stable to heat, light, acids and alkalis
- Functions: Red blood cells, metabolism of fatty acids and folic acid, nervous system
- RDA: Children 0.7–1.0µg, teenagers 1.0–1.4µg, adults 1.4µg, pregnant women 1.6µg, lactating women 1.9µg

Folic Acid
- Properties: Water-soluble, stable in acid, unstable to light, oxygen and heat
- Functions: Manufacture of DNA and RNA, red blood cell formation, prevent neural tube defects
- RDA: Children 100–200µg, teenagers 400µg, adults 300µg, pregnant and lactating women 400–500µg

B Group Vitamins: B_1, B_2, B_6, Niacin
- Properties: Water-soluble
- Functions: General good health, growth, metabolism of macro-nutrients, nervous system

Calcium
- Functions: Bone and teeth formation, blood clotting, muscle and nerve functioning, enzyme activity
- RDA: Children 800mg, teenagers 1200mg, adults 800mg, pregnant and lactating women 1200mg
- Absorption: Vitamin D, phosphorus, amino acids, lactose, oestrogen
- Inhibits absorption: Phytic acid, oxalic acid, fibre saturated fatty acids, lack of oestrogen, vitamin D

Iron
- Functions: Manufactures haemoglobin, transports oxygen, efficient enzyme function
- RDA: Children and men 10mg, teenagers and women 14mg, pregnant or lactating women 15mg
- Absorption: Vitamin C, hydrochloric acid
- Inhibits absorption: Phytic acid, oxalic acid, fibre, tannin

2: Diet and Health

●●● Learning Objectives

In this chapter you will learn about:
1. Energy
2. Current Nutritional Guidelines
3. Specific Dietary Requirements
4. Special Dietary Needs
5. Changes in Food and Eating Patterns in Ireland

Energy

- Energy is the body's capacity to do work.
- Energy in food is measured in kilocalories (kcal) or kilojoules (kJ). 1kcal = 4.18kJ (multiply calorie content × 4.184 = kJ)

Exam Hints

This section can be examined in conjunction with nutrients in Section B, question 1, or with food commodities in question 2.

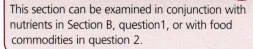

All foods contain energy in the form of protein, fats, carbohydrates (and alcohol).
1 gram protein   = 4kcal/17kJ
1 gram carbohydrate   = 4kcal/17kJ
1 gram fat   = 9kcal/37kJ
(1 gram alcohol   = 7kcal/29kJ)
                       (empty kilocalories)

Basal metabolic rate (BMR)

- Metabolism refers to the sum of all chemical reactions happening in the body.
- The basal metabolic rate is the least amount of energy required to keep your body functioning when resting, e.g. heart, lungs, brain.
- Each person's BMR is different, depending on age, size and gender.

Table 2.1 What determines your BMR?	
Age	Babies and young children need more energy than adults
Size	The larger a person is the greater the energy requirements
Gender	Males have higher energy requirements than females
Activity/occupation	The more active a person is the more energy is required
Pregnancy/lactation	More energy is needed for the developing foetus and breast-feeding
Climate	A warm climate requires less energy than a cold climate
State of health	Due to a reduction in activity less energy is required when ill

The role of energy in the body

Energy is needed for:
- Growth, especially during pregnancy and in children and adults.
- Physical activities, e.g. walking, studying and cycling.
- Metabolism of all body cells including BMR.
- Working of all internal organs, e.g. heart and lungs.
- Generating heat and maintaining a constant body temperature at 37°C.

How to balance energy intake and output
- To maintain your current body weight, the amount of kilocalories you take in food must equal what you use in activity and body function.
- If your intake of kilocalories is greater than your output you gain weight, which can lead to obesity.
- To lose weight, energy output should be greater than energy intake; this is achieved by extra physical activity, e.g. one hour of cycling = the energy supplied by a quarter-pound hamburger.

Table 2.2 Energy requirements		
	Daily energy requirements kcal	
	Male	Female
Children	1,500	1,400
Adolescents	2,800	2,300
Adult (sedentary)	2,400	2,150
Adult (active)	2,800	2,500
Pregnant		2,400
Lactating		2,800
Elderly	2,200	1,800

Current Nutritional Guidelines

The following organisations are responsible for dietary and nutritional guidelines in Ireland:
- Department of Health and Children
- Health Promotion Unit
- Health Service Executive (HSE)
- The Irish Nutrition and Dietetic Institute
- The National Nutritional Surveillance Centre

Current healthy eating guidelines

- Eat a wide variety of foods following the recommendations of the food pyramid.
- Increase intake of fruit and vegetables to at least four portions a day.
- Avoid highly processed food in the diet to reduce fat, salt and sugar intake.
- Replace saturated fats with polyunsaturated alternatives.
- Increase fibre intake to 30g per day.
- Reduce the amount of sugar in the diet.
- Reduce the salt intake in the diet.
- Water intake should be at least eight glasses a day.
- Alcohol, if consumed, should be kept within the recommended guidelines.
- Eat the correct quantity of food for your body size.

Balanced eating

Approximately $\frac{1}{6}$ of our diet should come from protein sources
$\frac{1}{6}$ from fat
$\frac{2}{3}$ from carbohydrates including fibre

If the food pyramid guidelines are followed, the correct proportion of nutrients to satisfy the nutritional needs of the general population is provided in a variety of foods. A balanced diet also contains all necessary vitamins and minerals.

RDA and DVR

The recommended daily allowance (RDA) figures which appear on food labelling display the nutrient requirements of the general population. These figures are decided on by the EU and adopted by each country. A more detailed analysis of food composition is available by referring to DRV (dietary reference values).

Table 2.3 Dietary reference values		
DRV incorporate the following:		
RNI	Reference nutrient intake	Measures protein, vitamins and minerals
EAR	Estimated average requirement	Refers to energy values
LTL	Lower threshold limit	Refers to people with low nutritional needs (most people require more)

DRV are used for:
- Evaluating and planning the diet of the general population.
- Evaluating and planning the diets of those with special dietary needs.
- Nutritional labelling such as RDA on foods.
- Providing information regarding large food supplies.
- Investigating the safe limits of a nutrient.

What are food composition tables?

- Food composition tables provide information regarding the nutrient content and energy values of a food.
- The figures refer to 100g of food, e.g. rice, and to 100ml of liquids, e.g. milk.
- The information from the food composition tables can be analysed and used by nutritionists to plan individual dietary needs.
- It is also used to provide nutritional labelling on convenience foods.
- It also allows you to evaluate the nutrient content of various foodstuffs.

Specific Dietary Requirements

Babies

1. A baby grows rapidly during the first six months of his/her life.
2. A baby can be bottle fed with dried formula milk, such as SMA, or he/she can be breast-fed with breast milk.
3. Breast-feeding is more beneficial to the baby as:
   - Breast-feeding helps the bonding between mother and child.
   - Breast milk is sterile, always at the correct temperature and contains antibodies which help fight infection.
   - Breast milk contains less fat than formula milk.
4. After six months a baby's diet needs to be supplemented with iron and vitamin C.
5. Weaning is the introduction of semi-solid food into the baby's diet.
6. Foods such as carrots and potatoes should be puréed or mashed to aid digestion.
7. Avoid sugar and salt.
8. Eventually all of the food groups should be included in the baby's diet.
9. Fresh homemade food with no additives provides the best nutrition for the baby.

Children

Children grow rapidly and need a balanced diet to get all the nutrients needed by the growth.

Table 2.4 Dietary requirements for children		
Nutrient	Function	Source
Protein	Needed for growth	Meat, fish, eggs, soya products
Calcium	Bone and teeth formation	Milk, cheese
Vitamin D	Absorption of calcium	Eggs, milk, liver, oily fish
Iron	For general good health and blood	Meat, dark green leafy vegetables
Vitamin C	Blood, healing of wounds	Fruit and vegetables
Avoid sugar	Can create a sweet tooth and result in tooth decay	
Avoid salt	Can increase risk of high blood pressure	

Adolescents

During the transition from childhood to adulthood growth spurts are evident. A healthy balanced diet is essential.

> Limit the amount of fat and fast foods. Current research has identified fat and sugar as the main nutrients in a child's diet. This imbalance has increased the number of children suffering from obesity to 1 in 5.

Table 2.5 Dietary requirements for adolescents		
Nutrient	**Function**	**Source**
Protein	Growth and hormone production	Meat, fish, eggs, soya products
Fibre	Prevents constipation and bowel disorders	Brown bread, rice, wholemeal pasta
Calcium	Healthy bones and teeth Prevents osteoporosis	Milk, cheese, tinned fish
Vitamin D	Helps absorption of calcium	Eggs, oily fish
Iron	Prevents anaemia, especially in teenage girls	Meat, dark green leafy vegetables
Vitamin C	Necessary for absorption of iron	Fruit and vegetables
Water	Healthy skin	Tap/bottled water, beverages

Fatty foods and processed/refined carbohydrate foods should be avoided or kept to a minimum. Excessive amounts of these foods could lead to obesity.

Eating disorders

An eating disorder is a serious disruption of a person's eating habits or appetite, which may reflect dissatisfaction with his or her physical appearance.

Eating disorders common to adolescents:
1. Obesity
2. Anorexia nervosa
3. Bulimia nervosa

Anorexia nervosa and bulimia nervosa are both psychological disorders characterised by a person's fear of becoming fat or obese. His/her self-image is distorted and unreal.
- Symptoms of anorexia nervosa include hair loss, growth of downy body hair, amenorrhoea (periods stop), death.
- Symptoms of bulimia nervosa include tooth decay, inflammation of the oesophagus, swollen salivary glands, dehydration.

Adults

Adults require a balanced and varied diet which should complement their lifestyle and level of activity. Gender and age influence the kilocalorie requirements.

Dietary requirements for adults

	Function	Source
	Repairs cells	Meat, fish, eggs, soya products
	Provide energy	Fruit and vegetables
	Prevents heart disease Prevents bowel disorders	Wholemeal products, e.g. brown bread, rice, pasta
(turated)	Prevent cholesterol build-up Reduce risk of coronary heart disease (CHD)	Lean meat, chicken, fish oils
Iron	Healthy blood Helps prevent anaemia, especially in women	Meat, dark green leafy vegetables
Vitamin C	Aids absorption of iron	Fruit and vegetables
Calcium	Healthy bone and teeth Increases bone mass	Milk, cheese, tinned fish
Vitamin D	Aids absorption of calcium	Sunlight, eggs, oily fish
Vitamin B	Aids cell metabolism	Variety of foods

It is also recommended to:
- Reduce salt intake to prevent hypertension (high blood pressure).
- Limit alcohol intake.
- Give up smoking.

Pregnant and breast-feeding women

During pregnancy a healthy, well-balanced diet is essential for the formation of new cells and tissues in the foetus and mother. Breast-feeding women should follow the same nutritional guidelines below and should also increase fluid intake.

Pregnant women should avoid:
- Salt as it can cause high blood pressure or oedema (water retention).
- Alcohol as it can cause foetal alcohol syndrome (FAS).
- Smoking as it causes a reduction in body weight of the baby.
- Raw eggs, unpasteurised cheese and pâté as a possible source of food poisoning through salmonella and listeria bacteria. An infection can increase the risk of miscarriage.

Table 2.7 Dietary requirements for pregnant and lactating women

Nutrient	Function	Source
Folate/folic acid (taken in supplement form for 12 weeks before and after conception)	Reduces risk of neural tube defects, e.g. spina bifida	Fortified cereals, oranges, eggs
Protein	New cells and tissues	Meat, fish, eggs, soya products
Calcium	Healthy bones and teeth. Increase intake by up to 40%	Milk, yoghurt, cheese
Vitamin D	Absorption of calcium	Sunlight, eggs
Iron	Healthy blood in mother. Prevents anaemia in baby	Meat, dark green leafy vegetables
Vitamin C	Absorption of iron	Fruit and vegetables
Fibre	Prevents constipation common during pregnancy	Wholemeal products, e.g. brown bread, rice, pasta
Fatty acids	Development of nervous system in baby	Oily fish, liver, eggs

Elderly people

- **Less active:** As people get older and often less active their daily diet changes.
- **Economical considerations:** Elderly people can be on a reduced income and so have to be economical when shopping.
- **Physical disability:** Such as arthritis which would make them less mobile and agile making it more difficult to cook or to shop.
- **Malnutrition:** This is a common problem among the elderly as they often live alone and may not cook healthy meals.

Table 2.8 Dietary requirements for the elderly

Nutrient	Function	Source
Protein	Repairs cells	Eggs, fish (easy to digest)
Calcium	Prevents osteoporosis. Healthy bones	Milk, cheese
Vitamin D	Absorption of calcium	Eggs and sunlight
Vitamin A	Healthy eyes and skin	Fish oils, liver, butter, eggs
Vitamin C	Healing of wounds. Iron absorption	Fruit and vegetables
Iron	Prevents anaemia	Red meat, offal, bread and flour
Fibre	Prevents bowel disorders. Prevents constipation	Wholemeal products; fruit and vegetables
Water	General good health	Tap or bottled water, beverages

Elderly people should:
- Continue to reduce fat, sugar and salt from their diet to reduce the risk of coronary heart disease, diabetes mellitus and high blood pressure.
- Avoid spicy food.

Convalescents

People recovering from an illness (convalescents) can be of any age, so follow the guidelines above for the relevant age and incorporate the guidelines below.

General guidelines for convalescents
- Increase water intake to prevent dehydration.
- Reduce calorie intake if necessary, to prevent weight gain due to reduced activity.
- Avoid spicy foods.
- Eat easy-to-digest foods, e.g. milk, fish and eggs.
- Eat high fibre foods to prevent constipation.
- Increase protein for repair of cells and to help the healing process.
- Ensure that strict hygiene guidelines are followed during food storage, preparation, cooking and serving.

Special Dietary Needs

An individual may have to follow a modified diet due to dietary excesses, medical conditions or choice. Diseases associated with dietary excesses include:
- Bowel disorders
- Obesity
- Coronary heart disease
- Dental diseases
- Diabetes

Bowel disorders

One of the main factors in the increase in bowel disorders is due to the reduced fibre intake in our diet and to its increased refined carbohydrate content. Study Table 2.9 for the main forms of bowel disorders.

Table 2.9 Bowel disorders

Disease	Symptoms	Dietary cause/Risk factor
1 Colon cancer	• Blood loss through the colon	• Reduced intake of fruit and vegetables • Diet high in fatty foods • Lack of high fibre food
2 IBS (irritable bowel syndrome)	• Extremely painful • Muscle cramps in the lower abdomen • Feeling bloated • Diarrhoea • Constipation	• Lack of high fibre food • Stress related
3 Diverticular diseases	• Pressure exerted on the intestinal wall when constipated creates small areas in the wall which fill with food that allows bacteria to grow. The pockets can become swollen and cause great pain	• Lack of fibre in the diet • Lack of fluids in daily diet
4 Haemorrhoids	• Swollen veins in the anus and rectum • Itchiness and blood loss • Can develop during pregnancy • Avoid excess exertion when excreting faeces	• Low fibre diet • Obesity
5 Constipation	• Irregular bowel movements which are often hard and difficult to excrete	• Low fibre diet

Fibre – non-starch polysaccharide (NSP)

How to increase fibre in the diet
- Use wholegrain or wholemeal varieties of flour, bread, cereal, pasta and rice.
- Increase fruit, vegetable and pulse intake.
- Drink plenty of water – eight glasses a day.
- Increase exercise to aid movement of the bowel.

Advantages of a high fibre diet
- Low in fat.
- Gives a feeling of fullness.
- Helps movement of food through the intestine.
- Assists lower blood cholesterol and reduces possibility of coronary heart disease.

urs when the bone mass is reduced, resulting in fragile and brittle (easily eak/ideal bone mass is achieved between 25 and 35 years of age. Achieving can significantly reduce the risk of osteoporosis in later life.

The following risk factors have been identified.

Gender	Women are more likely to develop osteoporosis
Age	Postmenopausal women due to lack of the hormone oestrogen Oestrogen helps bones maintain calcium
Family	Family history of osteoporosis
Diet	Inadequate intake of calcium and vitamin D
Lack of exercise	Contributes to weakening of the bone

- **Symptoms:** Brittle bones, fracture of bone especially hips, neck and back pain, loss in height, rounded shoulders, curved or humped back.

How to reduce the risk
- Increase intake of calcium and vitamin D in the diet, especially during the period of peak bone mass (25–35 years).
- Avoid smoking and keep alcohol to a minimum as it affects the absorption of calcium.
- Post menopausal women could use HRT (hormone replacement therapy) to compensate for oestrogen loss.
- Exercise regularly.

Obesity

- A person who is 20 per cent above his/her recommended weight for his/her height is described as obese.
- Obesity is the result of certain lifestyle choices where energy intake is greater than energy output.
- These habits need to be changed for a person to lose weight.

How does a person become obese?
- Calorie intake is greater than calorie output.
- Lack of exercise.
- Sedentary lifestyle, e.g. sitting at a desk all day.
- Increase in convenience foods and fast foods as a dietary option.
- Increase in consumption of foods high in saturated fat and sugar.
- Comfort-eating resulting from boredom or depression.
- Some medication or hormonal imbalance, e.g. in the thyroid gland, causing weight gain.

Obesity can create a number of health problems
- Heart disease and high blood pressure.
- Stroke: Due to high blood pressure or build-up of cholesterol.
- Diabetes, especially non-insulin-dependent (type 2) diabetes mellitus (NIDDM).
- Gallstones: Due to high cholesterol levels, and which can be extremely painful.
- Arthritis: Extreme pain in back and leg joints due to excess weight.
- Infertility and difficult childbirth: Due to extra weight.
- Psychological problems such as low self-esteem.

How to overcome obesity
The main aim should be to rectify the energy balance. This can be achieved by:
- Increasing exercise to 45-minute sessions most days of the week.
- Reducing high fat and calorie-laden foods such as sugar, refined/processed foods and fast foods.

> **Exam Hints**
> Prepare a set of daily menu plans for each diet and take into consideration the special nutritional needs of each individual diet, e.g. low cholesterol diet, CHD. Remember daily menus should include breakfast, lunch, dinner and beverages.

Ten dietary guidelines

1. Eat a well-balanced diet.
2. A slow weekly weight loss (1–2 lb a week) is far more efficient than extreme weight loss.
3. Eat plenty of fresh fruit and vegetables.
4. Drink at least eight glasses of water a day.
5. Increase intake of high fibre foods, e.g. wholemeal bread and rice.
6. Avoid foods high in saturated fats such as red meat, butter, biscuits, cakes and fast foods.
7. Avoid any refined carbohydrate or sugar-rich foods.
8. Avoid fast food meals and keep takeaways to a minimum.
9. Join a slimming club to provide support and motivation.
10. Remember to consult your doctor before commencing any dietary plan.

Coronary heart disease (CHD)

How does it develop?
The walls of the coronary arteries, which carry blood to and from the heart, become narrow due to a build-up of the fatty substance cholesterol. This blocks the flow of blood to the heart. This blockage or hardening of the arteries is called atherosclerosis. It develops gradually but can have serious consequences, e.g. angina and heart attack.

Risk factors associated with CHD
- Men over 45
- Women over 55
- Family history of CHD

- High cholesterol level and high blood pressure
- No exercise
- Smoking and excessive alcohol consumption
- Increased stress levels due to work or family circumstances
- Suffering from obesity and diabetes

Table 2.10 Lifestyle and dietary changes which help prevent CHD	
Lifestyle changes	**Dietary changes**
• Exercise regularly • Avoid smoking and alcohol • Reduce weight • Reduce stress levels	• Reduce salt and saturated fat intake • Increase use of polyunsaturated fats which help lower LDL • Increase fibre intake as it helps to lower LDL • Avoid refined carbohydrates, especially sugar • Eat low fat milk, cheese products, etc. • Increase intake of fruit and vegetables

About cholesterol

Cholesterol is produced in the liver and acquired from saturated fat in the diet. Cholesterol is needed in the body:

- To make new cell walls.
- To produce hormones for growth and reproduction.
- As a vital component of bile salts.
- To transport fat in the blood around the body.
- For attachment to a protein, creating lipoprotein.

> **Points to Note**
> There are two types of lipoprotein:
> 1 Low density lipoprotein (LDL) = A dangerous lipoprotein which leads to the build-up of cholesterol in the arteries.
> 2 High density lipoprotein (HDL) = A beneficial lipoprotein which eliminates excess cholesterol from the blood, therefore preventing a build-up in arteries.

Guidelines to reduce cholesterol levels

1 Reduce intake of foods high in cholesterol such as eggs and liver.
2 Reduce intake of saturated fats such as butter, cheese and red meat.
3 Increase intake of polyunsaturated fatty acids.
4 Have cholesterol levels monitored.

Dental diseases

Dental diseases which are connected to dietary excesses include:
1 Dental decay
2 Periodontal disease (gums and tissues around teeth become infected)

These conditions are mainly caused by a build-up of plaque, which results from the consumption of foods with a high sugar content. Plaque is found on teeth as a sticky substance, which is due to the reaction of bacteria and acid in the mouth.

How to reduce tooth decay
- Have a dental check-up twice a year.
- Avoid food with high sugar content.
- Brush teeth after each meal if possible; if not, twice a day.
- Floss daily to remove food lodged between the teeth.
- Use a mouthwash daily to prevent bacterial build-up and freshen breath.
- Use fluoride-based toothpaste.
- Use artificial sweeteners instead of sugar.
- Drink plenty of water and avoid fizzy drinks and sugar-laden fruit juices.
- Avoid sugar-based breakfast cereals and choose a fibre cereal instead.
- Read food labels in order to identify sugar content.

Diabetes mellitus

Diabetes mellitus is caused by the insufficient or absent production of insulin by the pancreas. Insulin is needed in the body to control the level of blood sugar (glucose), which is used for the production of energy.

There are two forms of diabetes mellitus called:
Type 1: Insulin-dependent diabetes mellitus (IDDM)
Type 2: Non-insulin-dependent diabetes mellitus (NIDDM)

	Table 2.11 Diabetes	
	Type 1: Insulin-dependent diabetes mellitus (IDDM)	**Type 2: Non-insulin-dependent diabetes mellitus (NIDDM)**
Information	• Pancreas does not produce insulin • Controlled by injections of insulin • Develops mainly in young children and adolescents • Often hereditary	• Insulin produced cannot be used by the body • Generally controlled by diet and medication • Mainly in overweight adults • Increasing number of young people between 25 and 45 years
Treatment	• Require insulin injections or oral medication	• Healthy diet and avoidance of high sugar food • Exercise

- **Symptoms:** Thirst, frequent urination, weight loss, tiredness and fatigue, blurred vision, potential to develop glaucoma. Kidney failure, heart disease and stroke can be a result of untreated/undiagnosed diabetes.

Dietary guidelines for diabetes sufferers
- Eliminate refined sugar products from the diet.
- Eat fruit with low sugar content.
- Increase intake of high fibre foods.
- Reduce intake of saturated fat in the diet to decrease risk of CHD and stroke.

- Eat three regular meals a day to stabilise blood sugar levels.
- Eat starch-based carbohydrate foods for slow energy release.
- Reduce alcohol intake.

Coeliac disease

What is coeliac disease?

Coeliac disease occurs in people who have an intolerance to the protein gluten. Gluten is found in wheat, rye, oats and barley. Gluten is a prolamine found in wheat.

What happens in the body?

- The body is deficient in the enzyme which is needed to digest gluten.
- The body's immune system identifies gluten as dangerous and this results in the inflammation of the small intestine.
- **Symptoms:** Weight loss, abdominal pain, anaemia due to iron deficiency, tiredness, slow growth in children, malabsorption of nutrients.

Dietary guidelines

- Follow a gluten-free diet.
- Read food labelling, especially for processed foods.
- Follow the dietician's recommendations.
- Use gluten-free products.
- Include naturally gluten-free foods, e.g. meat, fish, eggs and fruit.

Vegetarianism

A vegetarian is a person who eats a diet consisting primarily of plant foods.

Table 2.12 Types of vegetarianism	
Lacto-ovo vegetarian	Eat milk and eggs
Pesco-vegetarian	Eat fish
Pollo-vegetarian	Eat chicken
Lacto-vegetarian	Eat dairy produce
Vegan	Do not eat any animal produce or flesh

Why do people become vegetarian?

1. Religion: Some people believe it is wrong to kill animals, e.g. Buddhists.
2. Ethical reasons: Some people will not eat intensively produced meat.
3. Health: A healthier diet due to reduced saturated fat and increase in fibre
4. Aesthetic reasons: Some people do not like the smell, sight or taste of meat/fish flesh.
5. Financial reasons: Cheaper option than meat and fish.
6. Family influence: People often adapt to the eating pattern of their family.

Key factors of planning a vegetarian meal

1. Replace animal fats with vegetable oils.
2. Use vegetable stock cubes in soups and sauces.
3. Soya protein – in textured vegetable protein (TVP), tofu and Quorn – is a good alternative to meat.
4. For vegans, use alternative dairy foods, e.g. soya milk, soya yoghurt.
5. For lacto-vegetarians, incorporate milk, cheese and yoghurt for high protein and calcium levels.
6. Include all food groups in each meal.
7. Include wholegrain cereals such as rice and pasta for vitamin B group content.
8. Meet the nutritional needs of the person.
9. For vegans, use fortified products where available, e.g. breakfast cereals.
10. Use herbs and spices to add flavour to foods.

Advantages of a vegetarian diet

1. Healthier as it contains less saturated fat and more fibre, therefore reducing risk of CHD and bowel disease.
2. Helps lower blood pressure due to reduced levels of salt in diet.
3. Less likely to bring about obesity due to high fruit and vegetable content of diet.
4. Contains more fresh produce, therefore less food additives are consumed.
5. A smaller number of vegetarians develop diabetes.
6. Contains less sugar.

Vegan diet

The vegan diet consists of plant foods only; no dairy produce should be included.

A proper balanced diet normally provides most nutrients. A vegan's diet may be deficient in the following nutrients as they are mostly found in animal products.

Table 2.13 Nutrients needed in the vegan diet	
Nutrient	**Alternative source**
HBV protein	Seeds, nuts, soya protein
Calcium	Tofu, broccoli, spinach, baked beans, dried fruit, seeds
Iron	Bran flakes, baked beans, wholemeal bread, prunes, sesame seeds
Vitamin B_{12}	Bran flakes, yeast extract, TVP, vitamin supplements
Zinc	Wheat germ, whole grains, beans, seeds, lentils, tofu

Changes in Food and Eating Patterns in Ireland

The information needed to compare the dietary patterns in the Irish diet is obtained from:
1 National Nutritional Survey 1946–1948
2 Irish National Nutritional Survey 1990
- The establishment of the National Nutritional Surveillance Centre in 1992 has resulted in a detailed and continuous overview of trends in the Irish diet and how they reflect socio-economic trends.
- Slan (Survey of Lifestyle, Attitude and Nutrition) completed national nutritional surveys in 1998 and 2004.

Changes in the Irish diet

Availability of food and the eating patterns in Irish society have changed significantly over the last hundred years. These changes can be attributed to the following:

Table 2.14 Changes in food and eating patterns	
1 Development of transport links between towns and cities	Food could be transported between areas (Rural areas also send food to cities)
2 Establishment of state-run services, e.g. water supply and electricity	Clean water, new electrical appliances, e.g. fridge and cooker
3 Introduction of new agricultural practices due to technological development	Less labour intensive and greater yield
4 Continued growth and development in the food processing industry since the Industrial Revolution	Wider variety of foods available to buy in shops
5 World War I and II	Increase in food price. Rationing of food due to food shortages
6 Nutritional research has created healthy eating guidelines	People are becoming more aware of what they eat
7 Better transportation, people travelling more to other countries	Introduction of new food and different cooking methods

These changes can be divided into three main periods:

Table 2.15 History of the Irish diet			
Time	Regular diet	Nutrient content	Other changes
1900–1950	• Homemade bread, porridge, potatoes, some dairy produce, pork and poultry (special occasions), little processed food • From 1940 onwards importation of fresh fruit and vegetables	• Low in iron (anaemia was common) • Increase in sugar content • High in vitamin C • Increase in saturated fat • Adequate calcium (from milk) • High in carbohydrates	• Imports • During World War I and II unemployment, food shortages, rationing of food
1950–1990	• White bread, tea, bacon, eggs, processed foods • Decrease in potatoes, porridge and homemade produce • 1960 – introduction of Italian and Chinese foods to the Irish market	• Decrease in fibre, vitamins and, minerals • Increase in sugar • Increase in saturated fats, salt and food additives	• Availability of electricity and water • Increase in convenience and processed foods • First supermarkets opened • Increase in travel
1990–Present day	• Convenience and processed food • Varieties of bread, pasta, dairy produce, meat, fish, eggs, takeaways and fast foods confectionery, sweets, soft drinks	• Low in fibre • High in sugar and saturated fats • High in salt • Increase in HBV protein • Increase in additives • Low in iron and calcium	• Sedentary lifestyle, irregular eating times • TV dinners • Increase in eating out • Awareness of special dietary requirements • More health conscious due to increased awareness of food content

Does the Irish diet meet current dietary guidelines?

Observations of recent nutritional survey:
- A 3 per cent increase in foods eaten from the top shelf of the food pyramid reflects the recent findings of high fat and sugar in the diet.
- 83 per cent of those surveyed ate more than the recommended guidelines of less than three portions a day (from the top shelf of the food pyramid).
- Use of low fat/polyunsaturated fats has reduced from 59 per cent to 50.7 per cent.
- The use of saturated fats has decreased from 60 per cent to 48 per cent.
- 9.9 per cent of the population eat fried foods four or more times a week.
- Younger people are more inclined to grill or fry foods.
- With regard to vegetarian, vegan, diabetic and gluten-free diets, very little has changed since 1998.
- Low cholesterol diets among men have increased since 1998.
- Consumers are more concerned about food labels, and 66 per cent of the population read the labels for various pieces of information such as nutrition, ingredients and calories.

Recent trends in Ireland have led to a number of changes in eating patterns.

1. Economic growth has led to a more affluent society which can afford to eat processed foods and eat out regularly.
2. People are eating more food than is required, which can lead to weight gain.
3. People are consuming more alcohol than is recommended.
4. Increase in processed and convenience foods.
5. Increase in the establishment of farmers' markets where fresh organic products are sold.
6. Increase in consumer demand for free range/organic produce and a move away from processed foods. Supermarkets are increasing their range and supply of this type of product.
7. Traceability of meat and poultry has been introduced to create confidence in the food industry due to recent scares regarding BSE and foot and mouth disease.

Table 2.16 The Irish diet	
Low in	High in
Fibre	Saturated fat
Iron	Salt
Calcium	Sugar
Vitamin D and E	

Malnutrition

Due to the unbalanced nature of many Irish diets and the increase in convenience foods and those high in sugar and salt, many Irish people are now lacking important nutrients for a healthy body, e.g. calcium, protein and fibre.

Table 2.17 Problems in the Irish diet

Nutrient	Cause	Effect	Correction	Link up
Low in dietary fibre	• Low fibre intake • High intake of processed foods	• Bowel diseases, e.g. constipation, colon cancer	• Increase fibre intake • Increase fruit and vegetables • Increase water intake • Avoid processed foods	• Bowel disease
High in saturated fat	• Increase in fast foods, convenience foods and animal fats	• Obesity • CHD • Diabetes • High cholesterol	• Reduce intake of saturated fats • Use low fat products • Change cooking methods to steaming etc.	• CHD • Obesity • Cooking methods
Low in iron	• Inadequate intake of iron-rich foods • Lack of vitamin C for absorption • Menstruation • Increase in inhibiting factors, e.g. phytic acid	• Anaemia • Tiredness • Fatigue	• Increase intake of iron-rich foods • Increase vitamin C intake	
Low in calcium	• Insufficient intake of calcium-rich foods • Lack of vitamin D for absorption • Presence of inhibiting factors, e.g. fibre, oxalates and phytic acid	• Osteoporosis • Rickets • Dental decay	• Increase intake of calcium-rich foods, e.g. dairy, fish • Increase vitamin D intake	

Questions

1. (a) What is basal metabolic rate (BMR)? (3)
   (b) List three factors that affect energy requirements. (3)
   (2006, HL, Section A, 2)

2. (a) Define coeliac condition. (3)
   (b) Name three foods which should be avoided by a person with coeliac condition. (3)
   (2006, HL, Section A, 3)

3. Describe how osteoporosis affects the body and state 2 possible causes of this condition. (6)
   (2008, HL, Section A, 3)

Key Points

Energy
- Energy requirements are measured by BMR, kcal, kJ
- Factors determining BMR: Age, size, gender, activity, climate, health status, pregnancy
- The role of energy in the body: Growth, heat, metabolism

Current Nutritional Guidelines
- Reduce fat, sugar, salt and increase fibre intake
- Terminology: RDA, DRV, RNI, EAR, LTL

Specific Dietary Requirements
- Factors influencing dietary and food requirements: Baby, child, adolescent, adult, pregnancy, elderly and convalescents

Special Dietary Needs
- Diet-related problems: Bowel disorder, osteoporosis, obesity, coronary heart disease (CHD), dental decay and diabetes
- Modified diets for diabetes, CHD, coeliac disease, vegetarianism

Changes in Food and Eating Patterns in Ireland
- Development of better transport links and state-run services
- Technological advances in food production and agriculture
- Introduction of new food types and cooking methods

The Irish Diet and Current Dietary Review
- Increases in convenience foods, diet high in sugar, fats, salt
- Increase in obesity levels

Malnutrition
- Irish diet is low in fibre, iron, calcium, vitamins D and E
- High in saturated fat, salt and sugar

3: Food Commodities

●●● Learning Objectives
In this chapter you will learn about:
1. The Irish Food Industry
2. Role of Small Businesses and Home Enterprises
3. Career Opportunities in the Food Industry
4. Food Commodities: Meat, Poultry, Fish, Eggs, Protein Alternatives, Cereals, Vegetables, Fruit, Milk and Dairy Products, Cheese, Yoghurt, Fats and Oils (Lipids)

The Irish Food Industry

Table 3.1 Food agencies and government departments	
Agency	**Area**
The Department of Agriculture and Food	Promotes agri-food sector
Bord Bia	Promotes Irish food, drink and horticulture Information for consumer
Bord Iascaigh Mhara (BIM)	Irish seafood and Quality Seafood Programme
Department of Communications, Marine and Natural Resources	Irish fishing
Teagasc	Research centre for food and agriculture, training and advice
Enterprise Ireland	Supports new and existing agri-food businesses
Food Safety Authority of Ireland (FSAI)	Food legislation and safety

Food sectors
Imports and exports in Ireland within the food industry:
1. Dairy and ingredients
2. Beef
3. Lamb
4. Pig meat
5. Poultry
6. Edible horticulture
7. Mariculture
8. Beverages
9. Prepared consumer foods

Agri-food facts
- Irish companies export to over 170 countries worldwide.
- There are 678 food and drink companies in Ireland.
- Over 155,000 people are employed in this area (9.1%).
- The agri-food industry was worth 16.6 billion in 2004.
- The total amount of exports accounted for 7.15 billion in 2004 (8.4% of all exports).

The Love Irish Food label is used to idenify Irish manufactured food and drink. The logo can be seen beside or or the food product making it easy for the consumer to recognize the particular food as Irish. A strict set of criteria must be adhered to before a product has permission to use the love Irish food logo. www.loveirishfood.ie

Food imports

The majority of foods exported from Ireland are also imported when they are out of season in Ireland and when Irish producers cannot meet the demands of the consumer.

Role of Small Businesses and Home Enterprises

The majority of small businesses and home enterprises involve speciality foods and drinks. The following areas have been identified as speciality foods:

Table 3.2 Speciality foods	
Bakery	Biscuits, bread, puddings, gluten-free flour
Beverages	Mineral water, apple juice, beers
Condiments	Relishes, sauces, mustard, dressing
Confectionery	Sweets, chocolate, toffees, desserts
Dairy	Cheese, yoghurt, dairy spreads
Prepared foods	Frozen meals, vegetables, prepared salads and desserts
Preserves	Jam, chutney, marmalade
Speciality meat and fish	Smoked fish, black and white pudding, organic meats, spiced beef, ham, sausages

- Most of these businesses are family run and use natural local products.
- High standard of products, hygiene and presentation is expected.
- EU regulations regarding hygiene and safety are implemented.

Career Opportunities in the Food Industry

The food industry is a huge area as it extends from making and supplying the product to analysing the nutritional content of it. Some careers require specific qualifications such as a degree or diploma, while others, e.g. retailing, provide in-house training.
- Agricultural College: Farm management and practices
- Universities and ITs: Degrees, diplomas and certificates in nutrition, dietetics, hotel management, microbiology, teaching and lecturing
- Fáilte Ireland: Catering, hospitality, chef, waiter, receptionist. Full-time and part-time day release courses are available. Most of these courses are provided in local ITs
- Teagasc: Skills training and farm management

CHAPTER 3

Food Commodities

Food can be divided into the following groups.

Exam Hints

Each food commodity will be studied under all or some of the following headings: Classification; Nutritive and dietetic value; Structure; Processing; Effects of heat; Buying; Storing. Some commodities will have areas specific to them.

If you look at exam questions, you will find that these headings are often the keywords used in a food commodity question. Make sure that you fully understand the requirements of each.

Table 3.3 Food groups	
Meat and poultry	Milk and dairy products
Fish	Cereals
Eggs	Fats and oils
Protein alternatives	Fruit and vegetables

Meat

Table 3.4 Nutritional value of meat	
Protein	20–30% meat fibres contain myosin, actin and globulin The connective tissue contains elastin and collagen
Fat	10–30%, depends on type of animal – saturated, visible and invisible
Carbohydrate	0% NB. Potatoes
Vitamins	Vitamin A in offal, B_1 (thiamine), B_2 (riboflavin), B_{12} (cobalamin)
Minerals Iron (haem iron) Sulfur, potassium zinc, phosphorus	In myoglobin and haemoglobin of meat
Water	50–60%

Table 3.5 Dietetic value of meat		
Protein: high biological value protein	Needed for growth and repair of cells	Children, teenagers, pregnant women
Fat: saturated fat animal	Provides heat and energy Excess is stored as adipose tissue	Should be avoided/reduced by people with high cholesterol or at risk of coronary heart disease
Iron: haem iron Vitamin C	Easily absorbed by the body Prevents anaemia	Children, teenagers, adults, especially menstruating women
Lacking in carbohydrate, calcium and vitamin C		Serve with these foods for balanced eating

53

Structure of meat
- Lean meat is the muscle of the animal.
- Muscle contains small fibres.
- Fibres contain water protein (myosin and actin), minerals, vitamins and extractives. Actin is a globular protein. Myosin is a fibrous protein.

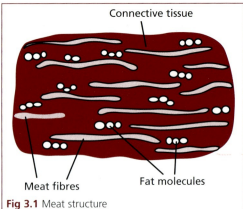

Fig 3.1 Meat structure

Table 3.6 What causes meat to be tough or tender?	
1 Age	• Older animals have longer and wider muscle fibres and more connective tissue • This results in tougher meat • Smaller muscle fibres provide tender meat • Therefore meat from younger animals such as lamb and veal is more tender
2 Activity	• The more active an area of the animal is, e.g. the neck or leg area, the longer the muscle fibre • Shorter fibres are found in less active parts (the back or rump) providing more tender pieces of meat
3 Treatment before or after slaughter	• Rest animals before slaughter to allow a build-up of glycogen in the muscles • After slaughter the glycogen changes to lactic acid and helps tenderise the meat during the hanging process • Meat is hung in a cold room (5°C) for between 7 and 14 days.
4 Method of cooking	• Tough cuts of meat require tenderisation during the cooking process • This is achieved by using slow, moist methods such as stewing or cooking (see also p. 55) • Quick methods of cooking such as frying or grilling toughen meat

Tenderising meat

Table 3.7 Meat tenderising methods

1	Proteolytic (protein splitting) enzyme	• Animals can be injected with proteolytic tenderising enzymes • Sprinkling raw meat with tenderising chemicals which contain proteolytic enzymes, e.g. papain from paw paw tree
2	Mechanically breaking the meat fibres	• Piercing with thin knives or needles • Pounding with a heavy object such as a meat hammer • Mincing meat
3	Marinating	• Steeping raw meat in a marinade containing lemon juice (acid), alcohol, oil and flavourings
4	Moist method of cooking	• Slow moist method of cooking, e.g. stewing or casseroling

Table 3.8 Effects of heat/cooking on meat

1	Protein	• Coagulates and becomes firmer • Decreases in size due to loss of meat juices
2	Fat	• Melts and adds flavour • Moistens the meat fibres
3	Collagen	• Converted to gelatine which results in the meat fibres loosening and becoming tender and easy to digest
4	Vitamins and minerals	• Water-soluble vitamins such as the B group could be lost in the cooking liquid
5	Bacteria	• Destroyed, making the food safer to eat
6	Colour	• Changes from red to brown due to the denaturation of myoglobin • Colour change due to Maillard reaction
7	Flavour	• Release of extractives form a tasty coating on the surface of the meat

Table 3.9 Buying and storing meat

Buying

- From clean hygienic premises
- Staff should be clean and hygienic
- Look for traceability symbols/information
- Raw and cooked meat should be stored and displayed separately to prevent cross-contamination
- Fresh meat should have good colour, moist flesh, fresh smell
- Avoid meat with fat or gristle
- Buy a cut of meat suitable for dish/cooking method used
- Cheaper cuts of meat contain the same nutrients as more expensive cuts, although they require longer cooking time

Storing

- Refrigerate meat after purchase, place below any cooked products to avoid dripping and cross-contamination
- Remove wrapping and place in a clean covered plate or bowl
- Cover, using cling film or greaseproof paper, allows air to circulate and prevents the meat drying out
- Use within 2 to 3 days
- Keep vacuum-packed meats such as bacon in wrapping until used

Table 3.10 Processing of meat

Type	Process	Changes	Examples
Freezing	• Meat is boned and the fat trimmed • Blast frozen commercially at −30°C, home freezing −25°C	• Loss of B group vitamins, otherwise no other changes	• Most meats
Vacuum packing	• Meat is boned, placed in polythene bags and sealed to remove any air • Storage 3–4 weeks • Keep refrigerated	• Little change in food value	• Bacon • Ham • Rashers
Canning	• All ingredients are heated to a high temperature, placed in sterile cans and sealed	• Loss of B group vitamins • Colour, flavour and texture change • Fat content can increase	• Meat stew • Meat balls • Corned beef
Dehydration	• Small pieces of meat are accelerated freeze-dried (AFD)	• Loss of moisture • B group vitamins are lost • Change in colour, texture and flavour	• Packet soups and sauces • Pasta sauces
Curing	• Preserving solutions such as brine (salt and water) are injected into the carcass • Soaked for a further 5 days to allow the colour to develop • Hung for 6 days to allow flavour to develop • Can be smoked or unsmoked	• Change in colour and flavour • Increase in salt content	• Bacon • Ham

Methods of cooking meat
- Frying, grilling, baking, stewing, casseroling, stir-frying and barbecuing.
- Meat products include: fresh, cooked and dried sausages; beef burgers; pâté; cold, cooked meats; gelatine.

Beef labelling – The Beef Quality Assurance Scheme
1. This is a combined scheme involving farmer, beef plant and retailer.
2. Only approved farmers are used by the beef plants.
3. A safety management system must be in place using HACCP (see p. 148) as a basis.
4. Audits are carried out by independent bodies contracted by Bord Bia.
5. If requirements are met the quality assured logo can be used on product/packing or point of sale.

Offal
Offal includes all the edible internal organs of an animal.

Table 3.11 Offal	
Nutritional value	
Protein	High biological value protein Most offal such as liver, kidney, heart
Fats	Most offal is low in fat
Carbohydrate	None
Vitamins	
Water-soluble	High in B group, especially B_{12}, folic acid, nicotinic acid Vitamin C found in most offal
Fat-soluble	Vitamins A and D high in liver and kidneys
Minerals	
Calcium	Similar to carcass meat, except for tripe
Iron	Very high in heart, kidney and liver
Buying and storing offal	
Buying	The same rules apply as for carcass meat
Storing	Best to use on day of purchase Refrigerate immediately Wash thoroughly, remove any blood vessels
Cooking method	Most offal can be fried, grilled, baked or used in stews

Poultry

Poultry is the collective name for all birds that are reared for meat and/or eggs. Chicken, turkey, geese and ducks are commonly described as poultry.

Table 3.12 Nutritional value of poultry	
1 Protein	High biological value protein
2 Fat	Saturated fat Percentage varies depending on the type of bird
3 Carbohydrate	None
4 Vitamins	B group vitamins B_1 (thiamine), B_2 (riboflavin), niacin
5 Minerals	Iron about half of that of meat Calcium traces
6 Water	Between 50% and 70%

Table 3.13 Dietetic value of poultry		
Protein	High biological value	Easy to digest Suitable for children, adolescents, elderly, convalescents
Fat	Skinless chicken and turkey are low in fat	Low calorie or low cholesterol diets
Carbohydrate	None	Serve with carbohydrate-rich food to provide balanced eating
Cooking	Poultry is a very versatile food and can be cooked in a variety of ways.	
Economic	It is relatively cheap	

Buying and storing poultry

Buying
1. Poultry can be free range, organic or factory reared.
2. It can be bought fresh, prepacked or frozen.
3. Buy from clean hygienic premises.
4. Check use-by-date if prepacked.
5. It should have a fresh, pleasant smell.
6. It should have no bruising or cuts on flesh.
7. Flesh should be firm and plump.
8. If frozen, it should be frozen solid (check temperature of freezer in shop).

Storing
1. Follow guidelines for meat.
2. If frozen, place in freezer immediately.

Fish

Table 3.14 Classification of fish		
1 Habitat (where fish live)	(a) Freshwater (rivers and lakes)	Salmon, trout
	(b) Saltwater (sea)	
	1 Demersal fish (living at the bottom of the sea)	1 Cod, plaice
	2 Pelagic fish (living near the surface)	2 Mackerel, tuna
	3 Farmed fish (aquaculture)	3 Salmon, trout, mussels, oysters
2 Shape	Flat	Sole, plaice
	Round	Salmon, trout
3 Nutritive value	White fish: Very low in fat. Fat in liver and is removed	Cod, plaice
	Oily fish: High in unsaturated fat. Fat is dispersed in flesh, hence darker colour	Salmon, tuna
	Shellfish: Low in fat, higher in cholesterol. Crustaceans can be difficult to digest	1 Molluscs: Outer shell, fish inside (mussels, oysters) 2 Crustaceans: Flesh on outside (prawns, lobster, crab)

Structure of fish

- Fish flesh is made up of bundles of short, thick fibres (actin and myosin) called myomeres.
- Connective tissue (collagen) is used to hold the myomeres together. This converts to gelatine during cooking.
- Fish has less connective tissue than meat.
- The fat in oily fish is distributed amongst the fibres.
- The outer skin of fish is made of scales.
- Shellfish fibres are tougher and therefore can be more difficult to digest.

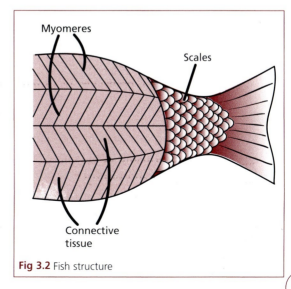

Fig 3.2 Fish structure

Table 3.15 Nutritional value of fish

Nutrient	Facts
Protein	High biological value (80–90%), collagen, actin and myosin
Fat	In white fish: stored in liver In oily fish: polyunsaturated fats (PUFA), especially omega-3 Contains EPA (eicosapentaenoic acid) and DHA (docosahexaenoic acid)
Carbohydrates	None NB
Vitamins	B group in all fish, vitamin C in oysters Vitamins A and D in oily fish
Minerals	Iodine in tinned fish such as salmon and tuna Phosphorus Calcium Iron in shellfish
Water	65–80% lower in oily fish

Table 3.16 Dietetic value of fish

1	Protein	High biological value Needed for growth in children and adolescents Easy to digest (convalescents)
2	Fat	Low in fat High in polyunsaturated fats, especially omega-3 and 6 Suitable for low calorie diet Helps reduce the risk of coronary heart disease
3	Carbohydrate NONE	Serve with carbohydrate-rich food, e.g. potatoes, rice, pasta
4	Variety	Huge variety of fish available
5	Versatile	Can be used for different cooking methods, e.g. frying, grilling, baking
6	Economical	Some fish is relatively cheap to buy, e.g. mackerel
7	Cooking time	Fish requires a relatively short cooking time so reduces the cost of energy
8	Calories	Low in calories and so ideal for a low calorie diet

Spoilage of fish

Fish is an exceptionally perishable food. There are three main types of spoilage:
1 **Oxidative rancidity:** Fish flesh reacts with oxygen in the air. Fat + oxygen
2 **Enzyme action:** Naturally occurring enzymes continue to work even at a reduced temperature.
3 **Bacteria:** When fish are caught they struggle. This uses up the glycogen stored in their muscles and liver. As there is very little glycogen left to convert to lactic acid on death, fish deteriorate very quickly due to the action of bacteria on the flesh. This produces a nitrogen-smelling compound called trimethylamine.

Buying
1. Buy from clean hygienic premises with knowledgeable hygiene-aware staff.
2. Fish should be stored on ice in a chilled unit.
3. Buy fish in season as it is cheaper and has a better flavour.
4. Choose medium sized pieces.
5. Fish can be bought whole or in cutlet, steak and fillet form.
6. Check for signs of freshness:
   - **Whole fish:**
     – Bright bulging eyes, gills should be bright red in colour
     – Skin should be moist and unbroken
     – Flesh should be firm and elastic
     – The scales should be tight
     – No unpleasant smell
   - **Shellfish:**
     – Molluscs shell should be closed or close when touched.
     – Crustaceans should be alive.

Storing
1. Refrigerate immediately and use within 24 hours.
2. Remove fish from wrapping, rinse and cover.
3. Place on a bed of ice in refrigerator, replace ice as it melts.
4. Frozen fish: Place in refrigerator immediately.
5. Check use-by-date.

Effects of cooking/heat on fish
- Protein coagulates and sets at between 60°C and 70°C.
- Collagen is converted to gelatine and the fish flesh separates easily (flakes).
- Fish shrinks slightly due to water loss.
- The appearance of the flesh changes from translucent to opaque.
- Overcooking results in tough rubbery flesh.
- Micro-organisms are destroyed.
- Cooked fish is easier to digest.
- Some vitamins and minerals are lost during cooking.

Preparation of fish for cooking
- In whole fish the scales, head, tail and fins are removed.
- The intestines are removed and the cavity is washed.
- The fish is then prepared in one of the following ways:
  – Filleted
  – Cut into steaks or cutlets
  – Cooked whole

Table 3.17 Processing fish		
Process	**Effect**	**Example**
1 Freezing • Commercial: blast frozen at −30°C • Home: fast freeze at −25°C • White fish can be stored for 6 months • Oily fish can be stored for 3 months	• Colour, flavour and texture remain unchanged • Micro-organisms are inactivated • Nutritional value unchanged unless fish is breaded/battered	• Breaded cod • Salmon steaks
2 Canning • Fish is heated to high temperature, placed in sterile cans and sealed • Fish can be placed in oil, brine or sauce	• Prevents microbial activity • Loss of B_1 • Increase in calcium • Calorie content can increase depending on sauce	• Salmon • Tuna • Sardines
3 Smoking • Creosote and formaldehyde are the chemicals used in smoking to prevent microbial activity • Placed in brine or rubbed with dry salt • Cold smoked at 27°C for longer • Hot smoked at 80°C	• Change in colour and flavour • Increase in salt	• Salmon • Herrings • Cod
4 Fish products	• Change in colour, flavour and texture • Calorie content can be increased	• Fish fingers • Fish cakes

Cooking methods

Stewing, poaching, casseroling, frying, grilling, stir-frying, baking, barbecuing.

Eggs

Structure of an egg

Eggs are made up of three main parts: shell, white and yolk.

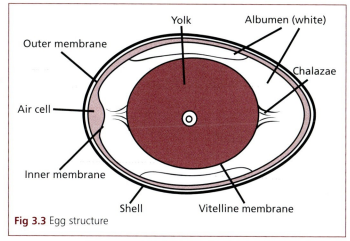

Fig 3.3 Egg structure

Table 3.18 Nutritional value of an egg	
Nutrient	**Facts**
Protein	High biological value protein (100%), ovalbumin, globulin, vitelin and livetin
Fat	Saturated fat in yolk, contains cholesterol, natural emulsifier lecithin
Carbohydrate	None
Vitamins	B_2 (riboflavin), B_{12} (cobalamin), vitamins A, D, E
Minerals	Iron, phosphorus, zinc, selenium
Water	74%

Table 3.19 Dietetic value of an egg	
Protein	• High biological value protein (100%), ovalbumin, globulin, vitelin and livetin • Excellent meat alternative • Ideal for the diet of children, adolescents and lacto-ovo vegetarians
Fat	• Saturated fat in yolk, contains cholesterol, natural emulsifier lecithin • Easy to digest • Should be restricted in diets of low cholesterol
Carbohydrate	• None • Serve with carbohydrate foods in order to achieve a balanced diet
Vitamins	• B_2 (riboflavin), B_{12} (cobalamin), vitamins A, D, E
Minerals	• Iron, phosphorus, zinc, selenium
Water	• 74%
Versatile	• Very versatile • Can be used in a variety of both sweet and savoury dishes
Cooking time	• Cooks very quickly and can be eaten on its own or as part of a dish, e.g. quiche

Grading and labelling eggs

Eggs are graded according to their weight and quality. All egg boxes must carry the following information:

- Country of origin, e.g. IE = Ireland
- Registration number of producer
- Class/Quality
- Use-by-date
- Quality assured mark
- Name and address of producer
- Quantity
- Week number (1–52)
- Storage instructions

Egg Quality Assurance Scheme (EQAS)

- This scheme was introduced to provide consumers with disease free (especially salmonella) monitored produce.
- It is implemented by the Department of Agriculture and Food and Bord Bia.
- Eggs that are produced and packed in accordance with set guidelines receive the EQAS symbol for use.
- It guarantees the traceability of the product.
- The EQAS mark is awarded by Bord Bia.

Table 3.20 Buying and storing eggs

Buying	Storing
1 Buy from a clean hygienic shop	1 Store in the egg compartment of the refrigerator
2 Look for the quality assurance logo	2 Store pointed end down; this prevents the chalazae from breaking
3 Check use-by-date and labelling	3 Avoid storing near strong flavoured foods due to porous nature of shell
4 Inspect shells; avoid purchasing broken or cracked eggs as they increase the risk of bacterial infection	4 Leftover egg white can be stored in an airtight container in the fridge
5 Eggs should be heavy for their size	5 Leftover egg yolk can be stored in water in the fridge
6 Free range and organic eggs are widely available	

Effects of heat/cooking on eggs

- Protein coagulates and sets between 65°C and 70°C.
- Bacteria such as salmonella are destroyed.
- Loss of B group vitamins.
- Egg white becomes opaque.
- At very high temperatures the egg could curdle.
- A green ring due to iron sulphide can be found around the egg yolk when overcooked.
- If overcooked the egg yolk becomes crumbly and the egg white rubbery.

Culinary uses of eggs

- As a whole food, e.g. as a cooked or poached egg, on its own.
- As part of a dish, e.g. in quiche, providing nourishment.

- **Binding**: Holding ingredients together, e.g. in burgers.
- **Glazing**: Giving a shine to carbohydrate-based foods, e.g. scones and pastry.
- **Coating**, e.g. fish and cheese.
- **Thickening**: Used for thickening quiche.
- **Emulsifying**: Contains the natural emulsifier lecithin, e.g. mayonnaise.
- **Aerating**: Used for meringues.
- **Clarifying**: Used for stock and jellies.
- **Garnish**: Used, e.g. for salad and kedgeree.

Table 3.21 Properties of eggs		
Property	Effects	Application in cooking
Coagulation	• Egg white sets at 60°C on cooking • Egg yolk sets at 65°C • Protein is denatured • Overcooking causes curdling	• Frying, boiling, poaching, binding, coating, glazing
Aeration/foaming	• Whisking of egg white/whole eggs entraps air • Friction created by whisking produces heat which temporarily sets the foam (slightly coagulates the albumin) • Further cooking permanently sets the foam	• Aerating cakes such as sponge cakes • Aerated egg whites are used for soufflés and meringues
Emulsifier	• Contains natural emulsifier lecithin • Enables two immiscible liquids to join together	• Blends fat and sugar in cakes • Blends oil and vinegar in mayonnaise

Protein alternatives (novel proteins)

The main sources of novel protein foods are:
- Plant foods, e.g. soya beans, grass, wheat, cotton seed
- Micro-organisms, e.g. fungi, yeast and bacteria

Protein alternatives from plant sources

Table 3.22 Nutritional value of soya beans	
Protein	• High biological value (74%)
Fat	• Cholesterol free • Low in saturated fats • High in the polyunsaturated fatty acid linoleic acid
Carbohydrate	• Contains starch and fibre
Vitamins	• B group vitamins
Minerals	• Non-haem iron • Calcium
Water	• Small quantity

Soya foods include tofu, tempeh, TVP, miso, soya sauce, soya oil, soya margarine, soya milk, soya margarine and soya yoghurt.

Textured vegetable protein (TVP)
- The oil is extracted from the soya bean.
- It is ground into flour and water is added.
- The mixture is spun and the carbohydrate is removed.
- The remaining protein is mixed with oil, flavouring and additives.
- It is dehydrated and made into chunks and granules.
- It is then fortified with vitamin B_{12} (cobalamin), weighed and packed.

Exam Hints

TVP is one of the food profiles you need to learn for the exam.

Table 3.23 Advantages and disadvantages of TVP		
Advantages	• Cheap nutritious alternative to meat • Long shelflife before reconstitution • Low in saturated fat • High in polyunsaturated fat • Little waste	• Ideal for vegetarians and vegans • Provides dietary fibre • No shrinkage during cooking • Can be used in a wide variety of dishes
Disadvantages	• Inferior in taste and texture to meat • Can be bland and needs extra flavouring when cooking	

Protein alternatives from micro-organisms
Mycoprotein
- Mycoprotein is made from the continuous fermentation of the fungus *Fusarium graminaurum*.
- Flavouring and colourings are added.
- The mixture is textured to resemble meat.
- It can be sliced, diced or shredded.
- It is used to make mycoprotein such as Quorn.
- It is used in curries, pies and casseroles or, as chunks, it can be grilled or fried.

Table 3.24 Nutritional value of mycoprotein	
Protein	High biological value protein but low in methionine
Fat	Low in saturated fat Cholesterol free
Carbohydrate	Excellent source of fibre
Vitamins	B group
Minerals	Iron, zinc
Water	Low water content

Cereals

The cereals available are wheat, barley, rye, oats, rice and maize.

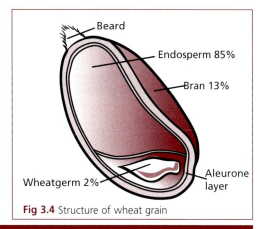

Fig 3.4 Structure of wheat grain

Wheat

Structure of the wheat grain:
- Bran (13%)
- Endosperm (85%)
- Germ (2%)

Table 3.25 Structure of the wheat grain

Part	Description	Nutrient content
1 Bran (13%)	• Tough outer fibrous skin • Contains layers of cellulose which are indigestible for humans	• Fibre
2 Endosperm (85%)	• Forms the largest part of the grain • Contains the starch reserve for the germ	• Protein (gluten) • B group vitamins • Starch • Aleurone layer is high in protein
3 Germ (2%)	• The seed of the grain which is found at its base	• Rich in protein • B group vitamins, vitamin E and any fat

Table 3.26 Nutritional value of the wheat grain

Protein	LBV, lysine, threonine, gluten
Fat	Polyunsaturated fat found in germ
Carbohydrate	High in starch and cellulose prior to processing
Vitamins	Thiamine and niacin, vitamin E
Minerals	Calcium, iron, phosphorus
Water	13%

Dietetic value

- Cereals provide energy and fibre for all age groups.
- Due to the high gluten content, cereals – especially wheat, oats, rye and barley – should be avoided by coeliacs.
- Cereals provide the staple foods in many countries, e.g. India.
- Cereals are economical, versatile and nutritious.
- Highly processed cereals should be avoided due to the loss of nutrients and the addition of sugar.

- Phytic acid in cereals can inhibit the absorption of calcium and iron.
- The lack of the essential amino acid tryptophan in maize can result in pellagra.
- The lack of thiamine in polished rice can lead to beriberi if rice is the staple food.

Table 3.27 Milling wheat	
Screening	Grain is sieved to remove any particles or metal
Sorting	Grain is sorted
Scrubbing	Grain is scoured to remove the beard on the outer layer
Washing	Dirt is removed
Conditioning	The moisture content of the wheat grain is adjusted to make rolling easier
Break rolling	Pairs of grooved rollers are used to separate the bran and the endosperm. This produces wholemeal flour
Sieving	Germ and bran are removed; these are sold separately
Rolling	Ensures bran and endosperm are completely removed
Smooth reduction rollers	The texture of the flour depends on how often it is passed through these rollers White flour production
Air classifying	Air is introduced to create a lighter product and to control protein quality by separating the particles
Additives	Bleaching agents, such as calcium carbonate improvers, and nutrients are added
Weighing, packaging, labelling	

Exam Hint
Milling wheat is a food profile.

Effects of heat/cooking on cereals
- Protein coagulates and sets bread and cakes.
- In moist heat, starch grains swell, burst and absorb liquids, e.g. gelatinisation.
- In dry heat, starch grains swell, burst and absorb fats or oil, e.g. pastry, popcorn.
- Fibre softens and absorbs moisture.
- Starch becomes more digestible.
- Surface starch is converted into dextrins, which browns the food (dextrinisation).
- Sugar on the surface of cakes caramelises.
- Loss of B group vitamins.

Buying and storing wheat
Buying
1 Buy in a clean, hygienic, well-ventilated shop.
2 Check use-by-date.
3 Packaging should be strong and clearly labelled.

Storing

1. Store in a cool, dry, well-ventilated area.
2. Once opened, transfer to an airtight container.
3. Wholegrain cereals have a shorter shelflife due to the fat content in the germ and can go rancid.

Table 3.28 Types of flour

Flour	Extraction rate	Characteristics	Use
1 Wholemeal flour	100%	• Brown in colour • High fibre content • Contains all of the wheat grain	• Bread • Scones
2 Stone ground flour	100%	• Rolled by stone rollers instead of metal rollers	• Bread • Scones
3 Wheatmeal/bran flour	83% Some of the bran is removed	• Brown in colour • Contains less fibre and less vitamin D	• Bread • Scones • Pastry
4 White flour (plain/cream flour)	75%	• Bran and germ are completely removed and used for other products • Endosperm remains in the flour • Loss of B group vitamins • Fortified with vitamins	• Cakes • Bread • Sauces • Pastry
5 Self-raising flour	75%	• Sodium bicarbonate and cream of tartar added as raising agents • Loss of B group vitamins • Fortified	• Cakes • Desserts
6 Strong flour		• High gluten content	• Used for yeast baking, e.g. bread
7 High-ratio flour	> 50%	• Low gluten content • Finely milled flour	• Used commercially by confectioneries
8 Gluten-free flour		• Starch is washed, which removes the gluten, and dehydrated	• Suitable for all baking products, although it lacks elasticity

Cereal products

Pasta
- Made from the semolina (endosperm) of durum wheat; high gluten content
- Mixed with water, salt, oil and eggs
- Available fresh or dried
- Add tomato or spinach to give flavour and colour

Breakfast cereals
- Wide variety in different formats
- Can be fortified with vitamins and minerals
- Some have high fibre content while others are high in sugar or salt

Rice

- Rice usually has its bran removed. This type of rice is called polished rice.
- It is low in nutritional value but very versatile and economical.
- The type of rice depends on:
  – The size and shape of the rice grain
  – Its region of origin
  – The degree of processing

Table 3.29 Types of rice		
	Type of rice	**Uses**
Size and shape of grain	• Short grain: plump and short • Medium grain: longer • Long grain: narrow and long	• Rice pudding • Risotto • Savoury dishes
Region of origin	• Basmati and Patna rice from India: long grain • From Carolina in North America: medium grain • Arborio rice from Northern Italy: short grain	• Accompaniment to dishes such as curry • Sweet and savoury dishes • Risotto
Degree of processing	• Brown rice: has only outer husk removed • Takes longer to cook	
	• White rice: polished (bran is removed) • Can be long, short or medium grain	
	• Pre-cooked/instant rice • Long-grain rice is cooked and dehydrated • Shorter cooking time	

- Other rice products are:
  - Rice flour: Used in shortbread
  - Wild rice: Seeds of an aquatic plant related to rice
  - Rice paper and rice cakes: Edible rice products

Oats, maize, barley and rye

Table 3.30 Other cereals		
Cereal	Characteristics	Uses
Oats	High in protein, fat and fibre	Oatmeal and rolled oats, e.g. porridge
Maize	Inferior to wheat	Corn, sweetcorn, cornflakes
Barley	Protein B group vitamins Starch	Vinegar, animal feed, brewing, soups, stews
Rye	Similar to wheat but darker Some protein and B group vitamins	Rye bread, rye biscuits

Vegetables

Table 3.31 Classification of vegetables	
Fruit	Tomato, cucumber
Seeds	French beans, runner beans
Flower	Cauliflower, broccoli
Leaves	Cabbages, spinach, kale
Stems	Asparagus, celery
Fungi	Mushroom, truffles
Tubers	Potatoes, sweet potatoes
Bulbs	Leeks, onions, shallots
Roots	Beetroot, carrots, turnips

Table 3.32 Nutritional value of vegetables	
Protein	• LBV except soya bean (HBV)
Fats	• No saturated fat • Small amount of polyunsaturated fat in olives and avocado
Carbohydrate	• Starch – high • Sugar, e.g. carrots contain small amount, high fibre, e.g. outer skins and flesh
Vitamins	• Water-soluble vitamins C and B • Fat-soluble vitamin A (beta-carotene)
Minerals	Calcium, iron, sodium
Water	High water content (70–95%)

Dietetic value of vegetables
- Vegetables are an excellent source of vitamins, minerals, fibre and water.
- Essential in the diet of all age groups.
- Provides antioxidants through vitamins A, C, E.
- Virtually fat free and therefore ideal for low calorie or low cholesterol diets.
- Cooking method can affect the fat and calorie content of the vegetable, e.g. chips, roast potatoes.
- Versatile: Can be eaten raw or cooked in a variety of ways.

- Economical and widely available.
- Should be served with foods high in vitamin D and B_{12}.
- Pulses provide essential protein for vegans.

Buying and storing vegetables
Buying
1. Buy only fresh vegetables. If vegetables are old they lose vitamin C and their flavour, colour and texture deteriorates.
2. Buy loose or netted vegetables to allow air circulation and prevent mould growth.
3. Buy in usable quantities.
4. It is more economical to buy vegetables in season.
5. Check use-by-date.

Storing
1. Remove plastic immediately.
2. Store in a cool, dry, well-ventilated area.
3. Store potatoes in a dark, dry, well-ventilated area.
4. Salad ingredients should be stored in the vegetable drawer of the refrigerator.
5. Use as soon as possible after purchase to retain vitamins.
6. Use gone off vegetables for compost bin.

Preparation
- Prepare just before use as this reduces loss of vitamin C.
- Remove dirt or damaged leaves.
- Avoid steeping in water.
- Always use a sharp knife when cutting vegetables.
- Wash to remove dirt and insects before cooking.

Cooking
- Cook in the minimum amount of water for the minimum amount of time.
- Place vegetables in boiling water.
- Avoid using copper saucepans.
- Keep the saucepan lid on.
- Cook vegetables *al dente* – with a bite.
- Do not overcook: Loss of vitamin C.
- Do not use bread soda as it destroys vitamin C.
- Use leftover cooking liquid for stock and sauces.
- Cooking methods: Boiling, steaming, baking, stir-frying, microwave, pressure cooker, grilling, barbecuing.

Effect of heat/cooking on vegetables and fruit
1 They become more digestible.
2 Micro-organisms are destroyed.
3 Colour, flavour, texture is altered.
4 Loss of water-soluble vitamins C and B group.
5 Loss of strong flavour of some vegetables.

Grading vegetables and fruit
Under EU regulations all vegetables and fruit sold in Ireland must be graded and labelled.
Grading system used:
Extra Class   Excellent quality, free of any defects
Class 1   Good quality, no bruising
Class 2   Reasonable quality, some minor defects in size and colour
Class 3   Marketable quality but may have blemishes in shape and colour

Table 3.33 Processing vegetables and fruit

Process	Vegetables	Fruit	Method	Effect
Freezing	• Most vegetables	• Raspberries • Apple • Strawberries	• Blanched first, blast frozen at −30°C to produce small ice crystals which result in less damage to the structure of the vegetable • Open freezing	• Some mineral and vitamin loss • Some change in texture • Micro-organisms are inactivated
Canning	• Carrots • Peas • Tomatoes	• Grapefruit • Strawberries • Pears	• High temperatures, sealed in containers	• Loss of water-soluble vitamins B and C • Change in colour, texture and flavour • Micro-organisms are destroyed • Sugar content can be increased if canned in syrup (sugar and water).
Dehydration (Drying)	• Beans • Lentils • Peas	• Currants • Raisins • Sultanas	• High temperature, moisture content is removed, prevents growth of micro-organisms	• Loss of B group vitamins and vitamins A and E • Dried fruit can be high in sugar

Irradiation
- Ionising radiation is used to preserve the food.
- Very strict controls in EU only.
- Herbs and spices are permitted and food must be labelled to inform the consumer.

Fruit

Fruit can be classified according to physical appearance.

Table 3.34 Classification of fruit

Berry	Strawberry, cranberry, gooseberry
Citrus	Lemon, lime, orange
Hard	Apple, pear
Stone	Apricot, peach, plum
Dried	Raisin, sultana, dates
Other	Melon, banana, pineapple, grapes

Table 3.35 Nutritional value of fruit

Nutrient	%	Information
Protein	0.5%	Low biological value
Fat	0%	Except for avocados which contain polyunsaturated fat
Carbohydrate	5–10%	Sugar, starch, fibre/cellulose
Vitamins		Raw: vitamins C and A (beta-carotene) in apricots/peaches
Minerals		Small amount of calcium, iron
Water	80–90%	Large quantity of water

Dietetic value of fruit
1. Fruit provides vitamin C which is needed for iron absorption.
2. Contains no fat so ideal for low calorie and low cholesterol diets.
3. Economical and versatile, can be used in a wide variety of sweet and savoury dishes.
4. Provides fibre.
5. Provides colour, flavour and texture to all dishes.
6. Can be eaten raw or cooked.
7. Diabetics need to be aware of sugar content of some fruits.

Buying and storing fruit

Buying
1. Buy in season.
2. Buy in clean hygienic shop.
3. Medium-sized fruit taste the best.
4. Buy loose or netted fruit.
5. Avoid fruit with discolouration.
6. Buy in useable quantities.
7. Check use-by-date.

Storing
1. Remove from wrapping immediately.
2. Allow air circulation to prevent mould growth.
3. Use quickly.
4. Remove damaged fruit.

CHAPTER 3

Preparing fruit
- Wash before use.
- Avoid peeling or steeping.

Effect of heat/cooking on fruit, see Vegetables page 73.

Culinary uses of fruit
- Raw
- As a drink, e.g. in smoothies, milkshakes, juice
- Snacks and in lunches
- Garnish and decoration
- Desserts
- Jams and jellies

Milk and dairy products

Milk
Milk usually comes from the dairy cow or goat; however, milk can be obtained from buffaloes, mares, sheep, camels and soya beans. Milk is used to manufacture butter, cheese, yoghurt and cream.

Table 3.36 Nutritional value of whole milk		
Nutrient	**Percentage**	**Information**
Protein	3.5%	• High biological value protein • It contains caseinogen, lactoalbumin and lactoglobulin
Fat	4%	• Saturated fat in the form of a fine emulsion makes it easier for digestion
Carbohydrate	4.5%	• Contains milk sugar lactose which is a disaccharide
Vitamins		• Fat-soluble vitamins A and some D; more in summer time • Water-soluble vitamins B_1 (thiamine), B_2 (riboflavin), niacin • Small amount of vitamin C lost during heat treatment
Minerals		• Calcium and small amount of phosphorus, potassium, iodine • Lacks iron
Minerals	87%	• High water content

Dietetic value of milk
- Easy to digest; ideal for babies, children and elderly.
- A complete food as it contains all the nutrients.
- Serve with carbohydrates, vitamin C and iron-rich foods for a balanced meal.
- Low fat or skimmed milk is ideal for those on a low calorie or low cholesterol diet.
- Economical food.
- Versatile; used in both sweet and savoury dishes, e.g. quiche.

Effects of heat/cooking on milk
- Protein coagulates and forms a skin on top of the milk.
- Milk curdles when mixed with acid ingredients such as lemon juice.
- Bacteria are destroyed.
- Flavour and colour change; the milk becomes sweeter due to the caramelisation of the lactose.
- Some loss of B group vitamins.
- Loss of vitamin C.

Buying and storing milk
Buying
1. Buy from clean hygienic premises.
2. Check use-before-date.

Storing
1. Store in a refrigerator.
2. Store at a temperature of 2–4°C; adjust according to season.
3. Use milk in rotation – first in, first out (FIFO).
4. Do not mix old and new milk.
5. Keep milk covered at all times.
6. Keep away from strong-smelling foods.
7. Keep milk in original sterile container/carton.

Processing milk
- Kills bacteria.
- Improves shelflife.
- Increases nutritive value.
- Makes milk more digestible.

> **Exam Hints**
> Milk is one of the food profiles suggested for the Leaving Certificate exam.

Table 3.37 Methods of processing milk

Method	Temperature/Time	Procedure	Effect
Homogenisation	60°C	• Milk is heated and forced through tiny holes under pressure (like a shower head) • The fat globules break down to one size and are dispersed	• Smoother milk • No nutrient loss
Pasteurisation	72°C for 15 seconds High temperature short time method (HTST)	• Cooled to 10°C and bottled	• Bacteria are destroyed, 10% loss of vitamin B_1 (thiamine) • Loss of vitamin C • Stay fresh for longer
Sterilisation	110°C for 20–40 minutes	• Milk is homogenised and placed in sealed bottles which are then heated to 110°C • Bottles are then cooled	• Pathogenic bacteria are destroyed • Loss of B_1, folic acid and vitamin C • Sweeter taste • Creamier appearance • Keeps for several weeks unopened
Ultraheat treatment (UHT)	132°C for 1 second	• Milk is homogenised, then heated • Packed in aseptic conditions	• Pathogenic bacteria are destroyed • Little change in colour or flavour • Loss of B group vitamins and vitamin C • Keeps for up to 6 months unrefrigerated
Dehydration	• Milk is first homogenised, pasteurised and heat treated • One of two methods is used: spray drying or roller drying	**Spray drying** • Milk is lightly sprayed into a hot air chamber • The water droplets evaporate from the milk and produce a fine uniform powder • Cooled and packaged in air-tight container **Roller drying** • The milk is poured onto heated revolving drums • On contact, the milk dries and sticks to the roller • A knife scrapes off the dried milk • Cooled and packed in airtight containers	• Loss of B group vitamins and vitamin C • Bacteria are killed • More expensive method but produces a better product • Reconstitutes easily • Uniform shape • Has a cooked taste • Loss of B group vitamins and vitamin C • Lumpy in shape • Does not mix well with water

Table 3.37 Methods of processing milk (cont.)			
Method	**Temperature/Time**	**Procedure**	**Effect**
Condensed	Homogenised and heated	• 15% sugar is added • Evaporated and reduced to one-third of its original volume • Cooled and sealed in cans	• Flavour and colour change • Nutrient content is changed (increase in sugar and loss of vitamins) • Bacteria are destroyed • Long shelflife • Sugar acts as a preservative
Evaporation	115°C for 20 minutes	• Homogenised and pasteurised • Placed in sealed cans and heat treated	• Loss of nutrients • Flavour and colour changes • Bacteria are destroyed • Long shelflife

Cheese

Table 3.38 Classification of cheese		
Hard	**Semi-Hard**	**Soft**
Parmesan	Port Salut	Mozzarella
Cheddar	Edam	Camembert

Table 3.39 Other cheeses	
Cottage	• Made from milk after cream has been separated • Low fat and often flavoured with herbs • Contains less than half the fat of original cheese
Processed	• Products made from cheese such as Cheddar Easy Singles
Cream	• Made from cream • Soft in texture
Vegetarian	• Made with non-animal rennet
Farmhouse	• Produced on a small domestic scale rather than in a factory

Production of Cheddar cheese

Most cheese production follows the basic procedure shown below with slight variations for each type.

- *Pasteurised* milk.
- A *started culture* such as *lactic acid* is added.
- This converts the *lactose to lactic acid* which acts as a preservative and adds flavour.
- The milk is heated to *30°C and rennet* is added.

Exam Hints

Production of Cheddar cheese is another food profile which is needed for your Leaving Certificate exam.

- Rennet contains the *enzyme rennin* which changes *caseinogens to casein*.
- The mixture is allowed to set for 40 minutes when it starts to *separate into curds* (solid) and *whey* (liquid).
- The *curd is cut* and the *whey is drained* off (the process for cottage cheese is complete here).
- *Scalding* involves the heating of the curd to 40°C.
- Curds are allowed to settle and are further *cut into blocks* and placed on top of each other.
- The curd is cut again and *2 per cent salt* can be added here.
- The *curds are pressed into moulds*. The longer the pressing the harder the cheese as the liquid is squeezed out.
- Finally, the *curds are sprayed with hot water* to form a skin for protection.
- The cheese is stored at *5–10°C*.
- The cheese is *wrapped* in polythene bags and left *to mature* for a number of months.
- The longer the maturing stage, the stronger the flavour of cheese.
- The cheese is *graded as* mild, medium or mature.
- It is cut into *retail size, packaged* and *labelled*.

The nutritional value varies depending on the type of Cheddar.

	Table 3.40 Nutritional value of Cheddar
Protein	• High biological value • Casein
Fat	• Saturated • Major source of energy
Carbohydrate	• Very little, in the form of lactose
Vitamins	• Fat-soluble vitamins A and D • Water-soluble vitamins B_2 (riboflavin), lack of vitamin C
Minerals	• High in calcium, very little iron
Water	• Between 37% and 79%, depending on the cheese

Dietetic value of cheese

1. Versatile and easy to use.
2. No cooking required.
3. High in saturated fat; should be restricted in low calorie and low cholesterol diets.
4. Economical with no waste.
5. Cottage cheese is a good alternative for low calorie diets.
6. Ideal for snacks and packed lunches.
7. Provides calcium for growth and bone formation, especially in babies, children, adolescents and pregnant women.
8. Pregnant women should avoid soft cheeses due to the risk of food poisoning from listeria.

Buying and storing cheese

Buying
1. Buy from a clean hygienic shop.
2. Check use-by-date of packed cheeses.

Storing
1. Fresh cut cheese should be refrigerated and used within 2 to 3 days.
2. Remove soft cheese from its wrapping and place in a polythene container in a fridge.
3. Wrap other cheese well to prevent drying out.
4. Serve at room temperature.

Effects of heat/cooking on cheese
- Protein coagulates and shrinks if overcooked.
- Becomes indigestible.
- No loss of any nutrients.
- Change of colour to brown.
- Carbonises if overcooked.

Yoghurt

Classification of yoghurt
- Set yoghurt
- Stirred yoghurt
- Drink yoghurt
- Frozen yoghurt

Table 3.41 Culinary uses of cheese	
Sauces	Cauliflower cheese, macaroni cheese
Salads	Diced, sliced or grated
Fillings	Baked potatoes, toasted sandwiches
Toppings	Pizza, lasagne
Desserts	Cheesecake, tiramisu
Baking	Cheese pastry, scones
Flans	Quiche Lorraine
Fondues	Cheese fondue
Sandwiches and snacks	On its own

Manufacture of stirred yoghurt
1. Milk is *homogenised* and *pasteurised* for 15–30 minutes at 85–95°C.
2. The milk is *inoculated* with the starter bacteria *Lactobacillus bulgaricus* and *Streptococcus thermophilus*.
3. The starter bacteria *ferment the lactose to lactic acid*.
4. The mixture is *incubated* at 37°C for 3–6 hours.
5. During this time the mixture *thickens* due to the coagulation of the protein and its distinct flavour develops.
6. The yoghurt is cooled *to 4.5°C*.
7. The *following additives are used*: Colouring, stabilisers, thickeners, preservatives, flavours (fruit) and sweeteners (sucrose).
8. The yoghurt is *packaged and labelled* and stored in a refrigerator.

> **Exam Hints**
> This is another food profile for the Leaving Certificate exam.

Table 3.42 Nutritional value of yoghurt	
Protein	High biological value (5%)
Fat	0.3–3.5% depending on type of yoghurt
Carbohydrate	Lactose (6%)
Vitamins	Water-soluble vitamins B_1 (thiamine), B_2 (riboflavin), niacin Small amount of fat-soluble vitamins A and D
Minerals	Calcium and small amount of potassium and phosphorus
Water	85–88%

Dietetic value of yoghurt

1. Good source of calcium and protein which is needed for growth in babies, children, adolescents and for pregnant or lactating mothers.
2. Low fat varieties make it suitable for those on a low calorie or low cholesterol diet.
3. Economical and versatile.
4. Easily digested; ideal for babies and convalescents.
5. Ideal for snacks or packed lunches.
6. Can be used as an alternative to cream in baking.
7. Addition of bacterial cultures such as acidophilus can aid digestion.

Buying

1. Buy from a clean, hygienic shop.
2. Check that it is stored in a chilled cabinet.
3. Check use-by-date.
4. Do not buy it if the centre of the lid is dome-shaped.

Storing

1. Store in refrigerator as soon as possible.
2. Do not eat after use-by-date.

Table 3.43 Culinary uses of yoghurt	
As a drink	In smoothies
Toppings	Moussaka, baked potatoes
Desserts	Cheesecake or with fruit
Salads	Dressing or dip
Garnish	In soups
As a cream alternative	
On its own	
With breakfast cereals	

Fats and oils (lipids)

Table 3.44 Classification of lipids

Animal fats	Saturated fat	Cream, suet, lard, butter, cheese, dripping
Plant oils	Polyunsaturated fat	Vegetables, nuts, seeds
Fish oils	Polyunsaturated fat	Cod liver oil, oily fish, e.g. tuna, herrings, sardines

Table 3.45 Nutritional value of fats and oils

Protein	Contain less than 1%
Fat	Fat content varies depending on the type of fat or oil, e.g. suet has 99% fat, while low fat spread has 40%
Carbohydrate	Only trace amounts in suet
Vitamins	Fat-soluble vitamins A and D Water-soluble vitamins: trace of B group vitamins, no vitamin C
Minerals	Low in calcium
Water	Depending on fat content
Energy (per 100g)	Butter 737kcal Low fat spread 365kcal

Dietetic value of lipids

1. Dietetic value depends on the type of oil/fat.
2. Everyone, but especially those on low calorie or low cholesterol diets, should reduce saturated fats.
3. Vegetable and fish oils provide polyunsaturated fats which are important in low cholesterol diets.
4. Fat provides heat and energy.
5. It provides fat-soluble vitamins A, D, E, K and essential fatty acids in the diet.

Vegetable oils

Processing of vegetable oil

- Vegetables oils are made from a variety of nuts, seeds and vegetables.
- The nuts/seeds/vegetables are washed, crushed and heated.
- The oil is extracted.
- A refining process removes any impurities from the fat. Impurities include free fatty acids.
- The oil is bleached with fuller's earth (bleaching earth that deodorises and clarifies).
- The mixture is filtered to produce a colourless liquid.

Exam Hints

The processing of oil and margarine manufacture are referred to as food profiles for the Leaving Certificate exam.

- Volatile odours are removed with deodorisers.
- The oil is filtered again and packaged.

Manufacture of margarine
1. Margarine is prepared using the *hydrogenation process*.
2. Oils and fats of vegetable, fish and animal origin are refined.
3. The oils are *hydrogenated* which creates *stability*.
4. *Hydrogen is added to the oil* and *nickel is used as a catalyst* which speeds up the reaction.
5. The oils are *refined again*.
6. *Other ingredients* such as skimmed milk, water, whey, salt, colouring, vitamins A and D and emulsifiers are added.
7. During *emulsification, liquids and fats* are mixed together in a votator which prevents the mixture from separating.
8. Mixing continues until the *desired consistency* is reached.
9. The margarine is *chilled and packed*.

Types of margarine
- Block margarine
- Soft margarine
- Low fat spread
- Functional dairy spreads

Culinary uses of fats and oils
- Add to the *flavour* of food, e.g. in baking or in salad dressing.
- Prevent cakes and biscuits from drying out and *improve the shelflife* of food.
- *Creaming*: Incorporates air into the fat, e.g. in cakes, which allows the product to rise.
- *Shortening agent*: Gives a crumbly texture to pastry and biscuits.
- *Form an emulsion* with water, e.g. in mayonnaise.
- Used for shallow or deep frying due to high temperatures reached.

Storage of fats
- Store oils in a cool dark place.
- Keep dairy spreads/margarine in a refrigerator.
- Keep away from strong smelling foods.
- Fats and oils go rancid when exposed to air.
- Check use-by-date.

Exam Hints
This whole section can appear as a Section A, short question, or Section B, question 1 or 2, combined with nutrients, food preservation and special dietary needs. Make sure that you know the link-up between all of these sections.

Questions

1. (a) List two career opportunities in the food industry. (2)
   (b) State two ways that the Food Safety Authority of Ireland (FSAI) supports the work of the food industry. (4)
   (2005, HL, Section A, 7)

2. Name three cereals grown for food production and give one example of a different product manufactured from each cereal. (6)
   (2008, HL, Section A, 5)

3. Discuss (a) the nutritional significance and (b) the contribution to the diet of fruit and vegetables. (20)
   (2008, HL, Section B, 2)

4. Classify fish and give one example of each class. (6)
   (2005, OL, Section A, 7)

5. Explain two factors that contribute to the spoilage of fish. (6)
   (2006, HL, Section A, 4)

6. (a) Name four nutrients found in eggs. (4)
   (b) List two effects of heat on eggs. (2)
   (2006, OL, Section A, 5)

7. State three uses of eggs in food preparation and give an example of each. (6)
   (2004, OL, Section A, 8)

8. Profile a food of your choice that has been processed to extend the shelflife. Refer to
   (a) Stages of production
   (b) Packaging
   (c) Labelling. (26)
   (2005, HL Section B, 2b)

9. Name the three main nutrients found in the endosperm of the wheat grain. (3)
   (2004, HL Section A, 4a)

10. (a) Classify vegetables and give one example of each class. (12)
    (b) Discuss four reasons why it is important to include an adequate amount of fruit and vegetables in the diet. (16)
    (2004, OL, Section B, 2)

11. Identify and explain two EU grading classes used for fruit and vegetables. (4)
    (2006, HL, Section A, 5a)

12. Name three classes of cheese and give one example of each class. (6)
    (2006, OL, Section A, 8)

13. Give details of the stages involved in the manufacture of yoghurt. (20)
    (2006, HL, Section B, 2)

Key Points

The Irish Food Industry
- Food Agencies: The Department of Agriculture and Food; Bord Bia; Bord Iascaigh Mhara (BIM); Department of Communications, Marine and Natural Resources; Teagasc; Enterprise Ireland; Food Safety Authority of Ireland
- The different food sectors: Dairy and ingredients; beef; lamb; pig meat; poultry; edible horticulture; mariculture; beverages; prepared consumer foods
- The role of small industries and home industries: Provide employment and high quality products
- Career opportunities within the Irish food Industry: Farm management; teaching; microbiology; hotel management; dietetics; catering

Meat
- Nutritional value: Protein high; fat varies; vitamins A, B_1, B_2, B_{12}; iron
- Dietetic value: HBV protein; contribute to CHD; serve with food rich in vitamin C; calcium, iron
- Toughness of meat: Age, activity, treatment before and after slaughter, method of cooking
- Tenderising meat: Proteolytic enzymes, mechanically, marinating, moist method of cooking
- Effects of cooking: Protein coagulates, fat melts, bacteria destroyed, flavour improves
- Processing meat: Freezing, vacuum packing, canning, dehydration, curing

Fish
- Classification: Habitat, shape, nutritive value
- Nutritional value: HBV protein; low in fat; vitamins B, C (oysters), A and D (oily); iodine, phosphorus, calcium, iron
- Dietetic value: HBV protein; low fat; reduce CHD; low in calories; source of omega-3
- Spoilage of fish: Oxidative rancidity, enzyme action, bacteria
- Processing: Freezing, canning, smoking, fish products

Eggs
- Nutritional value: Protein 100%; saturated fat in yolk; HBV; vitamins B_2, B_{12}, A, D, E; iron, phosphorus, zinc, selenium
- Dietetic value: HBV protein; high cholesterol; good source of vitamins and minerals
- Grading and labelling: Weight and quantity, quality assurance mark, week number
- Properties: Coagulation, aeration and emulsifier

Protein Alternatives (novel proteins)
- Sources: Plant foods, e.g. soya bean; micro-organisms, e.g. fungi
- Nutritional value of soya bean: HBV protein; low in fat; cholesterol free; starch and fibre; B group vitamins; non-haem iron, calcium
- Mycoprotein: Fermentation of fungus, flavourings and colourings added, textured; Quorn
- Nutritional value of mycoprotein: HBV protein; low fat; fibre; B group vitamins; iron, zinc

Key Points

Cereals
- Structure of wheat grain: Bran, endosperm, germ
- Nutritional value: LBV protein; fat small PUFA; carbohydrate; thiamine, niacin and vitamin E; calcium, iron, phosphorus
- Dietetic value: Provide energy and fibre, staple food

Vegetables
- Classification: Fruit, seeds, flower, leaves, stems, fungi, tubers, bulbs, roots
- Nutritional value: LBV protein; low fat; carbohydrate; fibre; vitamins C, B, A; calcium, iron, sodium
- Dietetic value: Good source of vitamins, minerals, fibre, water; antioxidants A, C, E; fat free
- Processing of fruit and vegetables: Freezing, canning, dehydration

Fruit
- Classification: Berry, citrus, hard, stone, dried
- Nutritional value: LBV protein; low fat; carbohydrates; vitamins C, A; calcium, iron
- Dietetic value: High vitamin C; no fat; high fibre; diabetics need to be aware of sugar content
- Culinary uses: Raw, drink, snack, garnish, desserts, jams and jellies

Milk and Dairy Products
- Nutritional value: HBV protein; saturated fat; carbohydrates; vitamins A, D, B_1, B_2; calcium phosphorus, potassium, iodine
- Dietetic value: Easy to digest; complete food; serve with vitamin C and iron-rich food
- Processing milk: Kills bacteria, increases shelflife and nutritive value, more digestible
- Types of processing: Homogenisation, pasteurisation, sterilisation, UHT, dehydration, condensed, evaporated

Cheese
- Classification: Hard, semi-hard, soft
- Other: Cottage, processed, cream, vegetarian, farmhouse
- Nutritional value of Cheddar cheese: HBV protein; saturated fat; vitamins A, D, B_2; calcium
- Dietetic value: Versatile, no cooking, restrict in low cholesterol diets, snacks
- Effects of cooking: Protein coagulates, indigestible, no nutrient loss, colour change

Yoghurt
- Classification: Set, stirred, drink, frozen
- Nutritional value: HBV protein; fat depends on type of yoghurt; lactose; vitamins B_1, B_2, niacin, A, D; calcium
- Dietetic value: Good source of calcium and protein; low fat varieties, easily digested, snacks
- Buying and storing: Clean hygienic shop, chilled cabinet, use-by-date, refrigerate
- Culinary uses: Drink, on own, desserts, salads, garnish, cream alternative, toppings

CHAPTER 3

Key Points

Fats and Oils
- Classification: Animal, plant, fish oils
- Nutritional value: Low protein; high fat, trace carbohydrates; vitamins A, D, trace B
- Dietetic value: Use vegetable or fish oils, fat-soluble vitamins A, D, E, K, essential fatty acids
- Types of margarine: Block, soft, low fat, functional dairy spreads
- Culinary uses: Add flavour; improve shelflife; creaming and shortening agent; form emulsion; used for cooking
- Storage: Cool dark place, refrigerate, avoid strong smelling foods, use-by-date

Your revision notes

4: Food Preparation and Cooking Processes

●●● Learning Objectives

In this chapter you will learn about:
1. Meal Planning and Management
2. Soups and Sauces
3. Pastry
4. Raising Agents
5. Selection, Safe Use and Care of Food Preparation Equipment
6. Aesthetic Awareness in Food Choice, Preparation and Presentation
7. Sensory Analysis
8. Recipe Modification

Meal Planning and Management

When planning a meal the following factors need to be considered in order to achieve a healthy balanced meal suitable for all who are eating it.

Table 4.1 Planning meals	
1 Current healthy eating guidelines	• Current healthy eating guidelines should influence the content of the meal • The meal should be low in fat, salt and sugar while high in fibre, polyunsaturated fats and water • Provide a balanced meal with the correct proportions of nutrients
2 Specific dietary requirements	• Depending on who the meal is prepared for a number of modifications may need to be made, e.g. coeliac – no gluten • The dietary requirements of a young child varies greatly from that of an elderly person
3 Knowledge and skills of cook	• The ability of the cook influences the type of meal planned
4 Resources available	• Money has a direct impact on the type of food eaten, e.g. lobster is expensive if a tight budget needs to be adhered to • Shopping in vegetable/food markets may provide better quality food at a cheaper price • The time available to prepare, cook and serve the food varies • Available food preparation equipment such as a food processor saves time when preparing a meal

Table 4.1 Planning meals (cont.)	
5 Choice of foods	• Food in season is cheaper and tastes better
6 Number of people eating	• The number of people eating influences the cost, the choice and complexity of the dish
7 Occasion	• If the meal is for a special occasion, e.g. a birthday or Christmas, more time, money and effort may be put into preparing the meal
8 Aesthetics of food	• The colour, flavour and texture of a meal make it more appealing, especially if effort is made in its presentation

Physical and chemical changes to food during preparation and cooking

Why do we cook food?
1 To improve the colour, flavour and texture of food.
2 To destroy any micro-organisms present.
3 To make the food more digestible.
4 To destroy enzymes.
5 To make the food more appetising.
6 To preserve food.
7 To add variety to our diet by combining different ingredients.

Table 4.2 Changes during food preparation	
Chemical changes	**Physical changes**
1 **Enzymic browning** Takes place when food is cut or damaged. The cells release an enzyme which reacts with the oxygen in the air. As a result the food changes colour, e.g. an apple turns brown and a banana black	1 **Nutrient loss** Vitamin C is an unstable vitamin and is lost if the cut food is steeped in water or exposed to air Vitamins A and B can be lost due to overexposure to light
2 **Tenderising of meat** Meat can be tenderised by using proteolytic enzymes or marinating in vinegar and flavourings	2 **Increase in size** Dried pulses and fruit absorb water when rehydrated and therefore increase in size
3 **Increase in size** In bread making the size of the dough increases due to the reactions of yeast	3 **Tenderising of meat** Meat is tenderised by using a meat hammer which breaks down the meat fibres

Table 4.3 Changes during cooking

Physical changes	Chemical changes
1 Colour change Meat turns from red to brown, pastry from pale to golden	**1 Colour change** Sugar changes its colour to brown when heated (caramelisation)
2 Meat is tenderised Collagen changes to gelatine which makes meat more digestible	**2 Increase in size** The addition of raising agents to cakes etc. causes the food to expand and set on heating
3 Destruction of enzymes and bacteria Enzymes and bacteria are destroyed or inactivated	**3 Maillard reaction (non-enzymic browning)** The reaction of certain amino acids with carbohydrates during cooking creates a tasty brown coating on food, e.g. roast potatoes
4 Loss of nutrients Vitamins C and some vitamins of the B group are lost at high temperatures	**4 Dextrinisation** During cooking long polysaccharide starch grains become shorter dextrins which change the colour of the food, e.g. toasting bread
5 Reduction in size Meat shrinks due to protein coagulation Vegetables shrink due to loss of water	
6 Texture changes Food becomes softer/crisper which can makes it more digestible	
7 Thickening and setting of food The addition of flour, roux or arrowroot thickens a sauce as the starch grains absorb the liquid (gelatinisation) Protein foods is used to set foods such as quiche due to coagulation. Gelatine is added to set desserts, e.g. cheesecake	
8 Increase in size The introduction of air to cakes, e.g. through sieving flour, increases size	

Points to Note

- Some cooking methods use more than one type of heat transfer.
- Boiling uses both conduction (heating of the saucepan) and convection (heating water and food).
- Roasting uses both conduction (heating the food molecules) and convection currents (heating the air in the oven).

Cooking methods

Food is cooked by applying and transferring heat. Heat can be transferred by:

1 Conduction
- Slow method of cooking.
- When molecules heat up they move around swiftly and pass on their heat to the next molecule until all are heated. The food being heated needs to be in direct contact with the heat source, where the saucepan or pan is on a hob, e.g. frying or boiling.

2 Convection
- Rapid transfer of heat through liquids and gases.
- As liquids or gases heat up they become less dense and rise.
- When they cool down, they lose density and fall, thereby creating convection currents.
- This movement of hot and cold gases/liquids creates an even temperature in the oven or saucepan, e.g. baking in the oven, boiling vegetables.

3 Radiation
- Very quick transfer of heat.
- Heat energy is transmitted directly from the heat source to the object without heating the space between them.
- The heat is transferred by electromagnetic waves.
- The food needs to be as close as possible to the heat rays, e.g. grilling, toasting.

Factors to consider when choosing a cooking method

- The density/thickness of the food.
- The time available (quick or slow method).
- Personal likes or dislikes (e.g. whether you like your steak rare or well done).
- The quantity/size of the food (how much has to be cooked).
- The equipment available (e.g. whether a cooker is available or only a grill).

Table 4.4 Methods of cooking

Moist methods	Dry methods	Frying
Boiling	Baking	Deep frying
Steaming	Grilling/barbecuing	Shallow frying
Stewing	Roasting	Dry frying
Poaching	Pot roasting	Stir-frying
Braising		
Pressure cooking		
Effect on food		
Loss of B group vitamins and vitamin C	Loss of B group vitamins and vitamin C	Increase in fat and calorie content
Cellulose becomes more digestible	Sugar melts and caramelises	More difficult to digest
Food is softer	Fat melts	Can be soggy due to absorption of fat
	Shrinkage of protein foods such as meat	Crispy, tasty finish
	Maillard reaction	

Table 4.5 Moist methods of cooking

Method	Principle/Application	Advantages	Disadvantages	Suitable foods
Boiling	• Combination of conduction and convection • Food is cooked in water at 100°C • Food simmers at 90°C • Cover saucepan and cook for the shortest time to retain nutrients	• Fast • Leftover liquid can be used for soups and sauces • Unlikely to burn	• Loss of flavour if overcooked • High nutrient loss	• Vegetables • Meat • Fish • Eggs • Pasta • Rice
Poaching	• Combination of conduction and convection • Food is cooked in liquid below simmering point • Food is only half covered	• Food is more digestible • Flavour can be added by using, e.g. stock or wine as poaching liquid	• Food suitable is limited • Food can be overcooked • Needs constant attention	• Fish • Eggs • Fruit
Steaming	• Food is cooked in the steam of boiling water, it does not touch the water • Steam needs to circulate around the food • Water must be boiling before food is placed in steamer	• Less nutrient loss • Economical • Food is easier to digest • Suitable for a variety of foods • Requires little attention	• Slow method • Can lack flavour • Uneconomical for puddings	• Fish • Vegetables • Chicken • Puddings, e.g. Christmas pudding
Stewing	• Combination of conduction and convection • Food is cooked in a small amount of liquid, simmering between 80°C and 90°C • Cooking liquid is served with the food • Cook in the oven or in a saucepan on the hob	• Economical • Cooks complete meal • Nutrients and flavouring • Suitable for tough cuts of meat	• Slow method • No contrast in texture • Some colour loss • If overcooked, food falls apart	• Tough cuts of meat • Fish • Chicken • Vegetables • Fruit
Braising	• Combines stewing, steaming and pot roasting • Food is cooked on a bed of fried root vegetables (mirepoix), covered in stock and basted • Cover pot with a lid	• Only small amount of nutrient loss • All food is used	• Slow method • Meat can lack colour • Brown meat before moist cooking or after cooking under the grill	• Tough cuts of meat • Chicken • Root vegetables
Pressure cooking	• Water boils at 100°C • If pressure is increased, it boils at a higher temperature • The steam inside the pressure cooker cannot escape and therefore increases the boiling temperature	• Saves time and energy • Vegetables retain more vitamins • Flavour and colour are retained • Complete meal cooked in one pot	• Moist methods of cooking only • Easy to overcook • Needs storage space • Can scald if not operated properly	• Vegetables • Stews • Jams • Bottling • Christmas puddings

Table 4.6 Dry methods (dry radiant heat) of cooking

Method	Principle/Application	Advantages	Disadvantages	Suitable foods
Baking	• Convection currents • Top shelf is the hottest shelf • Fan oven has even distribution of heat • Steam produced by food prevents it from drying out • Shortest time to retain nutrients	• A number of items can be cooked at the same time • Produces attractive flavour and colour	• Slow method	• Meat • Vegetables • Fish • Cakes
Grilling, barbecuing	• Radiation • Radiant heat from electric element or gas flame cooks the food	• Suitable for a variety of foods • Quick method • Reduces fat content • Produces appetising colour	• Food can overcook easily • Needs regular attention • Only suitable for thin pieces of food (approx. 25mm thick)	• Meat • Fish • Vegetables • Fruit • Sausages • Chicken
Roasting	• Combination of conduction and convection • Food cooks in the oven • Needs to be basted with fat regularly during cooking	• Economical • Good colour and flavour	• Requires a lot of attention • Meat can be tough/dry if overcooked	• Meat • Vegetables
Pot roasting	• Similar to roasting but on the hob • High temperature and food needs to be basted	• Convenient if you do not have an oven	• Requires a lot of attention • Burns easily	• Meat • Vegetables

Microwave cooking

Principle of microwave cooking
- Microwave ovens generate electromagnetic waves.
- The electromagnetic waves make the water molecules in the food vibrate rapidly, causing friction so that the food becomes hot and starts to cook.

Guidelines for microwave cooking
1. Follow manufacturer's instructions.
2. Time food accurately.
3. Allow standing time.

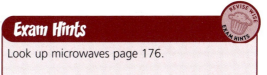

Exam Hints

Look up microwaves page 176.

4 The cooking time depends on:
- Whether the food is frozen or fresh
- The quantity (large amounts of food take longer)
- The density (less dense food cooks quicker)
- The size and shape of the food

Table 4.7 Microwave cooking	
Advantages of microwave cooking	**Disadvantages of microwave cooking**
Reduces cooking time and energy	Takes up work surface space
Reduces washing up	Unsuitable for cooking some foods, e.g. pastry
Microwave is easy to maintain and clean	Food overcooks easily
Good retention of colour and flavour	Requires special cookware
Good for defrosting	
Relatively inexpensive to buy	
Suitable for microwave cooking	**Unsuitable for microwave cooking**
Defrosting food	Baking
Reheating dishes, e.g. lasagne	Large quantities of food
Cooking vegetables	Food with high fat content
Heating milk	

Frying

- Quick method of cooking.
- Combination of conduction and convection.
- Increases calorie content of food.

Table 4.8 Frying		
Method	**Principle/Application**	**Suitable foods**
Shallow frying	• Food is fried in hot fat/oil in a shallow pan • Max. thickness of food: 25mm	• Sausages, rashers, steak, • Fish, onions, mushrooms
Deep frying	• Food is immersed in hot oil at 170–190°C • Food is often coated in batter or breadcrumbs • Thermostatically controlled electric deep fat fryer is safer than deep pan	• Potatoes and other vegetables • Fish • Cheese • Small sausages
Dry frying	• Food is fried in a non-stick pan with a sprayed-on coating of fat	• Pancakes • Rashers
Stir-frying	• Food is tossed in a small amount of oil heated in a wok • Quick healthy method of cooking	• Meat • Vegetables

Soups and Sauces

Soups

- A soup should be made from a good homemade stock.
- A stock is a well-flavoured liquid made by simmering meat, bones and vegetables in water.
- After the meat, bones and vegetables have been removed, the remaining liquid can be used as a base for soups and sauces.
- Stock can be frozen in ice cube trays for later use.
- Convenience stock cubes/powders made from meat, fish, chicken or vegetables are also available.

When to serve soup
- Starter, main part of a lunch, a snack, and refreshment in summer.

Nutritional value of soup
- The nutritional value of soup varies greatly depending on the ingredients and the consistency of the soup.

Table 4.9 Classification of soups

1 Thin soups	Characteristics	Examples
Clear soup	• Clear soup is made from a rich well-flavoured stock • It is clarified (cleared) by adding an egg white	• Consommé
Broth	• Broth is a thin unclarified soup made with pieces of meat and vegetables which are served with the soup • This soup can be thickened by adding whole cereals such as barley, rice, pasta and oats	• Chicken broth
2 Thick soups	**Characteristics**	**Examples**
Purée	• Soup is thickened by sieving or blending the ingredients after they have been cooked which gives the soup a smooth consistency	• Mushroom soup • Tomato soup
Thickened soup	• These soups are thickened with flour/cornflour • Chowders which usually include shellfish belong to this category	• Vegetable soup • Seafood chowder

Characteristics of a good soup
1. Good flavour with a dominant main ingredient (e.g. mushroom soup)
2. Good colour, texture and consistency
3. Free from grease showing on the surface
4. Well-seasoned
5. Served chilled or hot

How to thicken soups
- Soups can be thickened using a liaison (flour or cornflour or roux), beurre manié, eggs, cream or cereals, e.g. barley.
- Always allow the soup to continue cooking for at least 5 minutes after the starchy liaison has been added.

Convenience soups
- A wide variety of dehydrated, canned, frozen and cook-chill soups are available in most supermarkets.
- They are useful if time is short. However, they are expensive for the quantity bought and some contain artificial colours and flavouring.

Table 4.10 Garnishes and accompaniments for soups

Garnish	
Fresh herbs	Parsley, chives
Cream/yoghurt	A spoonful of cream/yoghurt is placed in the middle of the soup and swirled around
Grated orange/lemon rind	Used for colour on tomato, carrot and orange soup
Grated cheese (e.g. Parmesan)	Sprinkle on top of soup
Julienne strips of vegetables	Carrot, cucumber
Croutons	Fried cubes of bread added just before serving to provide texture
Crispy bacon	Bits of bacon sprinkled over soup. However, this increases the salt and calorie content of the soup.
Accompaniments	Slices of brown bread, herb bread rolls, white bread rolls, garlic bread, Melba toast

Sauces
1. A sauce is a well-flavoured liquid.
2. Sauces should not overpower the main ingredient of the dish.
3. Sauces can be served hot or cold.
4. They aid digestion.
5. Sauces add variety to the diet.

Why and how are sauces used

1 To improve flavour and colour.
2 To add nutrients.
3 To provide moisture.
4 To bind (panard) ingredients together (e.g. in rissoles).
5 As an accompaniment to a dish (e.g. cranberry sauce served with turkey).
6 As part of a dish (e.g. in stews).
7 As a coating on meat, fish and vegetables (e.g. on cauliflower).

Table 4.11 Classification of sauces

Type of sauce	Method	Examples
Simple	• Fruit or vegetables are puréed to a smooth consistency.	• Apple sauce • Cranberry sauce
Roux-based	• Equal amount of fat and flour with changing amounts of liquid • Can be made from white or brown flour	• Cheese sauce • Mushroom sauce
Egg-based	• Eggs are used to thicken sauces by coagulation or emulsification	• Mayonnaise • Hollandaise sauce
Cold sauces/dressings	• No cooking involved • Cold ingredients are combined	• Mint sauce • French dressing
Sweet	• These are often used with desserts to provide colour and flavour	• Chocolate sauce
Other sauces	• Variety of ingredients and methods • Strong international influence	• Curry sauce • Sweet and sour sauce • Tomato sauce

How to thicken a sauce

- Use a roux base, an egg yolk or reduction.

How to serve sauces

1 Most sauces are used as an accompaniment and can be served in a sauceboat.
2 Sauces can be served as part of a dish.
3 Sauces can be served under or over the food.
4 Do not cover the food completely with sauce.
5 Serve hot or cold.
6 Dessert sauces can provide a lot of variety to the presentation – feathered, dual sauce, etc.

Pastry

Basic ingredients used in pastry

- Pastry is a mixture of fat, flour and water.
- Rich pastry is made by adding eggs and sugar.
- The main difference between types of pastries is how the fat is added.

Characteristics of good pastry
1. Good pastry is fully cooked and not soggy.
2. It has a light golden colour.
3. It breaks easily when eaten.
4. It has a good crisp texture.
5. It is not greasy and the fat is dispersed evenly.

Table 4.12 Classification of pastry

Type of pastry	Use
1 Shortcrust pastry Wholemeal pastry Cheese pastry	• Apple tart, quiche, sausage rolls • Quiche, apple tart • Quiche, sausage rolls
2 Rich shortcrust/flan pastry	• Quiche, lemon meringue pie
3 Rough puff pastry	• Sausage rolls, vol-au-vents
4 Puff pastry	• Bouchées, cream cornets, sausage rolls
5 Flaky pastry	• Mince pies
6 Filo pastry	• Millefeuille, spring roll, baklava (Greek dessert)
7 Suet crust pastry	• Dumplings, steak and kidney pie
8 Choux pastry	• Eclairs, profiteroles, gougère (ring of pastry with meat/fish filling)

Guidelines for making pastry

- The main ingredients of pastry are plain flour, fat and water.
- The fat used could be butter, margarine, lard, cooking fat, oil or a mixture of fats.
- The water should be cold and just enough to bind the fat and flour together. Lemon juice can be added for flaky pastry.
- Egg can also be added.
- The raising agent is air.
- Keeping utensils, ingredients and the room cold is vital for successful pastry making.
- As a rule, shortcrust pastry uses half the amount of fat to flour, i.e. for 150g flour you need 75g fat.

Table 4.13 Preparing, cooking and serving pastry

Preparing	• Weigh all ingredients accurately • Preheat the oven to a high temperature • Chill all utensils before use • Line the tin and bake blind if necessary (see below) • Incorporate as much air as possible by sieving flour and rubbing in fat • Be careful when adding water. Add it slowly • Use a knife to mix water, flour and margarine. Handle pastry lightly • Knead and roll lightly. Do not overstretch the pastry • Chill before placing in the oven • Assemble the dish according to recipe
Cooking	• Cook pastry at a high temperature but be careful not to burn it • Reduce temperature after 10 minutes • During cooking the starch grains burst and absorb the fat
Serving	• Pastry can be served hot or cold depending on the dish • Savoury dishes such as quiche can be garnished with parsley or chives • Sweet dishes can be sieved with icing sugar or served with whipped cream or fruit coulis

Raising Agents

- Raising agents are used in baking to produce a light, more palatable pastry.
- Raising agents introduce air into the dough.

Points to Note

Baking blind
Baking blind is to bake the pastry case with no filling. It prevents the pastry from becoming soggy when the filling is added.

Classification of raising agents

There are three types of raising agent.

1 Mechanical raising agents
- Introduce air by physical means, e.g. beating, sieving, creaming, folding in, rubbing in.
- In batters and choux pastry steam acts as a raising agent.

2 Chemical raising agents
- The chemical reaction of an acid and alkali in the presence of liquid produces the gas CO_2 which acts as the raising agent.
- Acid + alkali + liquid = CO_2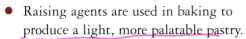

Examples
- Self-raising flour: Baking powder has been added during the processing
- Bread soda (bicarbonate of soda)
- Bread soda + butter milk = CO_2 gas

- Baking powder: A commercial raising agent which contains bicarbonate of soda (alkali), cream of tartar (acid) and filler (e.g. rice flour) which absorb the moisture and prevent the premature reaction of acid and alkali.

3 Biological raising agents
- Yeast is a living organism from the fungi family and produces CO_2 by fermentation.
- It is used as a raising agent in bread making.
- Yeast requires food, warmth and moisture to grow.

Food: Carbohydrate in flour and sugar which are broken down during fermentation
Warmth: Use warm utensils, as very hot temperatures would destroy the yeast cells
Moisture: Liquid ingredients such as milk, eggs, water

Yeast converts the carbohydrate in flour into alcohol and carbon dioxide by the action of enzymes (fermentation).
Glucose ($C_6H_{12}O_6$) + yeast fermentation (warmth and moisture) = alcohol ($2C_2H_5OH$) + $2CO_2$ (carbon dioxide)

Enzymes used in fermentation are:
- **Diastase (flour):** Changes starch to maltose.
- **Maltase (yeast):** Changes maltose to glucose.
- **Invertase (yeast):** Changes sucrose to glucose and fructose.
- **Zymase (yeast):** Changes glucose and fructose to carbon dioxide and alcohol.

Types of yeast
- Fresh yeast, dried yeast and fast action dried yeast

Chorleywood process
- The addition of vitamin C (ascorbic acid) to the yeast dough speeds up the fermentation time, as the vitamin acts as a reducing agent and reduces the time necessary for raising the dough.

Table 4.14 Guidelines for baking with yeast	
Yeast	Use fresh or dehydrated yeast
Flour	Use strong, plain white flour which has high gluten content
Sugar	Necessary for the growth of yeast. Too much sugar prevents growth
Fat	Prevents the growth of yeast so extra is needed
Salt	Used for flavour but too much salt can kill the yeast
Liquid	Water is the most suitable but milk gives a softer crust
Kneading	Helps the gluten develop
Rising	The dough needs to rise quickly in a warm environment, e.g. over oven, or overnight in a cool room
Warmth	Ingredients and utensils should be warm to encourage the yeast rising

Selection, Safe Use and Care of Food Preparation Equipment

Electric food preparation equipment

The following types of electrical food preparation equipment are available:
- Blender, food processor, food mixer, liquidiser, kettle, juice extractor

Table 4.15 Factors to consider when selecting food preparation equipment	
Budget	How much can you afford? Consider initial cost and running cost of the equipment
Quality	Buy a well-known reliable brand that offers a guarantee and good after sales service
Need	Do you really need the equipment and will you use it on a regular basis?
Time saving	Will it actually save time in food preparation?
Energy	Is it environmentally friendly and energy efficient? Check the labels
Space	The larger the equipment, the more space it will take up in the kitchen

Guidelines for the safe use of food preparation equipment
1. Follow the manufacturer's instructions.
2. Unplug all appliances before cleaning.
3. Never use wet hands when operating appliances.
4. If equipment such as a food processor has removable blades, be very careful when you detach or slot them in.
5. Only use equipment for what it is intended.
6. Do not overrun motor-based equipment. Pause regularly to prevent overheating.
7. Ensure handles are heat resistant.

Care of equipment
1. Follow the manufacturer's instructions.
2. Always unplug electrical equipment before cleaning.
3. Remove blades carefully.
4. Use a damp cloth to clean the outside of the equipment and the lead. Never immerse in water.
5. Wash and dry all detachable parts.
6. Store appliances unassembled and unplugged in a well-ventilated cupboard.

Aesthetic Awareness in Food Choice, Preparation and Presentation

- To make something aesthetically pleasing is to make it look good and appealing.
- The way food looks before and after cooking is vital to its palatability.
- Colour, texture, flavour, aroma and sound all contribute to how aesthetically pleasing a food is.
- All five senses are engaged in the sensory analysis of food.

Table 4.16 Aesthetic awareness in food choice	
1 Colour	• Food should have good vibrant colour, particularly fruit and vegetables • Actual colour should correspond to expected colour of food
2 Texture	• Fruit and vegetables should be crisp and fresh • Meat and eggs should be unblemished
3 Flavour and aroma	• Smell should correspond to the food, e.g. strawberries should smell like strawberries
4 Sound	• Food should sound crisp

Aesthetic awareness in food preparation

- If people are attracted by the colour, aroma and sound of food their appetite is stimulated.
- They begin to produce saliva which helps tasting by dissolving and diluting substances and controlling temperature. Saliva also aids digestion.

1 Colour/Sight

- The appearance of a food/meal (its size, shape, colour and surface appearance) is judged and appraised by sight.
- Colour is a fundamental element when deciding what food to eat.
- Naturally bright coloured food appeals to sight.
- Contrasting colours attract the eye and can be provided by using garnishes or sauces.
- The colour of the food is often an indicator for the freshness of the food, particularly in fruit and vegetables.
- Do not overcook food.
- Certain foods are expected to have a particular colour, e.g. bread should be white or brown and peas green.
- Food processing can lead to colour loss. Lack of colour is often substituted by artificial colouring.

Points to Note

Words to describe the appearance of food: fresh, moist, dry, bright, colourful, burnt, greasy, thick, smooth, watery.

2 Flavour

- Taste and aroma work together in establishing the flavour of a food.
- The tongue is responsible for our sense of taste.
- There should be a variety of flavours throughout a meal, e.g. an ideal meal should include something savoury and something sweet.
- Contrast flavours, e.g. sweet and sour, to stimulate the appetite. Avoid using overpowering flavours in a meal.
- Temperature intensifies the flavour of food.
- Use garnishes and decorations such as cream in soup to add extra flavour to food.
- Processed foods may lose flavour during processing. Flavour may be added artificially to make the food more appetising.

Points to Note
Words to describe the taste of food: bitter, sweet, sour, salty, spicy, smoky, bland, creamy, burnt, tasteless.

3 Aroma

- Smell receptors in the nasal cavity identify a smell or aroma.
- All foods have their own individual aroma. However, some such as garlic or oranges are more distinctive than others.
- To stimulate the awareness of smell a substance must be in a gaseous state.
- Smell is used to identify fresh, stale, rancid or poisonous food.
- Herbs and spices are added to improve the aroma of food.
- Overcooking can result in an unappetising burnt smell.
- Undercooked food lacks a stimulating aroma.
- Marketing techniques in supermarkets evoke the aroma of fresh bread to increase sales.

Points to Note
Words to describe the aroma of food: burnt, fruity, strong, spicy, fresh, aromatic, smoked, roasted.

4 Texture

- Texture is the consistency of food as perceived by the eyes and the mouth.
- It also relates to the feel of food in the mouth.
- Use various textures in a meal to add variety, e.g. tacos with chilli con carne.
- Specific foods are expected to have a certain texture, e.g. we expect cakes to be spongy, mayonnaise to be smooth and lettuce to be crisp.
- Overcooking can affect the natural texture of food.
- The texture of some foods can indicate whether the food is fresh or stale, e.g. a soft apple implies that it is not fresh any more.
- The texture of certain foods such as a lumpy sauce or burnt rashers can make them look unappetising.

Points to Note
Words to describe the texture of food: hard, soft, smooth, crispy, flaky, brittle, crunchy, lumpy, spongy, grainy, chewy, nutty.

- Additives are added to processed foods to improve the mouth feel of the food. Modified starch, e.g. increases the smoothness of food.

5 Sound: sizzling, fizzy, popping
- Our sense of hearing evaluates food during preparation and consumption.
- Certain foods are associated with a particular sound, e.g. fizz with fizzy drinks, sizzling with frying bacon and the pop with popcorn.

Aesthetic awareness in food presentation

Food presentation is a vital component in the aesthetics of food; it makes food more appetising and appealing.
- Serve hot foods hot and cold food chilled.
- Arrange food attractively on the plate.
- Use garnishes and accompaniments to enhance the presentation.
- Do not overload the plate with food.
- Clean the edge of the plate before serving.
- Savoury foods should be served on plain plates or dishes while sweet food can be served on more decorative plates.
- The tablecloth, napkins, cutlery and glasses all add to the presentation of food.
- Ensure the food is arranged balanced in colour, flavour and texture.

Sensory Analysis

Sensory analysis is used to distinguish food characteristics by measuring, analysing and evaluating the organoleptic properties of food. All five senses are used in the analysis and its interpretation.

What is sensory analysis used for?

- For developing new food products.
- For modifying recipes to meet consumer demands for less salt and less sugar, etc.
- In the classroom as part of evaluating food products for food assignments.

Sample Questions and Answers

(a) Give one reason why a food manufacturer might use sensory analysis testing. (2)
(b) Name two categories of sensory analysis tests. List one test from each category. (4)
(2005, HL, Section A, 5)

Answers
(a) A food manufacturer can use sensory analysis to develop new food products and to get consumer feedback on existing ones.

(b) Test 1 = Preference Tests, e.g. Paired Preference Test
Test 2 = Difference Tests, e.g. Triangle Test

Controlling the test conditions

1. Mid-morning or mid-afternoon are the best times for tests as tasters are more sensitive.
2. Avoid strongly flavoured food such as curry for 30 minutes prior to test.
3. The visual representation of all the samples should be the same:
   - Same quantity
   - Food containers similar in size, shape and colour
   - Colour should be white or colourless
4. The temperature of all samples should be the same.
5. Water for rinsing the mouth should be available for each taster.
6. The coding of samples should not indicate anything about the food, e.g. use A, B, C or 1, 2, 3.
7. The samples can be sequenced in one of the following ways:
   - Random: for larger number of samples
   - Balanced: for triangle tests A = control, B = sample, e.g. AAB, ABA
   - Combination of random and balanced sequencing

Sensory analysis tests

1 Preference tests

These tests are used to determine which product is preferred or if products are acceptable.

(a) Paired preference test
- Two samples of a product are given and the taster is asked to identify which he/she prefers.

(b) Hedonic ranking test
- One or more samples are ranked on a 5, 7 or 9 point verbal or facial scale to identify the degree of liking of a product.

2 Difference tests

Difference tests are used to determine small differences between sample products.

(a) Simple paired test
- Two samples are presented to the taster who states whether they are the same or different.

(b) Paired comparison test
- Pairs of samples are presented to the taster.

(c) Triangle test
- Three samples are presented to the taster, of which two are the same.

3 Grading or quality tests

These tests are used to rank specific organoleptic characteristics of food such as flavour, texture, odour and aftertaste.

(a) Ranking tests
- These tests are used to determine the order of a choice of foods (usually between two and 12 samples).
- These foods are ranked using hedonic rating or a particular characteristic.

(b) Rating tests
- These are used to determine how much a person likes/dislikes a food (hedonic rating).

Presentation of results

The results of the tests must be analysed and presented to reveal what changes need to be made.

The data can be presented as a pie chart, histogram or star diagram.

Recipe Modification

A recipe is modified when a dish is altered slightly by substituting or omitting certain ingredients or by changing the quantities required.

Why are recipes modified or adapted?

- To provide a dish suitable for people with special dietary needs such as coeliacs and vegetarians.
- To improve the nutritional value of the dish and follow healthy eating guidelines.
- To alter the number of portions required by increasing or decreasing quantities.
- To provide variety in a dish.
- To substitute unavailable, expensive or unhealthy ingredients with alternatives.

Table 4.17 Modification

	Modification
Less salt	• Omit salt from dish • Use low sodium alternative • Avoid convenience foods and stock cubes • Use herbs and spices to add flavour
Less sugar	• Reduce sugar in a recipe • Use artificial sweeteners instead • Use fruit juice and dried fruit in cakes and desserts
Less saturated fat	• Use low fat polyunsaturated spreads • Remove any visible fat from meat • Opt for low fat meat such as chicken and turkey • Use low fat milk, cream, yoghurt, cheese or a soya alternative • Change method of cooking, e.g. grill instead of frying
Increase fibre	• Use wholemeal products for flour, pasta, rice and bread • Add pulse vegetables to all-in-one dishes, e.g. stews • Avoid removing the skin of fruit and vegetables
Coeliac	• Use gluten-free ingredients
Vegan	• Use soya-based products • Use herbs and spices for flavour and variety
Allergies	• Be aware of individual allergies and provide a suitable alternative in the dish, e.g. replace milk with soya milk, goat's milk or coconut milk

Questions

1 Classify soups and give one example of each class. (6)
(2006, HL, Section A, 6)
2 (a) Discuss the influence of any three of the senses when choosing, buying or eating food. (15)
(b) Name three categories of Sensory Analysis tests and list one test from each category. (15)
(c) Set out the conditions necessary for conducting Sensory Analysis testing to ensure accurate results. (20)
(2007, HL, Section B, 3)

Key Points

Meal Planning and Management
- Current healthy eating guidelines
- Physical changes in food during preparation and cooking: Loss of nutrients, change in size, tenderising of meat, texture changes, thickening of food
- Chemical changes in food during preparation and cooking: Change in colour, enzymic browning, Maillard reaction, increase in size, bacteria destroyed

Reasons Why We Cook Food
- To improve the colour, flavour and texture of food
- To destroy any micro-organisms present
- To make the food more digestible and to destroy enzymes
- To make the food more appetising
- To preserve food
- To add variety to our diet by combining different ingredients

Three Methods of Heat Transfer
- Conduction: The heating of solid materials
- Convection: The heating of air or liquid
- Radiation: The transfer of heat without heating the space in between

Different Cooking Methods
- Moist method: Boiling, steaming, stewing, poaching, braising, pressure cooking
- Dry methods: Baking, grilling/barbecuing, roasting, pot roasting
- Frying: Deep frying, shallow frying, dry frying, stir-frying

Soups and Sauces
- Soup is made from stock
- Nutritional value of soup depends on ingredients used
- Classification of soups: Thin, thick soups
- Characteristics of a good soup: Good colour, flavour, texture, free from grease, well seasoned
- Garnishes and accompaniments: Fresh herbs, cream, yoghurt, grated cheese, croutons

Why Sauces Are Used
- Sauces improve flavour and colour, add nutrients and moisture
- Classification of sauces: Simple, roux, egg-based, cold dressings, sweet
- How to make a good sauce: Saucepan, correct proportions, fresh ingredients
- How to serve a sauce: In a sauceboat, as an accompaniment, part of a dish, over a dish, hot or cold

Pastry
- Basic ingredients used in pastry: Plain flour, fat, water, lemon juice, eggs
- Characteristics of a good pastry: Fully cooked, not soggy, light golden brown, crumbles easily, not greasy
- Types of pastry: Shortcrust, wholemeal, rich shortcrust, rough puff pastry, puff pastry, flaky pastry, filo pastry, suet crust pastry, choux pastry

Raising Agents
- Classification of raising agents: Mechanical, chemical, biological
- Types of yeast: Fresh yeast, dried yeast, fast action dried yeast
- Guidelines for baking with yeast

CHAPTER 4

Key Points

Selection, Safe Use and Care of Food Preparation Equipment
- Electric food preparation equipment
- Guidelines for the safe use of food preparation equipment
- Care of equipment

Aesthetic Awareness in Food Choice, Preparation and Presentation
- The importance of the five senses in food evaluation and appreciation
- The importance of colour, flavour, aroma, texture and sound in food preparation
- Vocabulary needed to describe food: Bright, dull, sizzling, runny, crisp

Sensory Analysis
- Sensory analysis is used to develop new food products, modify recipes
- How to control test conditions: Suitable time, avoid strong flavoured food prior to test, temperature of food, visual representation of food, water, sample and coding used
- Preference tests: Paired preference test, hedonic ranking test
- Difference tests: Simple paired test, paired comparison test, triangle test
- Grading or quality tests: Ranking tests or rating tests
- How to present results: Pie chart, histogram, star diagram

Recipes Modification
- Dietary needs: Coeliac, vegetarians, nutrition, weight loss
- Healthy eating guidelines, variety, provide an alternative food or substitute
- Modifications used: Low salt, less sugar, less saturated fat, increase fibre, coeliac, vegan, allergies

Your revision notes

5: Food Additives and Food Legislation

●●● Learning Objectives

In this chapter you will learn about:
1. Why Food Additives Are Used
2. Classification of Food Additives
3. Legal Control and Safety of Food Additives
4. Labelling Laws

Food additives are substances which are added to food to improve colour, flavour, texture, nutritional value and shelflife.

A food additive must have a useful and acceptable function before it can be added to the food.

Exam Hints

This topic can be examined in Section A or Section B of the Leaving Certificate paper. It could be asked in conjunction with a food preservation question or food profile, so remember to revise those at this stage as well.

Why Food Additives Are Used

Food additives:
- Act as a preservative in prolonging the shelflife of the food.
- Improve colour, flavour and texture of the food.
- Improve the nutritional value of the food.

Food additives must be avoided if:
1. They deceive the consumer.
2. Disguise faulty processing.
3. Decrease the nutritional value of the food.

Additives can be found in three forms:
1. Natural: Found in animals and plants, e.g. green colouring = chlorophyll.
2. Nature identical: Identical with a natural additive but synthetically made, e.g. ascorbic acid (identical with vitamin C).
3. Artificial: Synthetically made, e.g. esters.

Table 5.1 Advantages and disadvantages of food additives

Advantages	Disadvantages
Increase the shelflife of food	Possible side effects, e.g. allergies
Provide a greater variety of food	Colourings and polyphosphates may deceive the consumer
Improve the colour, flavour and texture of food	The accumulative effect of different additives on the body is unknown
Improve the nutritional value of the food	Research in animals suggests a possible link between food additives and cancer
Reduce waste	The toxicity of many food additives is still unknown
Reduce the risk of food poisoning	
Provide food suitable for diabetics	

Classification of Food Additives

1. Colourings
2. Preservatives
3. Flavourings
4. Sweeteners
5. Nutritive additives
6. Physical conditioning agents

The letter 'E' prefixes all tested and accepted additives in the EU.

Colourings E100 - E199

Function
1. Improve the colour of food.
2. Enhance the colour of processed food.
3. Replace colour lost during processing.
4. To meet consumer demands.

Examples:
- Natural: Chlorophyll (from plants) E140, caramel E150
- Synthetic: Tartrazine E102 (soft drinks), sunset yellow E110 (sweets)

Preservatives E200 - E299

Functions
1. Prevent the growth of micro-organisms.
2. Increase the shelflife of the food.
3. Provide food out of season.

4 Prevent food poisoning.

Examples:
- Natural: Salt, sugar, alcohol, vinegar, spices, smoke
- Synthetic: Sorbic acid E200 (cakes), sulphur dioxide E220 (sausages)

Flavourings

Flavourings do not have E numbers.

Function
1 Improve the flavour of food.
2 Increase the attractiveness of food.
3 Substitute and enhance the flavour of food.

Examples:
- Natural: Sugar (breakfast cereals), salt (cheese), spices, herbs
- Artificial: Esters (amyl acetate gives pear flavour to sweets), aldehydes (almond flavour)

Flavour enhancers
Function
1 Tasteless substances which can enhance, reduce or change the taste of food.

Example:
- Monosodium glutamate (MSG) E621: in soups, sauces, prepared meals, snack foods. MSG is not permitted in baby foods.

Sweeteners

Function
1 Sweeten food.
2 Used in low calorie/low sugar products.
3 Used in diabetic foods.

> **Points to Note**
> Some sweeteners have no limit on their use, e.g. mannitol and sorbitol, while others have a limit, e.g. saccharin and aspartame.

> **Points to Note**
> Diabetics do not need insulin to break down artificial sweeteners.

Examples:
- Natural: Sugar, glucose, fructose
- Artificial:
1 Intense sweeteners (much sweeter than natural sweeteners, only needed in small quantities), e.g.
   – Aspartame (NutraSweet): in soft drinks, desserts, yoghurt
   – Saccharin (Hermesetes): in soft drinks, as tablets for individual use
2 Bulk sweeteners (same sweetness as sugar, used in larger quantities), e.g.
   – Mannitol E421: in sugar-free confectionery, chewing gum
   – Sorbitol E420: in sugar-free confectionery, jam
   – Xylitol: in sugar-free gum

Nutritive additives

Function
1. Replace nutrients lost during processing.
2. Increase nutritional value.
3. To improve sales and meet consumer demands.

Examples:
- Vitamin D (margarine)
- Calcium (milk, flour)
- Vitamin B group (flour)

Physical conditioning agents

Function
Improve the texture and consistency of food.
1. Emulsifiers (used to form emulsions), e.g.
   – Lecithin (from eggs) E422 (mayonnaise), alginates E400 (ice cream)
2. Stabilisers (improve the stability of the emulsion)
   – Guar gum E412 (cakes)
3. Anticaking agents (prevent lumps forming in dehydrated food), e.g. flour, icing sugar
4. Humectants (prevent food from drying out by absorbing water)
5. Thickeners (improve the viscosity of food)
6. Buffers (stabilise the pH level of food)

Antioxidants E300 - E399

Function
1. Prevent oxidative rancidity of foods, especially fats and oils.
2. Prevent spoilage of certain foods exposed to oxygen.

Examples:
- Natural: Vitamin C (ascorbic acid) E300 used in fruit and jams
- Synthetic: Butylated hydroxytoluene (BHT) E320 used in chewing gum and butylated hydroxyanisole (BHA) E321 used in beef stock cubes

Legal Control and Safety of Food Additives

- A number of national and international agencies are responsible for the safe use of food additives.
- Before a food additive can be used it has to be tested and evaluated for its purity and safety level.
- The allocation of an E number ensures the safety of the additive.
- EU directives on additives do not include flavourings or nutritive additives.

Under EU regulations, additives:
- Must not reduce the nutrient content of the food
- Must not deceive the consumer
- Must not disguise faulty processing
- Must not be a health hazard
- Must be used in the smallest quantity

Agencies concerned with the regulation of food additives

- European Scientific Committee for Food (ESCF)
- Joint Expert Committee on Food Additives (JECFA)
- Food and Agricultural Organisation (FAO)
- World Health Organisation (WHO)
- Food Safety Authority of Ireland (FSAI)
- Department of Agriculture and Food

Control of residue levels

- The European Commission has established maximum residue levels (MRL), which show the maximum concentrate of a substance allowed for human consumption.
- Acceptable daily intake (ADI) is the amount allowed which has no ill effect on the body.

Labelling Laws

- All permitted food additives are identified by a name and an E prefix with a number.
- The category, e.g. 'colouring agent', and E number and/or the complete name of the additive must appear on the label.

Food legislation

Food Hygiene Regulations Act 1950–1989
- Governs all other legislation and is implemented by the Health Service Executive.
- Prohibits the sale of food that is diseased, contaminated or unfit for human consumption.
- Ensures precautions are taken at all stages of food processing, packaging and distribution to prevent contamination of food.
- Permission to destroy food unfit for human consumption.
- Requires the registration of certain food premises, dairy farms, butchers, etc.
- All mobile food stalls must apply for a licence annually.
- All food handlers must be aware of food hygiene practices.

CHAPTER 5

Table 5.2 Food legislation	
European Communities (Hygiene of Foodstuffs) Regulation 2000	• Requires food premises to be hygienic in all aspects of food preparation • Staff training in food hygiene and a hygiene management system such as HACCP must be adhered to
Sale of Food and Drugs Act 1875, 1879, 1899, 1936	• Protects the consumer against fraud and the corruption of food on sale • Under this act it is an offence to mix, colour or stain a food with any ingredient which would make it a hazard for human consumption • Sell any food which is not of the nature, substance and quality demanded by consumers
European Communities (Health Act 1947) Regulations 1991	Allow regulations to be made to: • Prevent danger to public health arising from the importation, distribution and sale of food • Regulate compositional standards for foods which are important to public health, e.g. milk
Health (Official Control of Foodstuffs) Regulations 1991	• Allow inspection of premises, provide guidelines for food hygiene from production through to selling
Labelling Regulations 1982 and 1991	• All labelling must be clear, legible and indelible, and must not mislead the consumer • Language understood by the consumer
European Communities (Labelling, Presentation and Advertising of Foodstuffs) Regulation 2002, Health (Nutrition Labelling For Foodstuffs) Regulation 1993	• Governs nutritional labelling • Nutritional labelling is only compulsory when a claim is made regarding the nutrient content of the food, e.g. on low fat food • Infant foods and formulas must display nutritional content

Sample Question and Answer

State one function of each of the food additives listed below.

Food Additive	Function
Flavour enhancer	Improves existing flavours and makes them stronger
Emulsifier	Improves the consistency of food by forcing oil and water to mix together without separating
Antioxidant	Reacts with oxygen and prevents rancidity of lipids therefore increasing shelflife of food

Key Points

Why Food Additives Are Used
- To prolong shelflife
- To improve colour, flavour and texture
- To improve nutritional value
- Additives can be natural, nature identical or artificial

Advantages of Food Additives
- To increase shelflife, to add variety, colour, flavour, texture and nutritional value
- To reduce waste and the risk of food poisoning

Disadvantages of Food Additives
- Allergies and other side effects
- The accumulating effect of additives and the deception of the consumer

Classification of Food Additives
- Colourings: Improve food colour, meet consumer demands; natural (chlorophyll) and synthetic (tartrazine E102)
- Preservatives: Inhibit growth of bacteria, increase shelflife, prevent food poisoning; natural (salt) and synthetic (sorbic acid E200)
- Flavourings: Improve food's flavour; natural (sugar) and synthetic (esters)
- Sweeteners: Sweeten food, used in low calorie and diabetic food; natural (glucose) and synthetic (aspartame and mannitol)
- Nutritive additives: Replace nutrients lost during processing, increase nutritional value
- Physical conditioning agents: Improve texture and consistency of food, e.g. emulsifiers, stabilisers, thickeners
- Antioxidants: Prevent oxidative rancidity, prevent food spoilage; natural (vitamin C) and synthetic BHT and BHA

Legal Control and Safety of Food Additives
- Agencies which regulate food additives: SCF, JECFA, FAO, WHO, FSAI, Department of Agriculture and Food

- Legislation: Food Hygiene Regulations Act 1950–89; European Communities (Hygiene of Foodstuffs) Regulation 2000; Sale of Food and Drugs Act 1875, 1879, 1899, 1936; European Communities (Health Act 1947) Regulations 1991, Health (Official Control of Foodstuffs) Regulations 1991; Labelling Regulations 1982, 1991; European Communities (Labelling, Presentation and Advertising of Foodstuffs) Regulation 2002; Health (Nutrition Labelling for Foodstuffs) Regulation 1993

Labelling Laws and the Use of the E Prefix
- Food additives are identified by a name and an E prefix with a number

6: Microbes and Food Spoilage

●●●Learning Objectives

In this chapter you will learn about:
1 Microbiology
2 Fungi (Yeast)
3 Bacteria
4 Food Spoilage

Microbiology

Micro-organisms

Exam Hints

A lot of the material in this section is examined at Higher Level only; this material has been identified by **I**. Remember when you are studying the different micro-organisms that you learn the necessary diagrams as well, e.g. structure, reproduction.

- Microbiology is the study of micro-organisms.
- Micro-organisms are tiny, single-celled living organisms.
- Micro-organisms vary in size from being visible to the naked eye to extremely small microbes unseen even by a microscope.
- Micro-organisms establish themselves in different environments, e.g. air, soil, water, plants, animals and food.
- Some micro-organisms can cause food poisoning. They are called pathogenic (disease causing) bacteria.
- Other micro-organisms are extremely beneficial to humans and provide vitamins, help decaying matter and are part of food production, e.g. in yoghurt and alcohol.

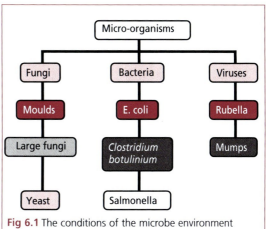

Fig 6.1 The conditions of the microbe environment

Classification of micro-organisms

What do microbes need for growth?
The conditions of the microbe environment influence how it grows.

Table 6.1 Conditions for microbes	
Condition	**Facts**
Food	Microbes can be classified as: 1 Saprophytic: feed on dead or decaying matter, e.g. fungi 2 Parasitic: feed on living matter
Oxygen	The presence or absence of oxygen will influence the survival of the microbe. There are three different types of microbes: 1 Aerobic: needs oxygen for its growth 2 Anaerobic: oxygen unnecessary for growth 3 Facultative: grow with or without oxygen
Temperature	All microbes have an ideal temperature for growth where cell multiplication is plentiful. There are three main groups: 1 Psychrophiles: prefer low temperatures between –5°C and 20°C 2 Mesophiles: most microbes are in this category. They thrive between 20°C and 45°C 3 Thermophiles: prefer temperatures above 45°C
Moisture	• Liquids or moisture are necessary for all microbes to metabolise • A low water content can reduce the growth of microbes in food
Correct pH (hydrogen ions)	• The pH of a food or liquid is calculated on a scale from 0 to 14, where 0 = acidic and 14 = alkaline (pH scale) • Most bacteria prefer a neutral pH of 7 • All microbes have their own preferred pH level for growth
Time	Micro-organisms need time to grow. However, over time they compete with each other for conditions of growth

Fungi

- Fungi can be divided into moulds, yeast and larger fungi.
- Fungi are very basic plants. However, as they do not have any chlorophyll (green pigment) they cannot produce their own food.
- Fungi can be saprophytic, i.e. feed on dead or decaying matter, or parasitic, i.e. feed on living matter.

Moulds

- Moulds are multi-cellular structures.
- They can contaminate many foodstuffs such as jam.
- Normally, the surface of food is only contaminated when mycotoxins are produced.

Structure of moulds
- A spore is a single cell.
- A spore locates a suitable medium to grow, e.g. food.
- If conditions are suitable it produces a threadlike filament called a hypha.
- The hypha grows down into the food source.
- The hypha continues to extend and branch out forming many hyphae called a mycelium.
- As the hyphae continue to grow some begin to grow upwards.
- The hyphae release enzymes that break down the nutrients present and help absorb them.

Reproduction of moulds
Moulds can reproduce by sexual or asexual means.

1 Asexual reproduction of a mould
- Asexual reproduction takes place when the mycelium is well established on the food source.
- The hyphae begin to grow upwards.
- The top of the hyphae enlarge to produce a sporangium (which is round in shape) or a conidia (chains of spores).
- When ripe, the sporangium bursts and releases spores.
- A conidia breaks away from the hyphae and releases the spores into the environment. These spores are carried by air or water.
- When the spores find a suitable medium the cycle starts again.

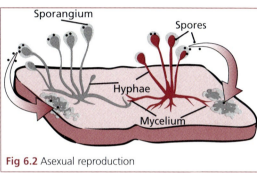

Fig 6.2 Asexual reproduction

2 Sexual reproduction of a mould
- Sexual reproduction of a mould occurs when conditions are unsuitable for the germination of the spore.
  1. Two hyphae grow towards each other.
  2. The two hyphae meet and fuse together.
  3. The dividing wall between the two hyphae disappear and a zygospore develops.
  4. The zygospore produces and stores spores.

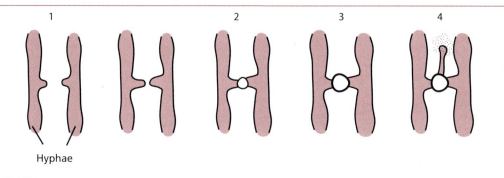

Fig 6.3 Sexual reproduction

- The zygospore has a thick wall and offers protection to the spores until suitable conditions emerge.
- The zygospore can survive for long periods of time.
- When conditions are suitable, the spores germinate and hyphae grow and extend from the zygospore.
- The spores are released into the air and the cycle begins again.

Table 6.2 Classification of moulds

1 Phycomycetes
- Reproduce sexually or asexually
- Produce sporangium
- Most favourable temperature at 30°C
- Generally are non–septae (have no dividing walls)

Example	Mucor	Rhizopus
Found on	<ul><li>Soil</li><li>Bread</li><li>Meat</li><li>Cheese</li></ul>	<ul><li>Soil</li><li>Bread</li><li>Soft rot on fruit and vegetables</li></ul>
Characteristics	<ul><li>Saprophyte</li><li>Sexual or asexual reproduction</li><li>White hyphae</li><li>Greyish sporangium</li></ul>	<ul><li>Saprophyte</li><li>Usually asexual reproduction</li><li>White mycelium</li><li>Black sporangium</li></ul>

2 Ascomycetes
- Optimum temperature between 20°C and 25°C
- Asexual reproduction
- Contain cross walls (septae)
- Produce conidia during reproduction

Example	Penicillium	Aspergillis
Found in	<ul><li>Cheese</li><li>Fruit</li><li>Bread</li></ul>	<ul><li>Fruit</li><li>Vegetables</li><li>Grain</li></ul>
Characteristics	<ul><li>Saprophyte</li><li>Crumbly green/blue mould</li></ul>	<ul><li>Saprophyte</li><li>Black or green mould</li></ul>
Use	<ul><li>For production of antibiotics</li><li>For ripening of cheese, e.g. Stilton</li></ul>	

Table 6.3 Growing conditions for moulds

Condition	Growth of mould
Food	Most moulds are saprophytic and develop on several types of food
Oxygen	Moulds are generally aerobic and grow on the surface of food
Temperature	Moulds are normally mesophile Temperatures below 15°C will retard their growth while freezing temperatures inactivate growth Temperature above 75°C destroy mould
Moisture	Moulds prefer moist and humid conditions
Correct pH	Moulds grow best in an acidic environment of pH 4–6
Time	Time is necessary for multiplication

Large fungi (Basidiomycetes)

- Large fungi are generally edible.
- They are visible to the naked eye.
- They include many varieties e.g.:
  - *Agaricus campestris* (field mushroom, e.g. oyster and button mushroom)
  - Truffles, a delicacy, are grown underground and located by special pigs sniffing the strong smell

Reproduction of Basidiomycetes

1. Mushrooms start as spores like other fungi.
2. They produce hyphae on a suitable medium such as soil. These hyphae grow and develop to produce mycelium.
3. The hyphae are packed really close together and grow upwards from the mycelium.
4. A tightly closed cap forms at the top of the hyphae.
5. This increases in size and opens as the mushroom develops.
6. Pink gills form underneath the cap. These change to brown as the mushroom gets older and spores are produced here.
7. When the mushrooms are ripe the spores are released.
8. If the spores find a suitable medium and the right conditions are present the cycle begins again.

Yeasts (Saccharomycetes)

1. Yeasts are single-celled.
2. Yeasts are saprophytic.
3. They are found in the air, soil and on fruit.
4. Yeasts can spoil fruit, jam, wine and meat.
5. Some foodstuffs such as bread, beer and vinegar rely on yeast for their production.

Structure of yeast

Yeast cells are usually oval in shape, have a thin outer wall, which is filled inside with cytoplasm that contains a nucleus and food vacuoles.

Reproduction of yeasts

1. In favourable conditions yeast cells reproduce asexually by budding. The parent cell develops a bulge.
2. The nucleus of the parent cell moves towards the bulge.
3. The nucleus divides into two.
4. A wall forms which separates the new bud from the parent cell.
5. The bud separates from the parent cell.
6. During quick growth in optimum conditions, a chain of yeast cells may develop. A bulge will form on the new cell before it has separated from the parent cell.
7. If conditions are not suitable for growth, a resistant spore forms and waits until conditions are suitable before reproducing again.

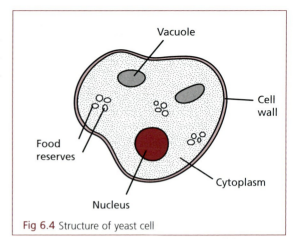

Fig 6.4 Structure of yeast cell

Exam Hints
Do not forget to learn the diagrams. Yeast could also be asked in conjunction with food preservation so check that section now as well.

Table 6.4 Growing conditions for yeasts (Saccharomycetes)	
Condition	Growth of yeast
Food	Yeasts feed on carbohydrate-based food, e.g. sugar
Oxygen	Yeasts are facultative microbes
Temperature	The ideal temperature for yeasts to grow is between 25°C and 30°C. Above 60°C yeasts are destroyed
Moisture	Yeasts prefer moist conditions
Correct pH (hydrogen ions)	Moulds grow better in an acidic environment of pH 4–5
Time	Yeasts need time to grow and multiply

Advantages of fungi

Moulds
1. Some moulds are used in the production of cheese, e.g. Stilton
2. Others are used for the production of antibiotics, e.g. penicillin.

Yeast
1 Used to produce food supplements as it is rich in vitamin B.
2 Used in the production of bread and in brewing.

Other fungi
1 Responsible for the decomposition of organic matter.
2 Many are edible and regarded as delicacies, e.g. truffles.
3 Some fungi are used in the production of novel protein foods, e.g. Quorn.

Disadvantages of fungi
1 Some fungi are poisonous if ingested, e.g. Amanita.
2 Fungi can cause human diseases, e.g. athlete's foot and ringworm.
3 Fungi can cause food spoilage. (See Food poisoning p. 129)
4 Fungi are responsible for some plant diseases, e.g. potato blight.

Bacteria

- Bacteria are single-celled micro-organisms.
- Bacteria are saprophytic or parasitic.
- Bacteria are found almost everywhere, e.g. in water, soil, air, plants, animals and humans.
- Bacteria are pathogenic (disease causing) or non-pathogenic.
- Some common bacteria cause whooping cough, meningitis, salmonella and listeria.

Structure of the bacterial cell

1 A bacterial cell has a rigid cell wall, which gives it structure.
2 It has a cell membrane, which incorporates the colourless cytoplasm.
3 Suspended in the cytoplasm are nuclear material, ribosome (manufacture protein) and food stores.

Variations in structure
- Some bacteria have a thick protective capsule which surrounds the cell wall.
- Flagellae are hair-like structures found in some bacterial cells, which assist the movement of the bacteria in liquid.

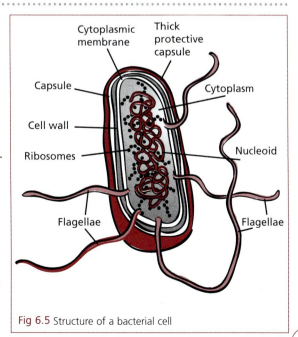

Fig 6.5 Structure of a bacterial cell

Reproduction of bacterial cells

Bacteria reproduce by binary fission, i.e. they divide into two. This is a method of asexual reproduction. In optimum conditions the bacterial cell, the bacterium, can reproduce every 20 minutes.

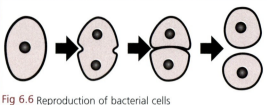

Fig 6.6 Reproduction of bacterial cells

1. The nuclear material in the bacterium divides in two.
2. A cell wall develops to separate the halves and to form two cells.
3. These two cells produce four cells in 20 minutes and so on.

- A colony is a large group of bacterial cells, which often becomes overcrowded.
- Overcrowding results in bacteria competing with each other for food, oxygen and space.
- The rapid growth stops and the production of waste toxins cause the death and decline of the bacteria.

Growth curve of a bacterial cell in ideal conditions

- Lag phase: Bacteria are getting used to their surroundings.
- Log phase: Bacteria begin to grow and multiply quickly.
- Stationary phase: Overcrowding begins and competition for nutrients etc. occurs.
- Decline phase: Build-up of waste products contributes to decline and death of bacteria.

Spore formation in bacteria

- Not all bacteria can produce spores.
- Bacilli and clostridia are two bacteria which can produce spores.
- Spores are only produced when conditions become unsuitable for growth.
- Spores are resistant to extreme heat, cold and certain chemicals.

Fig 6.7 Spore formation in bacteria

1. An endospore develops within the bacterium. This endospore will increase in size.
2. A thick protein wall starts to surround the spore.
3. The parent cell disintegrates.
4. The spore is released and will germinate when conditions are suitable for growth.

To destroy the endospore you need:
- Moist heat conditions at 121°C for 15 minutes, or
- Dry heat conditions at 150°C for 1 hour.

\	Table 6.5 Growing conditions for bacteria
Condition	Facts
Food	Bacteria can be: Saprophytic (feeding on dead or decaying matter) or Parasitic (feeding on living matter)
Oxygen	The presence or absence of oxygen will influence the survival of the microbe There are 3 different types: 1 Aerobic – oxygen is required for the growth of the microbe 2 Anaerobic – oxygen is not needed for growth 3 Facultative – these microbes grow with or without oxygen
Temperature	All microbes have an ideal temperature for growth where cell multiplication is plentiful. There are 3 main groups identified: 1 Psychrophiles – prefer low temperature –5°C to 20°C 2 Mesophile – most bacteria are in this category 20°C to 45°C 3 Thermophiles – prefer temperatures above 45°C
Moisture	Bacteria need liquids or moisture for metabolism
Correct pH	Most bacteria prefer a neutral pH of 7
Time	In ideal conditions bacteria can double in size every 20 minutes

Classification of bacteria

Bacteria can be grouped in many ways. The two most widely accepted ways of classification are shape and Gram staining.

Classification by Gram staining
What is Gram staining?
- Bacteria are classified depending on their reaction to a Gram stain test.
- Bacteria are classified as Gram positive when they stain blue and as Gram negative when they stain pink.

Testing bacteria
1 Place bacteria on an agar plate.
2 Crystal violet dye is poured over the bacteria, which then turn blue.
3 An iodine solution is poured over the bacteria – blue/black colour.
4 Pour alcohol over the bacterial cells and observe the results.

Table 6.6 Gram stain test		
	Gram +	Gram –
Colour	Blue/purple	Pink
Structure	Cell wall with one layer	Cell wall with two layers
Mobility	No flagellae	Flagellae
Reproduction	Produces spores	No spore production
Examples	Streptococci, *Clostridium perfringens*	Salmonella, E. coli

Table 6.7 Classification of bacteria by shape		
1 Cocci, spherical in shape		
• Coccus • Diplococci • Streptococci • Staphylococci	• Single bacterium • Pairs • Chains • Clusters/groups	• Meningitis • Pneumonia • Tonsillitis, sore throat • Food poisoning (caused by *Staphylococcus aureus*), boils
2 Bacillus		
• Bacilli • Clostridia	• Rod shaped (some have flagella for movement) • Chain-like	• Salmonella • E. coli • *Clostridium perfringens* • *Clostridium botulium*
3 Spiralla		
• Spiralla	• Spiral in shape, long, comma shaped	• Sexually transmitted diseases, e.g. syphilis
4 Vibrio		
• Vibrio	• Comma shaped	• Cholera

Table 6.8 Advantages and disadvantages of bacteria	
Advantages	**Disadvantages**
1 Production of vitamins B and K in the intestine	1 Can cause diseases in plants, in humans (e.g. cholera) and in animals (e.g. brucellosis)
2 Involved in food production, e.g. in yoghurt, cheese, vinegar	2 Responsible for food spoilage (e.g. causes sour milk)
3 Waste matter is decomposed by the action of the bacterial cell	3 Cause food poisoning
4 Synthetically produced bacteria are used to manufacture food supplement drugs	

Toxins

Toxins are poisonous substances. They can cause food poisoning. Bacteria produce most toxins. There are many different forms of toxins produced, some within food and others within the body:

1. Exotoxin
2. Endotoxin
3. Enterotoxin
4. Mycotoxin (moulds)

Table 6.9 Exotoxin and endotoxins	
1 Exotoxin	**2 Endotoxins**
• Produced during multiplication/growth of the bacteria in food • Secreted on the outside of the cell onto food • Produced before and after consumption of food • Bacterial cell may be dead but the toxin can still cause food poisoning, e.g. *Staphylococcus aureus* and *Bacillus cereus*	• Made inside the bacterial cell • Released when the bacterial cell dies • Require very high temperatures to be destroyed • Remain active after boiling • Cause infectious food poisoning, e.g. *Clostridium perfringens*

3 Enterotoxins
- Released by bacterial cells in the alimentary canal.
- Can cause gastroenteritis.
- Both exotoxins and endotoxins can be enterotoxins.

4 Mycotoxin
A toxin produced by some fungi.

Sample Questions and Answers

(a) State two uses of micro-organisms in food production. (4)

(b) Suggest one method of controlling enzymic spoilage in foods. (2)
(2005, HL, Section A, 6)

Answer (a)
Starter mould in cheese making, moulds in blue veined cheeses, fermentation of yoghurt, beer making, wine making, manufacturing meat substitutes, making yeast bread.

Answer (b)
Inactivated by heat, inactivated by addition of acids, blanching, low temperatures, correct storage, sulfur dioxide.

Food Spoilage

- Most foods are perishable, which means they will go through a natural process of decay/spoilage.
- When food has decayed it becomes inedible.
- At times food is contaminated with micro-organisms resulting in food poisoning.
- Other substances/contaminants can also spoil food and make it unsafe to eat.

> **Exam Hints**
> This section can be examined at both Higher and Ordinary Level in Sections A and B. The Higher Level material has been identified.

Causes of food spoilage are:
1. Enzymes
2. Dehydration/moisture loss
3. Contamination by microbes

Enzymes

- Enzymes occur naturally. They are proteins in nature.
- They are found in plants and animals.
- They are organic catalysts which speed up the rate of chemical reactions without changing themselves.
- A number of enzymes remain active even after harvesting (fruit and vegetables) and slaughtering (animals and fish).

Enzyme actions are ripening and browning.

1 Ripening
- Fruit and vegetables contain the enzymes necessary for ripening.
- Under-ripe (often inedible) to ripe (edible) to over-ripe (beginning of physical decay).
- During this process the colour, texture and aroma of fruit and vegetables change, e.g. a banana's colour changes from green to yellow to brown.

2 Browning
- Some fruit and vegetables become brown in colour when exposed to air during food preparation such as chopping or slicing.
- This is due to air reacting with enzymes such as oxidase in the food (oxidation).

Table 6.10 Prevention of enzymatic food spoilage	
Condition	Action/Results
Heat	• High temperatures inactivate enzymes • Prevent browning and ripening
Blanching	• Blanch before freezing food • Stops enzyme activity
Cold	• Place food in fridge • Cold temperatures slow down enzyme activity
Acids	• Turn apples in lemon juice • Prohibit enzyme activity and prevent browning (enzymes prefer a pH of 7)
Additives	• Sulfur dioxide preserves dried fruit and vegetables • Prevent action of enzymes

Moisture loss

- Moisture loss affects fruit and vegetables after they have been harvested.
- They no longer have the ability to absorb moisture from the soil through their roots, so they become dehydrated, which results in shrinkage, wrinkling and a limp appearance.
- Protein foods such as cheese and fish can also lose moisture through their surface when exposed to air.

Microbe contamination

- Food provides microbes with nutrients, moisture, pH, oxygen and warmth, the ideal environment for most microbes to grow and develop.
- Yeasts contaminate the exterior of food such as fruits.
- Moulds contaminate the exterior of food such as oranges and bread.
- Yeasts and moulds generally do not cause food poisoning as the food is not eaten.
- The mould *Aspergillus flavus*, which grows on peanuts and grains in humid conditions, produces alfa toxins. Alfa toxins are considered carcinogenic (cancer causing) and are linked to cancer of the liver.

Bacteria

- Bacteria are one of the main causes of food poisoning.
- Toxins produced by bacteria within food are invisible to the naked eye.
- Food containing these toxins is often consumed (eaten) unknowingly.

Food poisoning
- Food poisoning is an illness caused by food that contains harmful substances.
- It shows some or all of the following symptoms: abdominal pain, diarrhoea, nausea and vomiting, fever.

There are three categories of food poisoning.

1 Biological food poisoning
A number of foods produce toxins naturally which can cause food poisoning if eaten in large quantities.

Table 6.11 Examples of biological food poisoning		
Food	Toxin	Symptoms
Rhubarb	Oxalic acid	Affects calcium absorption
Tea, coffee, cola	Caffeine	Diuretic and stimulant

2 Chemical food poisoning
- Chemical food poisoning can be the result of harmful chemicals present in food.
- Chemicals from metals due to food storage and packing.
- Pesticides and antibiotics used in agriculture.

3 Bacterial food poisoning
- Bacterial food poisoning is the result of bacteria contaminating food.
- Presence of bacteria in food.

Table 6.12 Toxic and infectious food poisoning	
Toxic food poisoning	Infectious food poisoning
• Produces toxins outside the cell • Called exotoxin and can produce poisonous substances • Symptoms, e.g. vomiting and diarrhoea, occur within 2 hours • Boiling food for 30 minutes will destroy exotoxin	• Eating food that contains live bacteria results in the production of an endotoxin, which is released on death of bacteria • Symptoms occur within 12 hours • Symptoms are fever, vomiting, diarrhoea, headache • Heating destroys endotoxin
Examples of bacteria: *Clostridium perfringens*, *Staphylococcus aureus*	Examples of bacteria: salmonella, listeria
High risk foods: cream, milk, meat, poultry, eggs, soup, gravy, stock, reheated dishes	

Table 6.13 Toxic food poisoning bacteria	
1 Name	*Clostridium botulinum*
Description	• Rod shaped • Gram + • Produce spores
Environment	• Anaerobic • Acid pH • Ideal temperature 30–37°C • For destruction keep at 121°C for 15 minutes
Sources	• Soil • Vegetables • Intestine of fish and pig
Food	• Vacuumed packed food • Canned foods
Incubation period	12–36 hours
Duration	1–8 days
Symptoms	• Headache • Diarrhoea • Double vision • Slurred speech • Paralysis • Slow recovery • Death
2 Name	*Staphylococcus aureus*
Description	• Spherical • Gram + • No spores
Environment	• Facultative • Salt tolerant
Sources	• Nose • Throat • Skin of humans • Unwashed hands
Food	• Cold meat • Unpasteurised milk
Incubation period	3–6 hours
Duration	24 hours
Symptoms	• Vomiting • Cramps • Diarrhoea

Table 6.14 Infectious food poisoning bacteria	
1 Name	**Salmonella**
Description	Rod shaped, bacilli, no spores
Environment	Facultative, 37°C
Sources	Intestine of humans and animals, rodents, unwashed hands
Food	Poultry, meat, eggs
Incubation period	12–36 hours
Duration	1–7 days
Symptoms	Abdominal pain, fever, diarrhoea, vomiting, death in very young and elderly
2 Name	**E. coli 0157**
Description	Rod shaped, bacilli, Gram –
Environment	Aerobic
Sources	Excreta, polluted water, intestine of humans and animals, unwashed hands
Food	Raw meat, poultry
Incubation period	12–24 hours but can take up to 72 hours
Duration	1–5 days
Symptoms	Abdominal cramps, diarrhoea, nausea, fever, kidney failure in severe cases

Controlling microbial spoilage of food

Microbial spoilage of food can be curtailed by altering the specific requirements for growth of microbes, e.g. by removing the ideal conditions necessary for growth (see section 1).

Questions

1. List five conditions required for the growth of moulds. (6)
   (2006, HL, Section A, 7)

2. State one use of each of the following fungi in food production: Moulds, Yeast, Large Fungi. (6)
   (2008, HL, Section A, 6)

3. Give an account of the main causes of food spoilage. (16)
   (2005, OL, Section B, 3)

4. Name two main types of micro-organisms that are responsible for food spoilage. (4)
   (2004, OL, Section A, 7)

Key Points

Microbiology
- Micro-organisms are tiny, single-celled living organisms
- Conditions required for growth of micro-organisms: Food, oxygen, temperature, moisture, correct pH, time

Fungi
- Classification: Moulds, yeast, larger fungi
- Structure of moulds: Suitable conditions, spore, hypha, mycelium, grow upwards
- Reproduction: Asexual and sexual reproduction
- Classification of moulds: Phycomycetes = Mucor and Rhizopus; Ascomycetes = Penicillium and Aspergillis
- Conditions for growth: Food (saprophytic), oxygen (aerobic), temperature (mesophile), moisture, pH 4–6
- Larger fungi (Basidiomycetes): Edible, growth of mushroom
- Advantages: Production of food and antibiotics, food supplements, decompostion of organic matter, edible, production of novel protein foods
- Disadvantages: Poisonous, cause human and plant diseases, food spoilage

Yeast (Saccharomycetes)
- Structure: Cell wall, cytoplasm, nucleus, vacuoles
- Reproduction: Budding
- Conditions for growth: Food, oxygen (facultative) temperature (25–30°C), moist conditions, pH 4–5

Bacteria
- Structure: Cell wall, cytoplasmic membrane, ribosomes, nucleus, flagellae
- Reproduction: Binary fission
- Endospore formation: Resistant to extreme temperatures and some chemicals
- Conditions for growth: Food (saprophytic and parasitic), oxygen, temperature, moisture, pH 7
- Classification: Cocci, bacillus, spiralla, vibrio; Gram staining
- Advantages: Produce vitamins B and K, food production, decomposition of waste matter, food supplements
- Disadvantages: Cause diseases in plants, humans and animals, food spoilage, food poisoning
- Toxins: Exotoxin, endotoxins, enterotoxin, mycotoxin

Food Spoilage
- Different forms of food spoilage: Enzymes, dehydration and contamination
- Enzymes and how they spoil foods: Ripening and browning
- How to prevent enzymatic spoilage of food: Heat, blanching, cold temperature, acids, additives
- How microbes contaminate food: Yeast, moulds, bacteria
- Food poisoning: Biological, chemical and bacterial
- Toxic food poisoning bacteria: *Clostridium botulium*, *Staphylococcus aureus*
- Infectious food poisoning: Salmonella, E. coli 0157

7: Food Preservation

●●● Learning Objectives

In this chapter you will learn about:
1. Common Methods of Food Preservation
2. Commercial Freezing
3. Heat Treatments in the Home
4. Commercial Heat Treatments
5. Commercial Dehydration
6. Chemical Food Preservation
7. Irradiation
8. Comparative Evaluation of Foods

The main aim of food preservation is to have good quality, edible, pathogen-free food on a daily basis. The preservation of food is essential.

Exam Hints

Food preservation could be examined in Section A or B and in conjunction with microbiology, food profiles, food spoilage and food additives. Do not forget to highlight the link-ups as you go along, as this will make your revision easier and more successful.

The basic principles of food preservation

- To prevent microbial activity.
- To inhibit enzymic activity.
- To use sealed containers for storage to prevent the recontamination of the food.
- To maintain the original colour, taste, texture and nutritive value of food.

Food can be preserved by:
- A change in temperature to extreme heat or cold.
- Dehydration (removal of moisture).
- Using chemicals to aid preservation.
- Fermentation (use of lactic acid).
- Irradiation (use of gamma radiation rays to kill disease causing bacteria).

Advantages of food preservation

- Food preservation prevents waste by increasing the shelflife of food.
- Fresh fruit and vegetables are preserved to be used at a later date.
- Preserved food is economical.
- It is convenient, easy to use and useful in emergencies.
- Food preservation ensures that a wide variety of food is available throughout the year.

CHAPTER 7

Common Methods of Food Preservation

Home freezing

Freezing is the most common method of home preservation due to its simplicity and usefulness.

Principles of home freezing
- Warmth and moisture are two of the conditions required for microbial growth. Freezing removes both.
- Micro-organisms cannot utilise frozen water molecules.
- Freezing creates a hostile environment for microbes and enzymes which become inactivated or destroyed.
- If food such as vegetables are blanched enzymes are inactivated.

There are two types of home freezing:
1. Slow freezing
2. Quick freezing

Table 7.1 Slow and quick freezing			
Type	Temperature	Location	Effect
Slow freezing	0–24°C	In ice box	• Large ice crystals form • Damage to structure of food, loss of nutritive value, colour, flavour and texture
Quick freezing	–25°C or lower	Fast freeze section of freezer	• Small ice crystals form • Food structure and food value are unchanged

Table 7.2 Home freezing	
Advantages of home freezing	Disadvantages of home freezing
1. A wide variety of foods can be frozen 2. It is a simple and safe method of preserving food 3. It maintains the nutritive value, colour, flavour and texture of food 4. It prevents waste as leftover food can be frozen 5. Foods can be bulk frozen, saving time and energy 6. It allows food to be available out of season 7. It is economical to operate 8. Useful in emergencies	• Packaging needed for freezing can be expensive. Recycled plastic containers can be used instead • Bulk cooking and freezing of food is time-consuming and labour-intensive • Initial cost of freezer can be expensive • Availability of frozen convenience foods could result in the formation of unhealthy eating habits • As a full freezer is cheaper to operate it needs to be constantly restocked

Foods suitable for freezing
- Most fruit and vegetables
- Meat, fish, poultry (raw and cooked)
- Bread and pastries
- Convenience foods, e.g. pizza and chips
- Soups and sauces

Foods unsuitable for freezing
Any food with a high water content loses structure on thawing and becomes limp.
- Lettuce, tomatoes, cucumber, mayonnaise
- Bananas, strawberries
- Whole eggs (can be frozen if separated)

Guidelines for freezing food

1 Preparation
- Freeze only high-quality fresh food.
- 3–4 hours prior to freezing turn freezer to its lowest setting (−25°C/fast freeze).
- Do not freeze more than one-tenth of the freezer capacity at one time.
- Freeze food in useable quantities, e.g. in two portions.

2 Packaging
- Seal all packaging well. (See Packaging p. 137)
- Remove as much air as possible from the packaging.
- If freezing liquids such as soups allow head space for expansion.
- Use suitable packaging material (moisture and vapour proof, strong and airtight).
- Label all foods, recording the content, date and quantity.

3 Freezing
- Freeze all food in the fast freeze compartment at −25°C.
- Allow air to circulate.
- Remove from fast freeze compartment after 24 hours.
- Never refreeze thawed food unless it has been cooked first.
- Open freeze soft fruits such as berries or foods that might stick together, e.g. prawns. Place in a container after freezing.
- Return freezer temperature to normal at −18°C.

4 Storing
- Itemise contents of freezer.
- Use food within recommended time, e.g. bread should be used within 1 month, lamb within 6 months, other meat and vegetables within 12 months.
- Use food in rotation, following the FIFO (first in, first out) principle.

- Place similar foods together.
- Running costs of freezer are reduced if it is kept full.

5 Thawing
- Cook vegetables from frozen as it retains nutrients, colour, texture and flavour.
- Never refreeze thawed food without cooking it first.
- Frozen food should be thawed slowly and completely in the refrigerator.
- Use thawed food quickly to prevent microbial activity.
- Drips from thawing meat, poultry or fish could contaminate other cooked products.

Blanching
1. Prior to freezing, vegetables are placed in boiling water for approximately 1–8 minutes depending on the vegetable.
2. Enzymes and microbes are inactivated.
3. After blanching, immerse in cold water immediately for same amount of time.
4. Place in container and put in freezer.

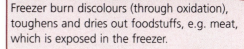

Points to Note

Freezer burn discolours (through oxidation), toughens and dries out foodstuffs, e.g. meat, which is exposed in the freezer.

Packaging

Packaging should be:
- Strong and sealable
- Vapour, water and greaseproof
- Easy to use
- Economical and reusable

Examples of packaging
Polythene freezer bags and containers, aluminium foil and containers, cling film, waxed cartons and freezer paper.

Commercial Freezing

Principles of commercial freezing

The same principles apply as for home freezing except that the quantities frozen and the methods used are different.

Types of commercial freezing

There are four methods used for commercial freezing.

Table 7.3 Commercial freezing	
Type 1	**Air blast freezing**
Temperature	−30°C to −40°C
Method	A blast of cold air circulates around the food as it passes through a tunnel on a conveyer belt Process takes 2–3 hours
Use	Most widely used method of commercial freezing Most foods can be frozen this way; ideal for awkward shaped foods
Type 2	**Plate/contact freezing**
Temperature	−30°C to −40°C
Method	Cartons with food are placed between two metal shelves On contact with the cold shelves the food is frozen
Use	Commonly used for foods packed in flat cartons, e.g. fish and burgers
Type 3	**Fluidised bed freezing**
Temperature	−30°C
Method	Method is similar to blast freezing but used to freeze smaller food products
Use	Example: peas which would otherwise stick together on freezing
Type 4	**Cryogenic freezing**
Temperature	−200°C
Method	Food is sprayed with liquid nitrogen
Use	Very quick but expensive method of freezing, e.g. strawberries and prawns

Heat Treatments in the Home

Heat treatments used in the home are: (i) jam-making (including sugar), (ii) chutney-making (including vinegar) and (iii) bottling.

The temperatures used for these methods of food preservation destroy most microbes. However, some bacteria produce heat resistant spores which require prolonged cooking.

Jam-making

Principles of jam-making
1. Fruit is boiled at 100°C to destroy any micro-organisms and to soften the fruit.
2. A high proportion of sugar (65%) is added to 35 per cent fruit to prevent microbial activity and to act as a preservative.
3. Pectin, acid and sugar are needed in the correct proportion to set the jam.

\multicolumn{2}{c}{Table 7.4 Ingredients needed for jam-making}
Ingredient	**Reason**
Fruit	• The pectin needed to set the jam is found in the skin • Ripe good-quality acidic fruit produce the best results, e.g. cooking apples, blackcurrants • Over-ripe fruit does not contain sufficient pectin for setting
Sugar	• Acts as a preservative and also sweetens the jam • Ensure the sugar is measured accurately as too much causes crystallisation • A well-made set jam contains 65% sugar concentration
Pectin	• Pectin is a polysaccharide; it is found in the cell wall of ripe fruit • Pectin is necessary for the setting of jam
Acid	• Acid is necessary to extract the pectin from the fruit • Lemon juice is often used in recipes • Acid enhances the colour and flavour of jam and helps prevent crystallisation

About pectin

There are three forms of pectin:

1 Pectose   In unripe fruit   Poor setting
2 Pectin   In ripe fruit   Good setting
3 Pectic acid   In over-ripe fruit   Very poor setting

The pectin content of different fruits varies.

Pectin content	Fruit
High	Apples, blackcurrants, oranges
Medium	Apricots, raspberries, plums
Low	Strawberries, pears, cherries

A simple test for pectin will determine if the jam will set.

Put 1 teaspoon of fruit juice and add 3 teaspoons of methylated spirits in a bowl. Mix and leave for 1 minute. Pour from one bowl to another and observe the clot formation.

- 1 firm clot = high in pectin
- 3–4 firm clots = medium amount of pectin
- Many soft clots = poor in pectin

If the pectin content is inadequate it can be improved by:
- Mixing a fruit that has a high pectin content such as cooking apples into the jam.
- Adding commercial liquid pectin.
- Using a special preserving sugar such as Sure Set.

Test for setting jam

1 Cold plate test
Place a little jam on a plate and allow to cool. Push the jam with your finger, a skin will have formed if the jam is set.

2 Flake test
Use a wooden spoon to remove some jam and cool. Turn spoon and observe the jam running off. If the jam runs off in one flake it is set.

3 Sugar thermometer
Warm thermometer slightly before placing in the jam. Jam sets at 104°C.

Chutney-making

- Chutney combines heat treatments and chemicals (acetic acid) as a method of food preservation.
- Chutney can be made from a combination of fruit, vegetables, sugar, spices and vinegar.

Principles of chutney-making
1. The high temperatures used inactivate or destroy any micro-organisms present.
2. The vinegar (5% acetic acid) reduces the pH level, therefore preventing micro-organisms from growing.
3. The sugar (brown) dehydrates the micro-organisms and thus prevents their growth.
4. The re-entry of microbes is prevented by sealing the jars and making them airtight.

Store the chutney for a couple of months before use to allow the flavour to develop and soften (mellow).

Commercial Heat Treatments

Commercial heat treatments are:
1. Bottling
2. Canning
3. Pasteurisation
4. Sterilisation
5. Ultra-heat treatment

Bottling and canning

Principles of canning and bottling
1. Bottling and canning are processes where food is sterilised in metal cans or glass bottles. The sealed can or bottle prevents recontamination.
2. The use of very high temperatures destroys any enzymes, micro-organisms and their spores.

3 Canning is used as a method of preservation for the following foods: vegetables, fruit, meat, fish, milk, soup

Method of canning

1 The food is prepared by washing and cleaning. Bones are removed from meat.
2 Meat or fish are cooked; vegetables are blanched.
3 Lacquered cans are filled with food. One of the following ingredients is added: syrup, brine (salt and water), sauce or oil.
4 All the air is removed and the can is sealed in a sterile environment.
5 Both the can and the food are sterilised.
6 The cans are labelled after cooling down.

Table 7.5 Types of canning	
Aseptic/HTST canning	• Ultra-high temperatures of 120–150°C are used for a short period of time to sterilise the food • Cans are sterilised separately • The sterilised food is put into the sterilised can and hermetically sealed • The cans are cooled and labelled

Pasteurisation, sterilisation and ultra-heat treatment

See Table 3.37, Methods of processing milk, p.77.

Commercial Dehydration

Principles of commercial dehydration

1 Dehydration removes the moisture content which is necessary for micro-organisms to grow.
2 Micro-organisms need moisture to metabolise. Dried foods normally contain less than 25 per cent moisture.
3 Mould and enzyme activity are also inhibited.

Methods of commercial dehydration

1 Spray drying: Used for liquid foods, e.g. milk (see p. 77)
2 Roller drying: Used for thickened food, e.g. baby food (see p. 77)
3 Sun drying: Used in hot climates (Australia, California), e.g. for tomatoes
   • Prone to contamination from air, soil and insects
4 Fluidised bed drying
5 Accelerated freeze drying (AFD)

Fluidised bed drying
- This method is often used to preserve vegetables.
- The vegetables are prepared and blanched.
- Hot air is circulated around the food, thus dehydrating it.
- The food is continuously moved around which prevents it from sticking.
- The vegetables are packed and labelled.

Accelerated freeze drying
- The food is first frozen so that tiny ice crystals are formed.
- The ice crystals are then evaporated in a vacuum chamber (sublimation) which produces a lightweight product with a longer shelflife.
- The process of sublimation allows the water to go from a solid state (ice) to a gas (steam) without going through the liquid state.

Chemical Food Preservation

For chemical preservation any one of the following substances are added to foods to inhibit microbial activity.

The use of commercial chemicals in food preservation is strictly tested and controlled. EU legislation limits the use of some chemical preservatives.

Table 7.6 Chemical preservatives	
Home preservation	**Commercial preservation**
Sugar	Sugar, sulfur dioxide
Vinegar	Salt, acetic acid
Salt	Antioxidants, sorbic acid

Principles of chemical preservation

1. The chemical dissolves in the water within the food and thereby changes its concentration. As a result any micro-organisms present are dehydrated.
2. Acids used in chemical preservation reduce the pH level and inhibit microbial or enzyme activity.
3. Alcohol denatures the protein in the bacteria.

> **Exam Hints**
> Chemical food preservation could be asked with food additives and food legislation.

Fermentation

Fermentation is the breakdown of organic substances by the action of bacteria or yeast. This process is used in the manufacturer of alcohol and in bread-making.

Fermentation

$$C_6H_{12}O_6 + \text{yeast} = 2C_2H_5OH + 2CO_2 + \text{energy}$$
$$\text{Glucose} + \text{yeast} = \text{alcohol} + \text{carbon dioxide} + \text{energy}$$

- The by-products of fermentation are used as preservatives, e.g. alcohol, acid.
- Yeast fermentation is used in the brewing and baking industries.
- Acid fermentation is used for the production of yoghurt, e.g. lactose is converted into lactic acid.

Irradiation

Principles of irradiation

1. Irradiation exposes food to low levels of radiation (gamma rays) in order to destroy micro-organisms.
2. Strict legislation governs the process and the type of food which can be irradiated.

Irradiation symbol Radura

Table 7.7 Advantages and disadvantages of irradiation

Advantages	Disadvantages
1 Destroys disease causing bacteria	1 Reduction in vitamins
2 Controls the growth of mould in soft fruits	2 Inadequate information whether food has been irradiated
3 Delays the ripening of fruit	3 Change in taste, particularly in eggs and dairy produce which can taste bad
4 Prevents sprouting of potatoes and other vegetables	4 Food production hygiene standards could be reduced
	5 Open to abuse by food manufacturers disguising stale food as fresh

Sample Questions and Answers

1. What is irradiated food? (2)
   (2004, HL, Section A, 5a)

Answer 1
The exposure of food to low levels of radiation to destroy micro-organisms.

2. State two effects of irradiation on food. (4)

Answer 2
Destroys disease causing bacteria, reduces nutrient content of food, delays ripening of fruit, controls growth of mould on soft fruits.

Table 7.8 Effects of food preservation	
Method of preservation	**Effect on food**
Freezing	• Loss of water-soluble vitamins B and C • Inhibits bacterial growth • Enzyme activity is prevented • Uncovered protein foods could suffer from freezer burn
Canning	• Loss of water-soluble vitamins B and C • Loss of colour, flavour and texture • Increased calorie content in some products due to the addition of sugar • Bacterial and enzyme activity are stopped
Dehydration	• Loss of vitamins B and C • Water loss • Bacterial growth is inhibited • Change of colour, texture and flavour
Chemical	• Loss of vitamins • Change in colour and taste • Bacterial growth is inhibited

Comparative Evaluation of Foods

A comparative evaluation of different methods of food preservation involves comparing the food using the following headings: Ingredients; Consumer information; Shelflife; Type of packaging; Effect of processing; Risk of spoilage; Method of processing; Name the method of processing; Cost per 100g; Use.

Questions

1. Outline the general rules to be followed when freezing fresh food. (16)
   (2006, OL, Section B, 2C)

2. Name two commercial methods of freezing and suggest a food suitable for each method. (6)
   (2006, HL, Section A, 8)

3. Suggest one method of food preservation which could be used to preserve a surplus of home grown fruit or vegetables. Explain the underlying principle of the method of preservation you have selected. (15)
   (2008, HL, Section B, 2)

Key Points

Food Preservation
- It prevents food spoilage
- It prevents microbial activity
- It inhibits enzymic activity

Common Methods of Food Preservation
- Types of food preservation: Freezing, dehydration, heat processing, chemical preservation, fermentation and irradiation

Home Freezing
- Slow freezing, quick freezing

Commercial Freezing
- Air blast freezing, plate/contact freezing
- Fluidised bed freezing, cryogenic freezing

Heat Treatments in the Home
- Jam-making (including sugar)
- Chutney-making (including vinegar)
- Bottling

Commercial Heat Treatments
- Bottling and canning
- Pasteurisation, sterilisation and ultra-heat treatment

Commercial Dehydration
- Spray drying, roller drying, sun drying
- Fluidised bed drying, accelerated freeze drying (AFD)

Chemical Food Preservation
- Home preservation: Uses sugar, vinegar, salt
- Commercial preservation: Uses sugar, sulfur dioxide, salt, acetic acid, antioxidants, sorbic acid

Irradiation
- Exposes food to low levels of radiation to destroy micro-organisms
- Governed by strict legislation

8: Food Safety and Hygiene

●●● Learning Objectives

In this chapter you will learn about:
1. Food Hygiene
2. Hazard Analysis Critical Control Point (HACCP)
3. Role of National Agencies in Food Safety

Food Hygiene

To reduce the risk of food poisoning extremely high standards of hygiene are necessary. To prevent contamination, food should be:

Exam Hints

In this section hygiene is looked at, and can be examined in Sections A and B of both levels.

- Prepared by hygienic staff.
- Prepared and cooked in a clean environment (utensils, work surfaces, floor).
- Stored and cooked at the correct temperature.
- Stored correctly.

Personal, kitchen and food hygiene are essential components of any food preparation area.

Personal hygiene of food handlers

1. Food handlers must wash their hands with hot water and soap on a regular basis and before handling food.
2. Extra care should be taken if the food handler has used the toilet, touched waste or animals, coughed or sneezed, or prepared raw food.
3. Clean protective clothing should be worn at all times.
4. Hair should be tied up and a hairnet worn.
5. Nails should be clean, trimmed and free of nail polish.
6. Any jewellery should be removed.
7. Smoking should be banned in the kitchen or the vicinity of food preparation and storage.
8. All cuts should be covered, using a bright coloured dressing/bandage.
9. If a food handler is ill (e.g. vomiting, diarrhoea) all contact with food should be avoided.
10. All food handlers should have some training in food hygiene procedure.

Kitchen hygiene

1. All surfaces such as floors, walls and units, in a kitchen should be easy to clean, non-absorbent and with no cracks on the surface where bacteria could lodge.
2. All surfaces should be washed and disinfected daily.
3. All access to pipe work (water) should be thoroughly sealed to prevent the entrance of vermin and insects.
4. A good lighting system should be in place.
5. An efficient ventilation system is necessary to circulate fresh air and remove odours from the kitchen.
6. All waste and recyclable waste should be stored in purpose-built containers.
7. All equipment should be washed and maintained following the manufacturer's instructions and hygiene guidelines.
8. All clothes should be disinfected or replaced on a regular basis.
9. A colour coded system for chopping boards and other equipment should be implemented to reduce the risk of cross-contamination of, for example, raw and cooked meats.
10. A clean water supply and an efficient drainage system should be in place.

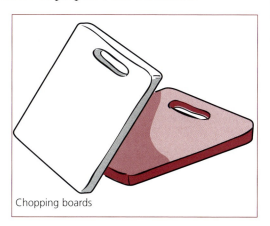
Chopping boards

Food storage

- All foods should be stored at a suitable temperature and in an appropriate container.
- Good ventilation is required in the storage area.
- Refrigerator and freezer should be at the correct temperature.
- Do not over pack the area, allow circulation of air.
- All foods should be covered during storage, especially strong smelling foods.

Points to Note

Cross-contamination of food is the biggest risk during preparation, handling and storage. The danger zone for contamination is between 5°C and 65°C.

Table 8.1 Guidelines for food storage		
Food type	**Example**	**Storage**
Perishable foods	• Meat • Fish • Eggs • Dairy	• Store in refrigerator for a short period of time (approx. 1–2 days)
Chilled foods	• Ready meals, e.g. lasagne • Fresh soup	• Store in refrigerator at 4°C • Do not over pack
Frozen foods	• Vegetables, convenience foods • Meat and fish products	• Store in freezer at –18°C • Never refreeze thawed food
Fresh fruit and vegetables	• Apples • Bananas • Carrots • Potatoes	• Store in cool well-ventilated space • Use as quickly as possible • Remove from trays and plastic containers
Non-perishables	• Dried, canned foods, e.g. fruit and fish	• Store in a well-ventilated larder • Check use-by-date

Guidelines for reheating food
- Use leftover food within two days.
- Only reheat food once.
- Ensure food is heated to 100°C to destroy any micro-organisms.
- A microwave or a conventional oven can be used for reheating.

Hazard Analysis Critical Control Point (HACCP)

A hazard is identified as anything that could cause harm to a customer. There are three potential forms of contamination.

Chemical contaminants
- Pesticides
- Insecticides
- Cleaning agents

Microbial contaminants
- Moulds
- Yeast
- Bacteria

Physical contaminants
- Glass
- Metal
- Dirt, hair

- A risk is the possibility of a hazard occurring. The risk potential can be high, medium or low.
- A CCP (critical control point) is an area in the food production where a hazard may occur which must be controlled or minimised.
- Some CCP areas are delivery, raw materials, preparing and storing food.

How to set up a HACCP system

1 A HACCP team is formed. The team members should be familiar with food processing and have some training in hygiene and safety.
2 The HACCP team develop a flow chart showing all areas of food production from raw materials to final product.
3 They recognise any potential hazards in the food processing.
4 A risk assessment is carried out to see how likely it is that the hazard would occur.
5 A system of control points is established to remove or reduce any microbial, physical or chemical contamination.
6 At each critical control point the team identifies:
   - What is to be done?
   - When is it to be done?
   - Who is to do it?
7 The food processing system is now monitored and controlled.
8 Written records of all stages of the HACCP system must be kept as evidence that the system has been implemented.
9 Action must be taken if required.
10 An evaluation of the system must be carried out annually, or if any point of the process has been altered.

Advantages of HACCP

1 HACCP helps reduce the risk of food contamination by identifying the hazards, therefore producing a safer product.
2 Food industry employees are aware of the importance of hygiene and safety during the production process.
3 Recorded evidence verifies food safety legislation is adhered to.
4 Records provide environmental health officers and food safety officers with a summary of the food production process.

ISO 9000

- ISO is an international organisation for standardisation.
- ISO is a group of global national standards agencies who establish standards to ensure good quality management systems.
- If a company receives the ISO 9000 award from the National Standards Authority of Ireland (NSAI) it means they have attained a standard of management which is accepted internationally.
- Food companies can be issued with the quality mark IS 343, commending a high standard of hygiene.

Role of National Agencies in Food Safety

There are a number of organisations and agencies in Ireland which control, monitor and enforce food safety regulations:

Government departments

1 Department of Agriculture and Food
The Department of Agriculture and Food monitors and controls:
- The use of pesticides and insecticides in vegetables, fruit and cereals.
- The use of antibiotics and other substances used in animal rearing.
- Abattoirs and meat processing factories.
- Animal testing for TB, brucellosis and BSE.
- The operation of the Beef Assurance Scheme which ensures full traceability and identification of meat.
- Dairies and milk processing plants.
- The implementation of EU legislation regarding poultry and egg production.

2 Department of Health and Children
It controls and monitors:
- The development of new food safety policies.
- Food safety and hygiene.
- Food labelling and food additives.
- Premises selling food to the public.
- Education of the consumer on food safety guidelines.

3 Department of Communications, Marine and Natural Resources
- The Department monitors and controls fresh fish transportation and fish processing.

4 Department of the Environment, Heritage and Local Government
- The Department controls and monitors public water safety and bottled water.

5 Local authorities
- Local authorities monitor and inspect abattoirs, meat processing plants and the licensing of farms for milk production in conjunction with veterinary officers.

6 Health Service Executive (HSE)
- Environmental health officers (EHO) from local HSE offices implement food legislation regarding nutritional labelling and food contamination and inspect food premises.
- Local HSE offices investigate incidences of food poisoning and contamination. They deal with emergency situations regarding contaminated food.

Specialised agencies

Food Safety Authority of Ireland (FSAI)
- The Food Safety Authority of Ireland was established to direct and regulate the implementation of food legislation for the safety and protection of the consumer.
- It was created under the Food Safety Authority of Ireland Act 1998.
- It is an independent body, working in conjunction with government departments and specialised agencies.

The main responsibilities of the FSAI are:
1. To put into practice and co-ordinate all food safety systems such as HACCP.
2. To provide advice and guidelines to food providers on food safety, nutrition, prevention of infection by bacteria, etc.
3. To organise emergency response to crises of food contamination, such as the contamination of food with Sudan 1 colouring, or outbreaks of food poisoning.
4. To inspect food premises and take appropriate action when food premises fail to meet legislation guidelines.
5. To monitor and control the introduction of new foodstuffs, such as genetically modified (GM) foods, or the application of irradiation as a method of food preservation.

Public Analyst Laboratories (PAL)
- PAL analyse food, drugs and water to ensure they comply with food legislation guidelines.
- They work in conjunction with environmental health officers.
- For a fee they also analyse food/water samples for the public.

National Consumer Agency
- The National Consumer Agency ensures EU legislation regarding food labelling and prepacked foods is followed.
- It has the responsibility to inspect food premises to make sure food labelling legislation is being implemented.
- It will examine complaints from the public regarding food labelling.

National Standards Authority of Ireland (NSAI)
- See ISO 9000, p.149.

Questions

1 List five guidelines that should be followed to ensure the safe preparation and storage of food in the home. (10)

2 (a) Explain how a Hazard Analysis Critical Control Point (HACCP) system can benefit a catering business in the prevention of food poisoning outbreaks. (12)
(b) Differentiate between (i) infectious food poisoning and (ii) toxic food poisoning. (8)
(c) Name and give a detailed account of any one type of food poisoning bacteria. Refer to
  (i) sources of infection
  (ii) high risk foods and
  (iii) symptoms. (20)
(2004, HL, Section B, 2)

Key Points

Food Hygiene
- To prevent food contamination: Good personal hygiene, clean environment, stored and cooked at correct temperatures
- Food storage guidelines: Good ventilation, refrigerator/freezer at correct temperature, do not over pack the area

Hazard Analysis Critical Control Point
- A hazard: Anything that could harm a customer
- Chemical contaminants: Pesticides, insecticides, cleaning agents
- Microbial contaminants: Moulds, yeast, bacteria
- Physical contaminants: Glass, metal, dirt, hair
- A critical control point (CCP) is an area in food production where a hazard may occur, which must be controlled
- Setting up a HACCP system: Team formed, flow chart, risk assessment, system of control points
- Advantages of HACCP: It helps reduce the risk of food contamination
- ISO 9000: International standardisation in good quality management systems

Role of National Agencies in Food Safety
- Department of Agriculture and Food
- Department of Health and Children
- Department of Communication, Marine and Natural Resources
- Department of the Environment, Heritage and Local Government
- Local authorities
- Health Services Executive (HSE)
- Specialised agencies
- Food Safety Authority of Ireland (FSAI) implements and directs food legislation in the food sector
- Public Analyst Laboratories (PAL)
- Office of the Director of Consumer Affairs
- National Standards Authority of Ireland

9: Family Resource Management

Learning Objectives

In this chapter you will learn about:
1. Family Resource Management
2. The Household as a Financial Unit within the Economy
3. Sources of Household Income
4. Household Expenditure
5. Saving
6. Insurance
7. Housing Finance

Family Resource Management

- Management is the skilful use of materials, time, money and other resources.
- Effective management of an organisation or situation will result in the desired outcome, e.g. saving money to buy a house.
- Resources such as time, money, technology or books are used to achieve goals, e.g. books, money and time are resources used in going to college.
- Family resource management involves organising, implementing and evaluating resources to accomplish the goals/needs of the family.

Purpose of family resource management

1. To achieve a better quality of life for the family.
2. To support the family in achieving goals.
3. To help individual family members achieve goals.
4. To use available resources efficiently to achieve goals.

> **Exam Hints**
>
> This chapter looks at a wide range of topics from family resource management to credit to savings, housing, finance and insurance. These topics appear regularly on the exam papers in Sections A and B at both Higher and Ordinary Levels. Some topics turn up more often than others.

The family as a managerial unit

- The management procedure is vital to the successful organisation within a family.
- Each family will have agreed aims/goals/priorities, such as a planned summer holiday, which will require management skills to implement.
- Each individual member will have his/her own goals to achieve.
- Most goals necessitate the interaction with other systems outside the family unit, e.g. go to college (education system), to improve health (health service).

Management skills are used in the following processes:
- Grocery shopping involves decision-making, e.g. making a shopping list, nutritional/dietary meal planning, knowledge about budget, transport and the environment.
- All management procedures should be evaluated and any changes implemented.

Components of management

Components of management are: (i) inputs (before); (ii) throughputs (during); (iii) output (the end result of inputs and throughputs).

Inputs

Inputs consist of the demands of the individual/family and resources available/needed to meet these demands.
- The demands include physical needs, social needs, goals and values of the family.
- The resources include food, shelter, money, love, security, environmental, e.g. space, temperature and equipment.

Throughputs

- Throughputs involve analysing the inputs, planning by gathering information, looking at the alternatives, drawing up a plan of action.
- Organising the implementation of the plan, allocating resources and people to tasks, and evaluating the whole procedure.

Outputs

- Outputs occur when inputs and throughputs have been completed.
- Evidence of whether the goals have been reached, the values have changed.
- Do resources, e.g. money, need to be replaced?

Evaluation

- Evaluation is looking back over the process/actions, seeing ways to improve it for the future, consider what went well and what did not.

The decision-making process

- Decision-making is making a choice between one or more options.
- Our values and goals will influence the choices we make.

The process of decision-making involves:
1. Defining the decision.
2. Collecting information.
3. Considering the possible alternatives.

4 Considering the consequences of each alternative.
5 Deciding on a solution.
6 Drawing up a resource list and a plan of action.
7 Implementing the plan.
8 Evaluating the process.

Communication

- Communication is the exchange of information between people.
- Effective communication means that the person receiving the information interprets it in the way the sender intended it.

Good communication within the family

- Communication is necessary to resolve conflict and any difficulties that may arise between family members.
- Communication involves talking and listening.

Social factors affecting management

1 Size and composition of the family, e.g. special needs, number of children.
2 Stages in the family lifecycle, e.g. with children, retired.
3 Employment patterns: Number employed, type of employment.
4 Socio-economic status: Education, opportunities.
5 Gender roles: Equality and fairness in home.
6 Culture: Acceptable social practices within society.
7 Values and standards: Influence decisions taken by family.

The Household as a Financial Unit within the Economy

Economic functions of the family

- The family provides finance for day-to-day living and long-term financial planning, e.g. children's education, retirement.
- Each household has varying degrees of available income depending on the size of the family and the age and employment status of each family member.
- Each person in paid employment contributes to the running of the country through the taxes and PRSI that they pay.

Social factors affecting household income

1 Age: Increase in wages due to promotion and age.
2 Gender: Employment Equality Act ensures equal pay and conditions for males and females.

3 **Socio-economic groups:** The group one belongs to can have a major impact on a person's income due to education and higher wages.
4 **Culture:** Every culture has different expectations on household income.

Sources of Household Income

Sources of household income are: (i) wages and salaries, (ii) pensions, (iii) state benefits, (iv) other incomes, e.g. investments.

Wages and salaries

- Income can be divided into gross income and net income.
- The gross income is the money a person earns before any deductions are made.
- The net income is the money available after deductions are made (see below).
1 *Compulsory deductions*: Income tax/Pay As You Earn (PAYE), Pay Related Social Insurance (PRSI)
2 *Voluntary deductions*: Private health insurance (VHI, Quinn Healthcare), pension contributions (superannuation), savings schemes, union subscriptions, loan repayments (e.g. for car)

Income tax

- Income tax has to be paid by everyone earning money.
- If income tax is not paid or avoided you might receive a fine or a prison sentence.
- There are two types of income tax:
1 *Pay As You Earn (PAYE)* for employees: The two tax bands for 2006 are standard rate 20%, higher rate 41%
2 *Self-assessment* income tax for the self-employed, e.g. farmers

- **P60 – certificate of pay, tax and PRSI**: Employers issue this certificate detailing the amounts paid by each employee at the end of each tax year. This certificate is often used as proof of income with financial institutions.
- **P45 – cessation certificate**: Employees receive a cessation certificate once they stop working for an employer.

> **Sample Question and Answer**
>
> Name and explain the two compulsory deductions taken from a person's gross income. (6)
> (2005, HL, Section A, 11)
>
> **Answer**
> PAYE – Pay As You Earn. The employer takes this deduction before a person receives any pay. This money is given to the Revenue Commissioners.
> PRSI – Pay Related Social Insurance. This is based on a percentage of the person's income and the rate will depend on it. Both the employee and employer contribute to this. This money is used to pay for social welfare payments and pensions.

Tax credits
- Tax credits help to minimise the tax payable by an individual.
- Income tax is calculated on the gross income and then any tax credits are deducted, therefore reducing the amount of tax paid.

Pay related social insurance (PRSI)
- Both the employee and the employer must contribute to the social insurance scheme.
- PRSI pays for unemployment benefit, disability allowance and state pensions.
- A minimum of 39 PRSI contributions must be paid in the year prior to any claim being made.
- The payment is calculated as a percentage of the claimer's income.

Pensions

A pension provides an income for people when they retire from work.

Social Welfare and Pensions Act 2005
- This act is based on the European Union Pensions Directive. Its aim is to protect the consumer and has the power to investigate pension schemes.

Types of pensions
There are three types of pensions: (i) personal pension; (ii) occupational pension; (iii) state pension. There are two types of state pensions:
1. Contributory pension: Paid at the age of 66. Not means tested.
2. Non-contributory pension: Paid at the age of 66. Means tested.

(Other state allowances: Living alone allowance (age 60 or over), fuel allowance, over 80 allowance.)

State benefits

The Department of Social and Family Affairs provides income in the form of benefits and assistance to a number of people. These benefits are:

1 Social insurance payments (contributory)
- These payments are made if a person has contributed the minimum amount of PRSI payments (39 weeks).
- These payments are not means tested.
- These social insurance payments include: Contributory old age pension; contributory widow(er)'s pension; disability allowance; jobseekers benefit.(The budget of April 2009 introduced a number of new criteria to claiming jobseekers benefit www.welfare.ie); injury benefit.

- A person may also be entitled to all or some of the following depending on their circumstances: Fuel allowance; medical card; free TV licence; electricity allowance, telephone rental allowance; living alone allowance; over 80 allowance.

2 Social assistance payments (non-contributory)
- Social assistance payments are paid to people who do not qualify for social insurance payments.
- These payments are means tested, e.g. savings, assets.
- Social assistance payments include the following: Non-contributory old age pension; non-contributory widow(er)'s pension; blind person's pension; one-parent family payment; Jobseekers allowance (New claimants of jobseekers allowance under the age of 20 will receive €100 per week from May 2009); carer's allowance; family income supplement (FIS); supplementary welfare allowances.

3 Universal payments
- Universal payments include child benefit, disability allowance and free travel for people aged over 66.

Household Expenditure

- Expenditure is the amount of money a family spends on a weekly/monthly basis.
- Expenditure can be essential or discretionary.

1 Essential expenditure
- Fixed: Mortgage, rent, loans, insurance, utility bills, e.g. gas, electricity, phone
- Irregular: Food, clothing, dentist, doctor, car

2 Discretionary expenditure
- Savings, luxury items, holidays, furniture, entertainment, leisure

Budgeting

- A budget is a plan for spending money.
- It is used to balance income and expenditure.
- A budget can be a weekly or monthly plan.

Advantages of a household budget
- Prevents overspending.
- Provides for unexpected expenses.
- Provides security and reduces stress.
- Allows for periods of increased expenditure, e.g. Christmas.

- Encourages both long- and short-term savings.
- Limits the use of credit and develops money management skills.

How to create a budget
- List all sources of income such as salaries/wages, children's allowance, pensions, social welfare benefits/allowances.
- Calculate the yearly expenditure on each bill. (Do this by dividing by 52 or 12.) This helps you calculate how much needs to be allocated for the item per week/month, e.g. health insurance = €1,200 per year = €100 per month.
- Incorporate both long-term and short-term savings.
- Allow extra finance for times of the year with high expenditure such as Christmas.
- Review budgets regularly or as your circumstances change, e.g. due to retirement, having children.

The following areas and percentages are accepted guidelines for planning a budget.

Guidelines for planning a budget
- Food 25%; housing 25%; household expense 15%; clothes 10%
- Transport 10%; health 5%; leisure 5%; savings 5%

Money Advice and Budgeting Service (MABS)
MABS advises people who are in financial difficulty due to poor money management skills, overspending and debt. It helps people to plan a realistic budget and repayment schedule.

Payment methods for household goods and services
1. **Cash:** Quick, convenient method of payment. No charges incurred for transaction.
2. **Cheque:** There is a charge for each cheque used. Safe method of payment.
3. **Debit cards (Laser card):** A current account with sufficient funds is needed.
4. **Credit cards:** A card with electromagnetic strip with a set credit limit. Chip and pin system now used for safety. Interest charged at various rates on purchases after 56 days.
5. **Direct debit (DD) and standing order (SO):** DD allows a variable payment. SO is a fixed payment to be made from one account to another designated account.
6. **Bill pay:** Available at post offices throughout the country.
7. **24-hour banking:** Customers have access to their current account and bill payment via the telephone.

> **Points to Note**
> 3V is a new financial product introduced in 2005 by the PTSB and Visa. A virtual value voucher is a prepaid voucher consisting of a 16 digit disposable number, e.g. used for Internet and mail order shopping.

8 **Credit transfer/bank giro:** Some utility bills, e.g. ESB, gas and phone bills provide customers with a giro slip.
9 **Online banking:** Provides customers with access to their current account around the clock via the Internet; bills and some transactions can be made.

Credit

Credit entails borrowing money to pay for purchases and repaying it with interest at a later date.

Table 9.1 The advantages and disadvantages of credit

Advantages	Disadvantages
- Have the use of the goods before they are paid for - Credit allows the purchase of large expensive items, e.g. houses and cars - No need to carry large sums of money around - Credit cards offer an interest free period of up to 56 days, i.e. no interest is paid if the bill is cleared on time - Use of credit encourages spending which is good for the economy as it provides employment	- It is easy for a person to get into debt if they have a lot of credit repayments - Goods can be repossessed if they are bought on hire purchase and the buyer fails to make the repayments - Goods are more expensive if bought on credit due to the interest rates charged - Credit promotes impulse buying and overspending, especially with credit cards

Annual percentage rate (APR)

The APR must appear on all credit advertisements and agreements. It allows the consumer to compare interest rates offered. The lower the interest rate, the lower the interest paid.

Forms of credit

- Personal/term loan: Banks, building societies, credit unions
- Overdraft: Banks, building societies
- Hire purchase: Large retailers, financial companies
- Credit cards/charge cards: Banks
- Store cards: Department stores
- Licensed money lenders

Hire purchase

- Hire purchase can be an expensive form of credit if high interest rates are charged.
- The consumer has use of the goods while making weekly/monthly instalments. However, they do not own the goods until the final instalment is made.
- If a consumer fails to make a repayment and less than one-third of the price has been paid, the goods can be repossessed.
- The Hire Purchase Act 1946, 1960 set out the conditions for a hire purchase

agreement to protect the consumer. These conditions are now incorporated into the Consumer Credit Act 1995, part VI, section 56.
- The hire purchase agreement must include the following:
  1. Name, address and signature of both parties
  2. A description of the goods
  3. A cash price and a hire purchase price of the goods
  4. The APR
  5. The cost of the credit, the number of instalments and the date of each payment
  6. A ten-day cooling off period during which the consumer can decide to end the agreement
  7. The rights of each individual to end the agreement or repossess the goods

Consumer Credit Act 1995

- The Consumer Credit Act incorporates all aspects of credit from advertising to contracts, e.g. hire purchase, leasing, mortgages.
- It is implemented by the National Consumer Agency.
- It provides protection for the consumer by stating that all credit agreements must be in writing, contain the APR, names, addresses and signatures of all concerned, any extra charges, the total cost of the credit and payment details.
- The act also highlights that credit advertising must contain the following information: APR, cost of credit, security or deposit required, instalments, details and any penalties incurred due to default in payment, e.g. a house may be repossessed if defaults occur on a mortgage or loan secured using the property.

Exam Hints
Look at the exam question 3 from 2004, Higher Level, Section B. It combines budgeting with insurance and the family as a financial unit. It is worth 50 marks.

Saving

- Saving is when money is put aside on a regular basis for use in the future.
- Saving can be long term and short term. The amount of money saved will depend on the individual circumstances.
- You can save at banks, building societies, credit unions, insurance companies and An Post.

Advantages of saving

- Saving provides security for the future.
- If savings can be used to pay for smaller items or contribute to the cost of larger items, they reduce the need for credit.
- Saving creates a financial record which could make future borrowing easier to obtain.
- Saving provides money for special occasions, e.g. weddings or luxury holidays.

Factors influencing your choice of saving scheme

T	Term	How long can you afford to invest the money for?
R	Risk	The less risk taken, the smaller the return
A	Access	How often do you need to access your money?
I	Interest	Interest will vary for each investment or saving scheme and depend on the conditions attached to the saving scheme
T	Tax	Deposit Interest Retention Tax (DIRT) is payable on interest earned in some savings scheme, while others are tax free

1. **Banks and building societies:** Offer similar saving schemes, e.g. demand deposit accounts, notice deposit accounts, special term accounts, savings accounts, stock market related saving plans.
2. **An Post:** Offers the following secure state-guaranteed saving schemes – deposit account, saving bonds, instalment saving scheme and saving certificates.
3. **Credit union:** Offer deposit accounts and share accounts.
4. **Insurance companies:** Offer many long- and short-term policies. Generally linked to stock market performance.

Insurance

- Insurance provides protection against risks.
- Insurance provides protection against events which could have disastrous financial implications for a person, a family or a business.
- A large number of people pay a relatively small premium to the insurance company to protect themselves against the risk of unforeseen events.
- These premiums are used to pay compensation to the few people who might make a claim on the policy.

Types of insurance
- Types of insurance include: Life assurance; house insurance; health insurance; motor insurance; travel insurance; Pay Related Social Insurance (PRSI).

Advantages of insurance
- Insurance provides security and peace of mind in the event of hospitalisation, car accident and death.
- It provides protection against big financial losses, e.g. in the event of a house fire.
- Some insurance such as endowment life assurance policies can be used as a means of saving.

A *policy* is the written evidence of the insurance scheme you are paying into. The *premium* is the amount of money you pay.

Life assurance

Life assurance provides financial security for dependants after the death of the insured. There are four types of life assurance: (i) term life; (ii) whole life; (iii) whole life assurance; (iv) endowment assurance.

1 Term life assurance
- A premium is paid for a set period of time, e.g. up to the age of 60 of the insured person.
- The insured person will only be covered for this period of time.
- Term life assurance is a cheap form of assurance.

2 Convertible term assurance
- Convertible term assurance allows people to change their term assurance to a *whole life* or *endowment policy* without losing the premiums they have already contributed.
- This assurance is slightly more expensive than basic term assurance.

3 Whole life assurance
- The insured person pays a premium for a set period of time; the insurance company pays out a lump sum at the end of this time.
- If the person dies before the time has lapsed the person's dependants/family receive the lump sum.

> **Points to Note**
>
> Mortgage protection policy is a term assurance most people have to take out when getting a mortgage. It protects the insured person for the life of the mortgage. If he/she dies prior to the mortgage being paid off the debt is cleared. Due to the recent increase in claims on these policies the premiums are now being increased, as there is a greater risk involved.

4 Endowment assurance
- The insured person pays a premium for a set period of time. The insurance company will pay out a lump sum at the end of this time whether the person is alive or dead. This policy can be cashed in at any time.

House insurance

House insurance consists of three types: (i) buildings insurance; (ii) contents insurance; (iii) all risks.

> **Exam Hints**
>
> Take a look at the exam question from 2005, OL, Section B, question 4 it combines budgeting for a family savings scheme and the Consumer Credit Act 1995.

Health insurance

Health insurance provides protection in case of hospitalisation or other medical treatment. There are two basic types of health insurance:
1. Private health insurance: VHI, Quinn Healthcare.
2. Permanent health insurance: A 2 per cent levy is deducted from salaries over a certain income.
   - Other health related insurance is serious illness cover and salary/income protection insurance.

Motor insurance

Motor insurance is a legal requirement when driving a motor vehicle in Ireland. The premium is paid annually and depends on the age of the driver, the car engine's size, and the insured's driving history. There are three types of motor insurance:
1. Third party
2. Third party, fire and theft
3. Fully comprehensive

Travel insurance

Travel insurance provides protection against medical expenses, loss of luggage and delayed flights while abroad. Insurance can be purchased for single trips or multi-trips.

Housing Finance

Mortgages

When most people purchase a house they borrow the money to do so from lending institutions over a long period of time. You can get a mortgage at: (i) bank; (ii) building society; (iii) local authority; (iv) insurance companies.

The following factors should be considered prior to borrowing: (i) amount to borrow; (ii) deposit; (iii) income; (iv) credit history; (v) interest; (vi) insurance; (vii) type of property.

Interest rates vary from lender to lender. However, due to competition for business the rates should be comparable. The types of interest available are:
1. **Variable:** The variable interest rate fluctuates, generally following European Central Bank rates.
2. **Fixed:** The interest rate is fixed generally for 1–5 years. Usually, the fixed interest rate is higher than a variable interest rate being offered at a given time.
3. **Combination:** This allows you to divide your borrowings between the two interest rates above.
4. **Tracker interest rate:** This rate changes at a fixed rate above European Central Bank rates.

Types of mortgage
There are three main types of mortgages:
1 **Repayment/annuity mortgage:** The most popular and flexible type of mortgage.
   - Repayments can be made weekly, fortnightly or monthly to suit the needs of the individual.
2 **Endowment mortgages:** One part of each repayment pays the interest on the capital and the other part a premium to an insurance company.
   - The insurance company invests this premium and should provide enough money to pay off the capital at the end of the term. Any surplus money can be used by the person for other needs.
3 **Pension mortgage:** Used by the self-employed or by individuals who are not part of a company pension scheme.
   - It is similar to the endowment mortgage where the interest is paid and the premium is put into a pension fund.

Tax relief is available on the interest paid on a mortgage.

Local authority housing finance

- Local authorities provide housing (rented or purchased) for individuals/families who cannot obtain/afford a mortgage from a financial institution and meet a set list of criteria.
- Points are allocated depending on each situation and the houses are given out accordingly.
- Local authorities help to provide accommodation through:
  1 Rental subsidy scheme
  2 House purchase loan
  3 Tenant purchase scheme
  4 Shared ownership scheme
  5 Mortgage allowance scheme
  6 Affordable housing scheme

1 **Rental subsidy scheme:** Available to individuals on an income below €28,500.
2 **House purchase loan/mortgage:** The local authority lends 97% of the purchase price over 25 years up to a limit of €185,000 as long as the repayments are less than 35% of total income of the individual/couple.
3 **Tenant purchase scheme:** Allows tenants of local authority housing of one year or more to purchase their house. The cost of the house is the market value minus discounts.
4 **Shared ownership scheme:** Available to people who cannot purchase a house with their own resources. The individual purchases 40% of the house (through a mortgage) while the local authority purchases 60%, which the individual rents back.
5 **Mortgage allowance scheme:** Facilitates individuals who wish to move from rented local authority housing to the private sector.
6 **Affordable housing scheme:** If an individual does not qualify for a mortgage from a financial institution and earns less than €40,000 gross for a single person, or €100,000 gross for a couple (gross income of higher earner × 2.5 plus gross income of second earner), the local authority will provide a 95% mortgage repayable over 25 years.
   - The houses are purchased at a reduced price and offered to individuals at this price. (Figures may change, check with your teacher.)

Housing choice

Table 9.2 Factors influencing housing choice	
1 Size and income of the family	• Number of people sharing the house • How much the repayments will be • What the requirements of the family are
2 Stage of family life	• A young couple with small children will require more space than a retired couple with no children
3 Location of the house	• Close proximity to school, work, amenities, shops, transport links
4 Money available	• How much money the family can afford to spend on the house
5 Special needs	• Any special requirements due to disability, e.g. wheelchair access
6 Personal preference	• Style and type of house, e.g. bungalow, apartment, detached house • The size of garden and the ease of maintenance • Situated in a village or town

National housing policy

The national housing policy is devised by the Department of the Environment, Heritage and Local Government. The policy provides the legislation regarding adequate housing in Ireland. It incorporates the following areas:

- Local authority housing, homeless shelters, Travellers' accommodation, sale of local authority housing to tenants
- Legislation for rented accommodation, improvement and restoration grants

Points to Note
Part 5 of the Planning and Development Act 2000–02 states that in any new development of five units or more 20% must be allocated to social and affordable housing.

Trends in housing development

- Development of larger housing estates.
- Increase in apartment living, especially in urban areas.
- A mix of housing types in estates, e.g. detached, semi-detached, terraced, apartment, duplex.
- Redevelopment of inner city areas.
- Exclusive houses are built in small estates (10–12 houses).
- Individuals buy larger houses in the suburbs and choose to commute to work.
- New houses are becoming more environmentally friendly through materials used, better insulation and meeting the BEG requirements.

- All estates must be provided with adequate open green spaces, walled entrances and amenities.
- Houses are much smaller than those of previous generations.
- Individuals are buying land and designing and building their own homes, usually at a reduced cost.

Availability of housing
- Financial circumstances dictate the type of property a person can afford.
- Due to the current economic situation (2009) and the downturn in the property market there is an over supply of new houses in Ireland.
- Renting is often the only option available in many cities.
- Social and affordable housing is limited and prioritised.

Sample Question and Answer

Identify three recent housing developments in Ireland. (6)
(2005, HL, Section A, 12)

Answer
1. People are building further away from cities and commuting to work.
2. Due to land costs smaller houses are being built, e.g. two-bed townhouses.
3. People are encouraged to build more environmentally friendly houses, e.g. solar heating.

Questions

1. (a) State the purpose of family resource management. (2)
   (b) List two factors that affect the management of family resources. (4)
   (2005, OL, Section A, 9a)

2. In relation to the management process explain and give an example of each of the following:
   (a) input, (b) output. (6)
   (2005, HL, Section A, 10)

3. (a) Identify and elaborate on the general terms and conditions that have to be fulfilled before a mortgage is granted. (20)
   (b) Explain the term mortgage protection and state why mortgage protection is necessary. (10)
   (2008, HL, Section B, 4)

4. Name two methods of paying for goods and services. State one advantage and one disadvantage of each method. (6)
   (2004, OL, Section A, 9)

5. (a) State three advantages of credit buying. (3)
   (b) Identify three areas controlled by the Consumer Credit Act (1995). (3)
   (2004, HL, Section A, 10)

6. Outline the protection provided to the consumer by the Hire Purchase Act 1960. (8)
   (2005, HL, Section B, 3c)

7. (a) Outline the advantages to the householder of having adequate insurance cover. (12)
   (b) Name and describe two different types of household insurance. (14)
   (2004, OL, Section B, 3a)

Key Points

Family Resource Management
- Purpose of resource management: Organising, implementing and evaluation of resources
- Components of management: Inputs, throughputs, outputs
- Evaluation: Considering decisions made and changes that might be made in the future
- Decision-making: Choice between different options, process of decision-making
- Communication: Effective communication
- Factors affecting management: Needs, wants, goals, available resources, decision-making process

Household as a Financial Unit within the Economy
- Economic functions of the family: Day-to-day living expenses, available income, level of debt and impact on family
- Social factors that impact on household income: Age, gender, socio-economic group, culture

Household Income
- The different types of income: Wages, salaries, pensions, state benefits
- The income tax bands and tax credits available: High 41%, low 20%
- Types of pensions: Personal, occupational, state
- Social welfare allowances and benefits: Unemployment, disability, blind persons

Household Expenditure
- Different types of expenditure: Essential and discretionary
- How to create a written budget: Weekly and monthly
- Different methods of bill payments: Cash and credit card, bank giro, Internet banking
- Different forms of credit and their uses: Term loans, credit cards, store cards, overdraft, charge cards
- Hire Purchase Act 1946, 1960 and Consumer Credit Act 1995

Saving
- Factors influencing the choice of saving scheme: Term, interest, risk, access, tax
- Different types of saving accounts: Term accounts, notice deposit accounts, An Post saving schemes
- Life assurance: Term life, convertible term, whole life, endowment
- Health insurance: Private, permanent, serious illness cover, salary/income protection insurance
- House insurance: Buildings, contents, all risks
- Motor insurance: Third party, third party fire and theft, comprehensive
- Travel insurance: Single and multi-trip

Housing Finance
- Types of mortgage available: Annuity/repayment, endowment, pension
- Assessment of mortgage procedure: Deposit, credit history, property, income
- Types of interest rates: Fixed, variable, combination, tracker
- Local authority housing finance provide: Rental subsidy scheme, house purchase loan, tenant purchase scheme, shared ownership scheme, mortgage allowance scheme, affordable housing scheme
- Factors influencing housing choice: Socio-economic factors, national housing policy, trends in housing development, availability of housing

10: Household Technology and Home Management

●●● Learning Objectives
In this chapter you will learn about:
1. The Use and Benefits of Technology in the Home
2. Selecting Household Appliances
3. Categories of Household Appliances

The Use and Benefits of Technology in the Home

Technology has:
- Reduced the workload in the home.
- Reduced the time needed to carry out tasks.
- Increased efficiency in the home.
- Improved communications and security in the home.
- Provided more durable and hygienic surfaces and materials.

Table 10.1 Technology in the home	
Food preparation	Food processor, mixer, juice extractor, kettle
Cooking	Fan oven, hob, microwave
Food storage	Refrigerator, freezer
Cleaning	Dishwasher, washing machine, vacuum cleaner
Automation	Timers, intelligent appliances, lighting
Security and communication	House alarm, phone, computer (Internet), lights
Surfaces	Plastics and other durable finishes make appliances more durable, easy to clean and aesthetically pleasing
Garden and DIY	Electric tools, electric lawnmowers, electric cutters

Selecting Household Appliances

Criteria for selecting household appliances are:
- **Cost:** How much can you afford? What are the installation costs? What are the running costs? Keep within budget.
- **Safety:** Check for safety labels.

- **Reliability/brand name:** Is it a reliable, well-known brand? Is it a reputable shop?
- **Energy efficiency:** The appliances are rated from A to G, with A being the most efficient.
- **Needs of the individual/family:** The size of the family and the amount of use the appliance gets dictates the type of appliance needed.
- **Space available:** What size is the appliance? Will it fit into the existing space? Check dimensions before purchasing the appliance.
- **Design:** Variety in colour and shape, such as brushed steel or retro style, allow the coordination of appliances in the home.
- **Construction:** Ensure the appliance is well made, durable and easy to operate.
- **Guarantee and after sales service:** A guarantee protects the consumer against faulty goods. Check for local or national after sales service.
- **Ease of cleaning:** A complex design can make cleaning difficult. The material of the appliance should be durable and stain resistant.

The following sources provide information regarding household appliances:
- Advertisements
- Newspaper and magazine articles
- Manufacturers' leaflets and brochures
- Sales staff
- Word of mouth
- Consumer magazines
- TV programmes

Categories of Household Appliances

Household appliances can be divided into two basic categories: (i) appliances with a motor (ii) appliances with a heating element.

Table 10.2 Household appliances	
Appliances with a motor	**Appliances with a heating element**
• Food processor • Carving knife • Liquidiser • Juice extractor	• Kettle • Sandwich maker • Deep fat fryer • Contact grill • Iron

Some appliances combine a motor with a heating element, e.g. dishwasher, washing machine.

Small household appliance with a motor: food processor

A food processor makes the preparation of many foods much easier. It can reduce time and energy in preparing soup, chopping vegetables, etc.

Design and construction
- A food processor is made up of a base unit and many detachable parts including a bowl, blades and discs.
- The motor is housed in a strong plastic casing.
- A transparent plastic bowl sits on a spindle and has a lockable lid with a feeder funnel.
- A control switch with various speeds, including a pulsating speed, is found on the plastic casing.
- A flex and a three-pin plug bring electricity to the appliance.

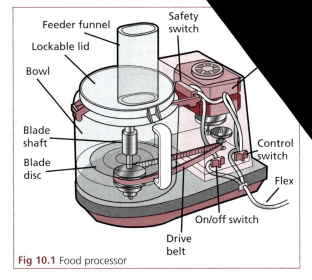

Fig 10.1 Food processor

All food processors will have some or all of the following attachments:

Table 10.3 Atttachments for food processors	
Attachment	**Usage**
Chopping blades	Soups, sauces, meat
Whisks	Cakes, meringues
Grating disc	Vegetables, potatoes, cheese
Dough hook	Pastry, bread
Juice extractor	Juice made from citrus fruits
Liquidiser	Soups, sauces

Working principle of a food processor
- A blade or disc is placed on the spindle.
- The food is placed in the bowl and the lid is locked into place.
- If the feeder funnel is being used, the lid is locked into place before the food is fed through the funnel.
- The food processor is plugged in and the motor which is powered by electricity causes the spindle to rotate.
- There are a number of control speeds on the casing.
- The capacity of most food processors is 2 litres. However, smaller ones are also available.

Food processor

...manufacturer's instructions.
...be fitted correctly.
...guidelines when preparing food.
...fingers in the feeder funnel when the disc/blade is rotating.
...with food.
...and scrape down the sides of the bowl.

Guidelines for the care and cleaning of a food processor
- Always unplug the appliance before cleaning.
- Wash all removable parts in hot soapy water and dry thoroughly.
- Be extremely careful when removing, washing and drying the blades or discs.
- Never immerse the motor/plastic casing in water. Clean the outside and the flex with a warm damp cloth.
- Place the dismantled food processor in a well-ventilated cupboard to allow good air circulation.

Small household appliance with a heating element: kettle

A kettle is used to heat water quickly and efficiently.

Design and construction
- The traditional kettle is dome shaped; modern versions are often jug shaped.
- Kettles are made from a number of materials including stainless steel, plastic and copper.

Fig 10.2 Kettle

- Kettles are available in a variety of colours which allows colour coordination with other appliances in the kitchen.
- A heating element is found inside the base of the kettle.
- The spout or a removable lid can be used for filling the kettle with water.
- Cordless kettles are placed on a base with a plug that connects to the plug at the bottom of the kettle.
- Traditional kettles have a plug and lead which is plugged directly into the wall socket.
- All kettles have a maximum and minimum water level.
- The handle is manufactured from wood or heat resistant plastic.
- Most electric kettles are automatic and contain a thermostat which automatically turns off the kettle on boiling.
- The standard kettle holds 1.7 litres of water.
- An indicator light is often used to show the kettle has been switched on.

Working principle of a kettle
- The kettle is plugged in and the electricity flows to the element where it meets resistance.
- This resistance creates friction which in turn heats the element.
- The element heats the water through convection currents.
- When boiling point is reached the thermostat automatically switches the kettle off.

Guidelines for use of a kettle
- Follow the manufacturer's instructions.
- Unplug the kettle before filling it with water.
- Make sure the element is covered with the minimum amount of water, but be careful not to overfill the kettle.

Guidelines for the care and cleaning of a kettle
- Use only for boiling water.
- Unplug before cleaning.
- Wipe outside with a damp cloth and polish dry.
- Never immerse the kettle in water.
- In hard water areas a build-up of limescale on the element needs to be removed regularly.
- Avoid using abrasives on the outside.

Large appliances: refrigerator

- A refrigerator is used to maintain the quality of perishable foods in a cold environment for a specific amount of time.
- The cold environment inhibits the growth of micro-organisms.

Design and construction
- The basic construction of the refrigerator includes an outer casing of enamelled steel and moulded polystyrene for the interior and the door.
- Insulating material is placed between the enamelled steel and the polystyrene.
- The door has a rubber gasket and magnetic strip which form a seal when the door is closed.
- A thermostat controls the temperature. It can be adjusted during hot or cold weather.
- A switch automatically switches on the light when the door is opened.
- The inside contains a number of glass shelves as well as half-shelves to accommodate milk cartons and larger bottles.
- Two plastic vegetable drawers are at the base of the fridge.
- Most fridges have an icebox at the top of the fridge.
- The doors contains adjustable bottle holders, cheese and egg compartments.
- Control switches indicate if defrosting is necessary.
- Refrigerators are available in a variety of colours and styles.

Table 10.4 Modern features	
Different designs and materials used	Frost free refrigerators
Ice makers/dispensers	Juice or drink dispensers
Integrated models	Automatic defrosting
Zoned refrigeration – different temperature for different compartments of fridge	
Large American style refrigerators and retro style are very popular.	

Working principle of a compressor refrigerator

Points to Note
When a liquid evaporates it draws heat from the surrounding area, thereby cooling it.

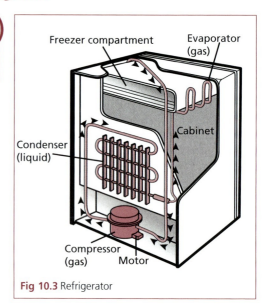

Fig 10.3 Refrigerator

- The compressor at the base of the fridge contains a gaseous refrigerant (Freon 12 or liquid ammonia).
- The compressor is turned on by the motor which forces the refrigerant into the condenser.
- The condenser cools the refrigerant, changing it into a liquid.
- The refrigerant then goes to the evaporator where it is converted back into a gas.
- The liquid refrigerant evaporates by taking heat from the fridge cabinet, thereby keeping it cool.
- The refrigerant returns to the compressor and the cycle starts again.
- A thermostat controls the temperature internally.

Guidelines for use of a refrigerator
- Check the temperature inside the fridge regularly.
- Avoid opening the fridge door unnecessarily as this will increase the temperature inside.
- Store raw meat on the bottom shelf and cooked foods on a higher shelf.
- Ensure all foods are covered and labelled.
- Never place hot food in the fridge as this increases the overall temperature.
- Do not overfill the fridge – to allow circulation of air between foods.
- Defrost regularly unless there is an automatic defrost.

Guidelines for the care and cleaning of a refrigerator

- Never place the fridge near a heat source such as a cooker or
- Allow sufficient circulation of air behind the fridge and dust
- Clean fridge interior weekly. Wipe up any spills immediately
- Wash interior with warm water and bicarbonate of soda; avoi smelling detergents.
- Use a damp cloth wrung out in hot soapy water to clean the e the rubber seal.

Table 10.5 Star rating

Each refrigerator has a star rating indicating the temperature in the icebox.

	Star	Temperature	Storage time
*	1 star	– 6°C	1 week
**	2 star	–12°C	1 month
***	3 star	–18°C	3 months
****	4 star	–18 to –25°C	Up to 12 months

A freezer works like a fridge except that the temperature is lower. A fridge freezer has a condenser, two compressors and evaporators.

Sample Question and Answer

State the function of each of the following parts of a refrigerator,
(a) the thermostat,
(b) the refrigerant. (6)
(2005, HL, Section A, 9)

Answer
(a) The thermostat controls the temperature within the cabinet.
(b) The refrigerant is the liquid in the refrigerator that evaporates by drawing heat from within the cabinet, therefore cooling it.

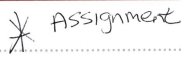

Cooking appliance: microwave oven

There are three main types of microwave ovens:
- **Conventional microwave:** Used for cooking, reheating and defrosting.
- **Combination microwave:** Combines oven, grill and microwave; can brown food.
- **Microwave with grill:** Cooks, reheats, defrosts and browns food.

construction

A microwave oven consists of:
- A metal-lined steel box with an enamelled exterior.
- A glass door with a perforated metal layer to stop microwaves from escaping.
- A seal and a safety lock on the door.
- A manual or digital control panel with an on/off switch, time and defrost facility and programme settings.
- A light inside the oven which illuminates the food during cooking.
- A flex and a plug.

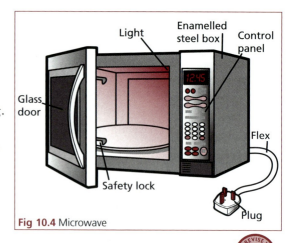

Fig 10.4 Microwave

Enclosed in the metal casing is:
- A *magnetron* which converts electricity to microwave/electromagnetic energy.
- A *transformer* which increases the domestic voltage.
- A *wave guide/stirrer* which distributes the microwaves evenly.
- A *glass turntable* to ensure the even cooking of the food.

Exam Hints
Remember each of these and what they do.

Microwaves are available in different colours and as integrated appliances.

Working principle of a microwave oven
- Microwave ovens use *electromagnetic energy* to cook food.
- The *magnetron converts electricity to microwave/electromagnetic* energy.
- The microwave/electromagnetic energy travels into the oven space via the wave guide where it is *evenly distributed by the turntable* or wave stirrer.
- The microwaves will *penetrate the food to a depth of 5cm.*
- The water molecules in the food attract and absorb the microwave/electromagnetic energy.
- The *water molecules now vibrate* at high speed (over 2,000 million times per second).
- This *vibration causes friction* which creates heat and thereby cooks the food.
- Food cooked in the microwave does not colour so a grill may be used to brown the food.

How are electromagnetic waves distributed?
The electromagnetic waves in the microwave oven are:
1 Reflected
2 Transmitted
3 Absorbed

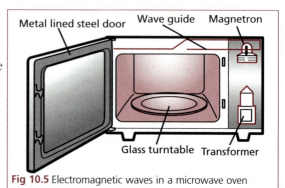

Fig 10.5 Electromagnetic waves in a microwave oven

Guidelines for use of a microwave oven
- Follow the manufacturer's instructions.
- The oven may be used to cook, reheat or defrost food.
- Never place metal or metal trim containers or dishes in the microwave oven.
- Use appropriate cookware made from paper, glass, plastic and ceramic.
- Cover food with cling film or kitchen paper to help retain moisture and speed up the cooking time.
- Arrange foods in a circle to ensure even distribution.
- Stir liquid foods occasionally during cooking, e.g. to prevent hot spots in soup.
- Allow foods to stand for the recommended time after cooking.
- Microwave ovens are generally unsuitable for cooking large quantities of food.

Guidelines for the care and cleaning of a microwave oven
- Follow the manufacturer's instructions.
- Always unplug the microwave before cleaning.
- Avoid moving the microwave oven as it may damage the magnetron.
- Turn off oven before opening the door.
- Wipe up spills immediately.
- Remove the glass turntable and clean regularly.
- Wipe the outside of the oven and the rubber door seal with a damp cloth wrung out in hot soapy water. Avoid using abrasives.
- If any fault occurs get a qualified person to rectify it.

Remember to look up cooking methods on page 94 for advantages and disadvantages, suitable foods and unsuitable foods for the microwave.

Questions

1. Outline 3 factors that should be taken into consideration when choosing large electrical appliances for the home. (6)
(2006, OL, Section A, 9)

2. Set out details of a study you have undertaken on a refrigeration appliance. Refer to (a) the general criteria to be considered when selecting the appliance, (b) guidelines for use, (c) two modern design features. (34)
(2005, OL, Section B, 3b)

3. (a) Set out details of a study you have carried out on a microwave cooker. Refer to (i) working principle, (ii) modern design features, (iii) guidelines for using the appliance. (30)
   (b) Evaluate the contribution of the microwave cooker to modern food preparation and cooking practices. (12)
(2005, HL, Section B, 3a)

4. Set out details of a study that you have undertaken on a household appliance with a heating element. Refer to (a) working principle, (b) guidelines for using the appliance, (c) energy efficiency. (18)
(2004, HL, Section B, 4c)

Key Points

The Use and Benefits of Technology in the Home
- In the home technology has: Reduced the workload and the time needed to carry out tasks; increased efficiency; improved communications and security; provided more durable and hygienic materials

Selecting Household Appliances
- Criteria: Cost, safety, reliability, energy efficiency, need, space available, design, guarantee, ease of cleaning

Categories of Household Appliances
- Appliance with a motor: Food processor
- Appliance with a heating element: Kettle
- Large appliance: Refrigerator
- Cooking appliance: Microwave oven

Your revision notes

11: Textiles in the Home

●●●Learning Objectives

In this chapter you will learn about:
1. The Use of Textiles in the Home
2. How to Choose Textiles
3. Textile Care and Scientific Principles
4. Types of Fabric
5. Safety and Textiles

The Use of Textiles in the Home

- Textiles (fabrics) are used widely in the home.
- Textiles are needed for clothing and household items, e.g. carpet, upholstery, cushions, duvets, curtains.

Table 11.1 Functions of clothing	
Function	**Application**
Identification	A uniform or a particular piece of clothing indicates where people work or their job, e.g. police, nurses, judges
Protection	Clothes protect us from the weather, e.g. from rain, wind or sun
Safety	Clothes can protect from fire, infection or chemicals, e.g. fire fighters, chemical workers
Self-expression	Clothes may reflect a person's personality or emotional state, e.g. wedding clothes, hippy-style clothes
Modesty	Society expects a certain amount of clothing, which can vary in different countries
Impression on others	Clothes can make an impact on how people are perceived, e.g. designer clothes, interview clothes
Hygiene	In all areas of catering and food production particular clothing items need to be worn for hygiene reasons, e.g. hats, hairnets, aprons

Table 11.2 Functions of household textiles	
Functions	Application
To provide comfort	Duvets, cushions, carpets
To provide warmth	Curtains, blankets, carpets
To provide insulation	Curtains, blinds, rugs
To absorb sound	Upholstered furniture, rugs, carpets
To absorb moisture	Towels, dish clothes, tea towels
To provide privacy	Blinds, curtains
To provide protection	Oven gloves, non-slip floors, textiles with flame retardant finish
To decorate	Household textiles play a fundamental role in decorating a house due to the variety of colour, pattern and texture available

How to Choose Textiles

The following points should be considered prior to choosing a textile.

1 **Suitability:** The fabric's suitability depends on its properties and on the intended use, e.g. rainwear needs to be waterproof.
2 **Cost:** The amount of money available determines the quality of the fabric. Natural fibres, e.g. silk and wool, are generally more expensive than synthetic fibres.
3 **Properties:** The properties of a fabric have a big influence on whether or not the fabric can be used for a particular purpose, e.g. crease resistant.
4 **Personal choice:** Personal likes or dislikes regarding colour, texture, pattern and the budget influence the choice of fabric.
5 **Aesthetic appeal:** How attractive and appealing a fabric appears is often influenced by personal choice and the properties of the fabric. The appearance, drape, weight, texture, resilience, lustre and durability of a fabric all contribute to its aesthetic appeal.
6 **Care:** It is important to consider the cleaning and care a fabric requires. Is it washable or does it need to be dry cleaned? Is it stain resistant?
7 **Safety:** Fabrics need to be flame retardant for certain uses, especially for upholstery, children's clothing and nightwear.

Textile Care and Scientific Principles

- The care of a textile will depend on the fibre, fabric construction and any finishes used.
- The care label of each textile item describes accurately how the textile should be cared for.
- Each fabric type has different cleaning specifications.

Table 11.3 Care labels

Symbol		Instructions	Fabric
Washing			
Wash at 95°C	〔95〕		Cotton and linen
Wash at 60°C	〔60〕		Cotton, linen and viscose which are colour fast, i.e. colours do not run
Wash at 40°C	〔40〕	Medium action wash	Acrylics, polyester/wool blends
Wash at 30°C	〔30〕	Minimum action wash	Wool
Hand wash	✋		
Do not wash	⊠		
Tumble drying			
Tumble dry	⊙		
Do not tumble dry	⊠		
Drying			
Line drying	⊓		
Drip drying	⫼		
Dry flat	⊟		
Ironing			
Do not iron	⊠		
Cool iron	⌁		Nylon, acrylic, polyester
Warm iron	⌁		Wool/polyester mixtures
Hot iron	⌁		Cotton, linen, viscose
Dry cleaning			
Dry clean in all solvents	Ⓐ		
Do not dry clean	⊗		
Bleach			
Do not bleach	⊠		
Use of chlorine	△cl		

The following factors are all part of cleaning textiles:
1. **Water:** Type of water, e.g. hard makes it difficult to create a lather.
2. **Temperature:** Correct temperature for fabric, e.g. wool shrinks at high temperature.
3. **Detergent:** Suitable for fabric, contains surfactants, bleach, conditioner, enzymes.
4. **Level of agitation:** Dislodges dirt, amount needed depends on fabric.
5. **Water removal:** Wringing out, drip drying, spin drying, drying flat, tumble drying.
6. **Use of conditioner:** Reduce static build-up, soften fabric, make ironing easier and fabric smell nicer.

Care labels

- A care label is permanently attached to a garment or fabric and tells us how to care for it.
- Each care label contains instructions on how to wash, dry, dry clean and iron the item and which (if any) bleach to use.

Types of Fabric

- Fabrics can be divided into two categories: (i) natural fabrics and (ii) man-made fabrics.
- Regenerated fabrics are made from natural fibres to which chemicals are added. The care of these fabrics depends on their properties.
1. **Natural fabrics:** Wool, silk, cotton, linen
2. **Man-made fabrics:** Synthetic, polyester, nylon
3. **Regenerated fabrics:** Viscose, rayon

Table 11.4 Natural fabrics

Fibre	Property	Care	Use
Wool	• Absorbent and soft • Weak when wet • Scorches easily • Pills • Shrinks at high temperatures	• Wash at low temperature (40°C) • Dry flat • Suitable for dry cleaning • Unsuitable for bleach • Warm iron • Do not tumble dry	• Blankets • Jumpers • Trousers • Carpets
Silk	• Absorbent • Easily damaged by high temperatures, moths and bleach	• Suitable for hand washing and dry cleaning • Cool iron • Do not bleach or tumble dry	• Shirts • Dresses • Curtains • Cushions
Cotton	• Absorbent • Strong • Shrinks easily • Easily creased • Scorches • Dyes easily	• Hand or machine wash • Hot iron • Bleach can be used • Temperatures as high as 95°C	• Clothes • Curtains • Upholstery • Towels

Table 11.5 Man-made fabrics

Fibre	Property	Care	Use
Synthetic (polyester)	• Quick to dry • Easy to wash • Prone to static build-up • Strong • Crease resistant	• Machine wash at 50°C • Cool iron • Chlorine bleach	• Shirts • Duvet covers • Sports wear
Regenerated (viscose)	• Absorbent • Creases • Weak when wet • Shrinks at high temperatures	• Machine wash at 50°C • Cool iron • Do not wring out	• Clothes • Curtains

Sample Question and Answer

List two desirable properties of a fabric for upholstered furniture. (2)
(2004, Section A, 11a)

Answer
(a) Strong
(b) Crease resistant

Table 11.6 Types of finishes

Finish	Fabric
Stain resistant	Many fabrics
Antistatic	Synthetic
Shrink resistant	Wool
Crease resistant	Cotton, viscose
Flame retardant	Many fabrics
Water proofing	Polyester, cotton
Mercerising	Cotton

Safety and Textiles

Safety considerations when selecting household textiles

- The majority of fabrics are flammable.
- However, some smoulder or melt, while others ignite and produce toxic fumes which can cause choking.
- Fabrics can be treated to alter their reaction to flames and to make them less harmful.
- Many fabrics contain a flame retardant finish such as Proban which self-extinguishes.
- Some upholstery fillings can also produce toxic fumes when on fire.
- To minimise the risk, check that the upholstery fabric has been treated with a flame retardant and that the filling/foam is *combustion modified high resilience foam* (CMHR).
- Some fabrics pose a greater risk than others due to their construction.
- High-risk fibres are cotton and acrylic, which are both fast burning.
- Low-risk fibres are wool, which will smoulder and extinguish, and polyester which will melt and light gradually.

Flame retardant finishes and fabrics

- Flame retardant fabrics and fibres are used in textile production to minimise the risk of fire and flames.
- Fabric can be coated on the outside which is cheaper but less durable.
- Fibres can be treated prior to the making of the fabric; this is more expensive and needs extra care but is more durable.

A flame retardant finish – Proban
- Proban is used on cotton and cellulose fibres.
- It protects the fabric by adding an invisible layer of phosphorus and nitrogen to the fibre structure.
- On ignition, an insulating substance forms around the fabric with no melting, smouldering or after-flame, and the flame will self-extinguish.

Fire Safety (Domestic Furniture) Order 1988, 1995 (amended)
- This order protects consumers from the risk of fire from textiles in their home.
- It covers the following items: beds, upholstery such as sofas, armchairs, cots, pushchairs, pillows and loose chair covers.
- The order states that fillings used must be combustion modified high resilience (CMHR).
- Fabrics are subject to a cigarette test and a match test.

Safety labels used in household textiles

All household textiles should contain the following labels:

1 Permanent label
The permanent label is normally stitched to the fabric. It should contain the following information:
- Name and address of the manufacturer or importer
- Manufacturer's identification number and batch number
- Description of filling and cover material used
- Type of fire resistant interliner
- The warning mark 'Carelessness causes fire'

Swing label

2 Display or swing label
- A display or swing label signifies that the filling and the covering meet all safety requirements.
- It symbolises that the filling meets the safety requirements, while the cover is fire resistant but does not pass the match test.

Questions

1. What information does the following label convey to the consumer? (4)
   (2004, HL Section A, 11b)

2. Recommend two fabrics suitable for living room curtains and state one property of each fabric. (6)
   (2006, OL, Section A, 11)

3. (a) Identify two safety considerations that should be considered when selecting textiles for household purposes. (4)
   (b) Name one fire retardant finish used on household furnishings. (2)
   (2006, HL, Section A, 12)

Display or swing labels

4. Suggest a reason why two of the properties listed below are considered important when caring for fabrics. (6)
   (a) Crease resistant
   (b) Strong when wet
   (c) Colour fast
   (2005, OL, Section A, 10)

Key Points

The Use of Textiles in the Home
- The functions of clothes: Identification, protection, safety, self-expression, modesty, impression on others, hygiene
- The functions of textiles: To provide warmth, insulation, privacy and protection; to absorb sound and moisture; to decorate

How to Choose Textiles
- Criteria for choosing textiles: Suitability, cost, properties, personal choice, aesthetic appeal, care, safety

Textile Care and Scientific Principles
- How to care for textiles: Depends on the fibre, fabric construction and finishes, read instructions

Types of Fabric
- Natural fabrics: Wool, silk, cotton, linen
- Man-made fabrics: Synthetic, polyester, nylon, viscose, rayon

Safety and Textiles
- The safety of household textiles: Flame retardant finish – Proban
- Fire Safety (Domestic Furniture) Order 1988, 1995
- Safety labels on household textiles: Permanent label, display or swing labels

12: Consumer Studies

●●●Learning Objectives

In this chapter you will learn about:
1. Consumer Choices
2. The Purchasing Process
3. Consumer Rights and Responsibilities
4. Consumer Responsibility towards the Environment
5. Consumer Protection

Consumer Choices

A consumer is someone who purchases goods or services for his/her own use.

Table 12.1 Factors influencing consumer decision-making	
1 Available income	• The amount of disposable income impacts on consumer behaviour • A family budget may reduce the amount of goods purchased
2 Personal preferences	• Personal and family likes or dislikes, values, needs and wants influence the type of goods that are purchased
3 Merchandising	• Techniques include discount offers and displays to draw the consumer's attention to a product • Includes loyalty schemes, e.g. Tesco and Dunnes Stores club cards
4 Advertising	• Purpose is to convince consumers that they need the advertised product and should buy it • It creates a desire for the product • Must attract the consumer's attention, e.g. through the use of strong bold colours, a popular song or product promoted by a celebrity
5 Word of mouth	• Family and friends often influence us whether or not to buy a product • Word of mouth can influence us positively and negatively
6 Sales people	• Provide consumers with details regarding a product • They may influence consumers by giving their personal opinion
7 Packaging and labelling	• These two factors are linked, as labels are attached to the packaging • Packaging has to appeal immediately to the consumer • There is competition between brands and the type of packaging used

The Purchasing Process

The following factors all play a part in deciding what and where to buy:
1. Type of retail outlet
2. Retail psychology
3. Shopping patterns
4. Consumer research

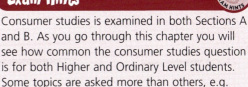

Exam Hints

Consumer studies is examined in both Sections A and B. As you go through this chapter you will see how common the consumer studies question is for both Higher and Ordinary Level students. Some topics are asked more than others, e.g. consumer rights and responsibilities, the environment.

Table 12.2 Classification of retail outlets

Type	Examples	Characteristics
Supermarkets	• Tesco • Superquinn	• Large open plan, self-service • Wide variety of products, e.g. food, household items, clothes • Optional Internet shopping
Voluntary supermarkets	• SuperValu • Centra	• Amalgamation of independent grocery shops • Similar to supermarkets but independently owned outlets • Association with a large group offers greater benefits
Hypermarkets		• Similar to supermarkets but much larger in size • Located in suburbs • Free parking • Huge variety of stock • Cheaper • Common in Europe
Independent shops	• Murphy's Shoes	• Family-owned small shops. Limited stock • Often specialise in certain products, e.g. shoes, furniture
Department stores	• Brown Thomas • Debenhams	• Large shops. Wide variety of products • Divided into various departments, e.g. clothing, household • Generally offer good value for money
Multiple chain stores	• Penneys • Dunnes Stores	• One company with many branches • Large self-service shops • Competitive prices, offer good value for money • Layout and style of all stores the same • Located in cities and large towns
Discount stores	• Argos • Marlin	• Orders from a catalogue • Take away purchase on same day • Limited stock in shop. Generally cheaper • Goods are prepacked • Generally good returns policy

Retail psychology

- Retail psychology studies the behaviour and experience of the consumer.
- All advertising and marketing techniques are influenced by retail psychology to ensure they are effective in achieving their aim.
- Retailers use a number of techniques to encourage and promote consumer spending.

Points to Note

Other types of shopping outlets include: mail order, Internet shopping, vending machines, auctions, TV shopping.

Table 12.3 Techniques used in retail psychology	
Technique	**Description**
Store layout	• The overall size influences how long the consumer remains in the store • **Free flow layout:** Unstructured layout allows movement and access to all areas • **Grid layout:** Structured layout with aisles; consumer follows the flow of movement
In-store stimuli	• Everything from lighting and background music to aromas can influence the consumer to buy
Product placement	• Essentials are often placed at the back of the store • Fresh and colourful fruit and vegetable displays are placed at the entrance to encourage spending • Products grouped by association • Sweets placed beside checkouts • Special offers placed at the end of the aisles
Shelf position	• Products at eye level sell more, e.g. luxury items • Products placed on other shelves tend to be essentials
Pricing	• This is to make consumers feel they are getting bargains or products cheaper, e.g. €4.99 is cheaper than €5 • Multiple buys, e.g. 3 for €1.50
Loyalty schemes	• Some stores offer a loyalty scheme, e.g. club card from Tesco • Collection of tokens for household products, e.g. from SuperValu
Merchandising	• Offers in supermarkets, e.g. 3 for the price of 2 • Encourages the consumer to buy more

Shopping patterns

Factors which can influence shopping patterns are:
- **Income:** Family income will dictate available money.
- **Size of household:** More planning is needed in a larger household, e.g. meals.

- **Available time:** Limited time for shopping, increase in on-line shopping and 24-hour shops.
- **Shopping centres:** One-stop shopping facility, free car parking, variety of shops.
- **24-hour shopping:** Many supermarkets open 24 hours.
- **Retail parks:** Demand for DIY and consumer durables.
- **Transport:** Delivery service which is convenient.
- **Customer expectations:** Customers demand good quality service and products.

Consumer research

- Consumer research investigates the needs and wants of the consumer.
- The analysis of this information provides the manufacturers with a greater understanding of what the consumer needs and wants.
- Consumer research can be carried out through field research and desk research.

Advantages of consumer research
- Consumer research identifies consumers, and their wants and expectations.
- It creates consumer profiles, e.g. according to age, gender or income.
- It recognises the competition, advertising and marketing techniques.
- It highlights market trends and what is successful.
- It identifies the market size or potential markets.

Consumer Rights and Responsibilities

Table 12.4 Consumer rights and responsibilities	
Rights	**Responsibilities**
Choice: Variety of products and services creates competition and avoids monopolies	**To inform themselves:** To know rights, safety and quality symbols
Information: Truthful information about a product	**To follow instructions:** To read and follow specific instructions to ensure safe use, care of product
Value for money: Should get value for money spent	**To complain:** If a product or service is faulty, complaining ensures better standards in the future
Safety: Goods should be safe to use and harmless; safety legislation, safety symbols, quality marks, warnings and instructions	**To use resources responsibly:** Be aware of the damage excess waste can have on the environment
Redress: To complain and receive compensation, e.g. refund, repair, replacement	**To be aware of quality and value:** Assess if quality corresponds to the price being paid. Over-priced goods do not mean better quality

Sample Questions and Answers

(a) State two consumer responsibilities. (4)
(b) Name one voluntary agency concerned with consumer protection. (2)
  (2005, OL, Section A, 11a)

Answers
(a) (i) To complain if they are unhappy with a product or service.
   (ii) To be informed of products, pricing, quality and safety of products.

(b) Consumer Association of Ireland (CAI).

Quality and safety symbols

Consumer rights and responsibilities can be aided by the use of quality marks and safety labels on products.

Table 12.5 Quality symbols	
EIQA	Approved Quality System/Quality Irish
(guaranteed)	Guaranteed Irish
(Design Centre)	Design Centre
nsai	National Standards Authority of Ireland (NSAI)
(BSI kitemark)	British Standards Institution
(eye symbol)	Irish Standards Mark (Caighdeán Éireannach)
Safety symbols	
CE	Communauté Européenne
(eye symbol)	Irish Mark of Electrical Conformity
▢	Doubly Insulated
Other symbols	
♻	Recyclable
(arrow circle)	Green Dot
(people symbol)	National Consumer Agency
Hazardous material or substances	
☠	Toxic
🔥	Flammable
✖	Harmful and irritant
(corrosive symbol)	Corrosive

CHAPTER 12

Consumer Responsibility towards the Environment

Environmental management

While many changes need to be made globally, an integrated local management system will:
- Emphasise waste prevention
- Minimise landfills
- Maximise recycling

Mismanagement of the environment results in:
- Climate change or global warming
- Exhaustion of non-renewable sources of energy
- Depletion of the ozone layer
- Degeneration of the tropical forests
- Loss of species

Sustainable development

Sustainable development is very important, as it will ensure the least amount of damage is done to the earth's environment and it promotes the use of renewable energy sources.

Effective waste management
- The current waste management system in Ireland is based on the following waste hierarchy: Prevent, minimise, reuse, recycle, recover energy and landfill.
- Consumers should reduce, reuse and recycle.

Table 12.6 Reduce, reuse, recycle	
Reuse	Shopping bags, plastic containers, newspapers, clothes, furniture
Reduce	Amount of packaging, disposable products, use of cars
Recycle	Plastic, metal, paper, cardboard Use a compost bin Purchase goods made from recycled material, e.g. toilet paper, nappies

Ten steps to making a difference

1. Shop for the environment: Avoid over packaged products, look for EU eco label.
2. Get into recycling: Separate bottles, cans and recycle.
3. Say no to plastic bags: Buy reusable bags for shopping.
4. Compost your waste: Dispose of your kitchen waste in a compost bin in your garden.
5. Do not litter and do not tolerate those who do.
6. Water is life: Water is a valuable commodity and goes through an expensive process. before it is safe for us to use. Do not waste it.

7 Dispose of waste liquids correctly, e.g. household cleaners, paints and weed killers.
8 Do you need to use the car for short journeys? Car emissions pollute the air and damage the environment.
9 Turn down and switch off: Don't over heat your home; turn off lights when leaving a room.
10 Become label conscious: Choose energy labels A or B when buying a new washer, dryer, fridge or freezer saves energy and money.

(Adapted from *A better place to live – your home and the environment*, source ENFO, p. 2)

Renewable and non-renewable resources

Table 12.7 Renewable resources	
Type	**Energy won from**
Hydropower	Flowing water
Biomass	Plants
Solar power	Sunrays
Wind power	Wind
Geothermal	Heat produced within the earth's centre

Renewable resources
- Renewable resources are expensive, although government grants are available to install some forms of renewable energy in domestic homes.
- Are sustainable, clean and efficient.
- Provide electricity and heating.
- Produce little pollution and are on the increase.

Non-renewable resources
- Non-renewable resources include coal, gas and oil.
- Non-renewable resources are cheaper.
- Are in limited supply.
- Cannot be replenished.
- Cause air pollution.
- Provide electricity.

Air, water and noise pollution

Air, water and noise pollution are different types of pollution, all of which have detrimental effects on the environment.

	Table 12.8 Types of pollution		
	Water pollution	**Air pollution**	**Noise pollution**
Cause	• Factory waste • Sewage • Farm waste • Fertiliser and pesticides • Chemical waste • Detergents containing phosphates	• Smoke from the burning of fossil fuels, e.g. coal • Chlorofluorocarbon (CFC) emissions • Carbon monoxide emissions	• Music systems and TV • Construction sites • Traffic, e.g. trains, cars, aeroplanes • Lawnmowers
Result	• Kills fish and marine life • Affects tourism and fishing industry • Makes water unsafe to drink	• Global warming • Decline in ozone layer • Increase in medical conditions and allergies	• Headaches • Pain • Sleeplessness
How to reduce	• Use phosphate-free detergents • Monitor and control factory waste disposal • Reduce use of chemicals, fertilisers and pesticides • Implement efficient sewage treatment system	• Use renewable energy resources • Avoid products containing CFCs • Use smokeless fuels • Car share or use public transport	• Reduce volume of TV and music • Install noise proof windows • Avoid living close to entertainment venues and flight paths of planes, train lines and motorways

Consumer Protection

Consumer rights are protected by the following acts:
- Sale of Goods and Supply of Services Act 1980
- Consumer Information Act 1978 (Consumer Protection Bill 2006)

Sale of Goods and Supply of Services Act 1980

The act states that:
- Goods should be of merchantable quality, e.g. reasonable quality, durable and useable.
- Goods should be fit for the purpose intended, e.g. a washing machine should wash clothes as intended.
- Goods should be as described, e.g. they should correspond to the description on the label, to a salesperson's description or a brochure, e.g. if bread is described as gluten-free it has to be free of gluten.
- Goods should correspond to the sample, e.g. the paint in a can should be the same as the colour in the sample shown.
- Services should be provided by a skilled person, with care and diligence and using proper materials.

- A consumer is entitled to redress, which generally takes the form of a refund, repair or replacement.

The Sale of Goods and Supply of Services Act 1980 includes legislation regarding guarantees.
- A guarantee does not affect your legal rights under the act.
- A guarantee is a contract between the manufacturer and the consumer.
- The guarantee usually has a time limit, e.g. 6 months or 1 year.
- During this time the manufacturer agrees to replace or repair any faulty goods.
- There may be some exclusion to the guarantee, e.g. certain parts of an appliance, labour costs, or postage may be excluded.
- A guarantee should be clearly legible and state:
  - The name of the product
  - The name and address of the manufacturer/company offering the guarantee
  - The duration of the guarantee
  - The procedure to follow when making a claim
  - The length of time it should take
  - What the manufacturer will do
  - Any charges the consumer may incur

Consumer Protection Act 2007 (Consumer Information Act 1978)

- The consumer Protection Act 2007 provide the National Consumer agencies with a lot more power regarding consumer issues. www.nca.ie
- This act provides protection for the consumer against false or misleading claims about goods, services and prices.
- Under this act it is an offence to mislead the consumer by making false claims either verbally, e.g. through a sales assistant, or in a catalogue or in advertising. For example, if a product is said to be guaranteed Irish, it has to be produced in Ireland.
- The act prohibits false or misleading claims about services and the person providing the service, e.g. a 24-hour service has to deliver around the clock.
- It prohibits false or misleading claims regarding price, previous price or recommended retail price (RRP).
- Extra costs should be stated on the price tag. If the price of a lawnmower does not include the box, the extra cost has to be stated clearly.
- It prohibits the seller from giving inaccurate sales prices. The stated previous price must be true. For example, if it is stated that an item 'Was €40 now €20', the item must have been for sale in the premises at that price for 28 consecutive days in the previous 3 months.

WAS €40 NOW €20

Points to Note
When you shop online the Electronic Commerce Act 2000 protects you.

Statutory and voluntary consumer protection agencies

There are a number of statutory and voluntary agencies which protect the consumer. A statutory agency is an agency which is established by the government.

Table 12.9 Statutory and voluntary agencies

Statutory agencies	Voluntary agencies
1 National Consumer Agency	1 Consumers' Association of Ireland
2 Ombudsman	2 Advertising Standards Authority of Ireland
3 European Consumer Centre	
4 National Standards Authority of Ireland (NSAI)	
5 Comhairle	
6 Financial Regulator	

Statutory agencies

1 National Consumer Agency

- It aims to create consumer awareness with regards to consumer rights.
- It checks that products are consistent with safety standards.
- It checks that advertisements and labelling are truthful and accurate.
- It investigates complaints regarding false or misleading advertisements.
- It advises the government on changes regarding consumer issues.
- It instigates legal proceedings against offenders.

Formation of National Consumer Agency (NCA)

- The Consumer Strategy Group was established in 2005.
- Its main aim was to make recommendations for a national consumer policy strategy.
- The group recommended establishing the National Consumer Agency (NCA) as a new consumer agency.
- This recommendation was supported by the Minister for Enterprise, Trade and Employment.
- The NCA was established in 2006 and replaces the Office of the Director of Consumer Affairs when the Consumer Protection (National Consumer Agency) Bill 2006 becomes law in 2007.
- The NCA has a broader remit than the ODCA, while still carrying out the same functions.
- The overall functions include advocacy, research, information, enforcement, education and awareness.

2 Ombudsman
- The ombudsman investigates complaints made by the public against government departments, insurance companies and credit institutions.
- Attempts should be made to resolve the issue locally first. The ombudsman should be a last resort.
- The ombudsman will examine the case and make a recommendation.
- The ombudsman's actions are not legal procedures.

3 European Consumer Centre
- The European Consumer Centre was established in conjunction with the Director of Consumer Affairs and the European Commission.
- It is a walk-in advice centre providing consumers with information regarding consumer rights and protection both in the EU and Ireland.

4 National Standards Authority of Ireland (NSAI)
- The NSAI establishes standards in relation to safety and quality in products.
- These standards are implemented in the Irish industry in order to provide better and safer products for the consumer.

5 Comhairle
- Comhairle runs Citizen Information Centres (CIC) around the country.
- It is a state-run agency providing the public with information regarding their rights and entitlements, e.g. unemployment benefits and housing issues within the social services.
- It also advises the public on consumer issues.

6 Financial Regulator
- The Office of the Financial Regulator was established in May 2003.
- It is responsible for the regulation of all financial services in Ireland.
- It protects the consumer by ensuring that financial legislation is adhered to and that financial institutions are solvent, protecting the consumer from losing money.

Voluntary bodies
1 Consumers' Association of Ireland
- This is a non-profit-making independent voluntary organisation.
- It carries out research and surveys in order to provide objective information on consumer products and services.
- It produces the monthly magazine *Consumer Choice*.
- It petitions the government on consumer issues.
- It represents consumers on many private and public bodies and organisations such as the FSAI and the ASAI.

2 Advertising Standards Authority of Ireland (ASAI)
- The ASAI is a voluntary self-regulating body within the advertising industry.

- It ensures all advertisements are legal and truthful.
- It investigates complaints made by the public regarding advertisements, e.g. false claims made or offensive contents of advertisements.

How to make a complaint

- Once you identify a fault stop using the item.
- Return the item to the retailer/supplier with the receipt if you have it.
- Ask to speak with the manager and outline the fault in the product.
- If the retailer is cooperative they should offer some form of redress (repair, refund or replacement) which is acceptable to you.
- If the retailer is uncooperative and unwilling to find a satisfactory solution, put your complaint in writing to the retailer. (Do not include the original copy of your receipt. Photocopy it!)
- If no satisfactory solution can be found, seek advice from the National Consumer Agency helpline.
- If you are still dissatisfied you may then proceed to make a claim at the Small Claims Court (claims up to €2,000).

Small Claims Court

- The Small Claims Court is part of the District Court system.
- It deals quickly and inexpensively with consumer disputes.
- No solicitor is required.
- Consumer claims have to be below €2,000.
- Applications forms are available from the District Court Registrar.
- The application costs €15.
- The claimant is the person making the claim and the respondent is the person/company the claim is against.

How does the Small Claims Court operate?
- The claimant completes the application form. He/she needs to fill in:
  - Name and address of the claimant
  - Name and address of the respondent
  - Amount claimed
  - Details of claim
  - Date and signature of claimant and include the fee
- A copy of the claim (Notice of Claim) is sent to the respondent.
- A respondent can decide to do one of the following:
  - Accept the claim
  - Challenge the claim
  - Counterclaim
  - Ignore the claim
- If the claim is disputed the registrar will try to resolve the issue.

- If it cannot be resolved it will be referred to the courts.
- If the respondent does not reply/refute the claim within 15 days, the claim is settled in favour of the claimant.
- The respondent has 28 days to comply with the judgement.

Questions

1 (a) Name one law that protects the rights of the consumer. (2)
(b) State the function of the small claims procedure (2).
(2004, OL, Section A, 12a)

2 (a) List three consumer responsibilities. (9)
(b) Compile a set of guidelines outlining how the consumer can protect the environment. (12)
(c) Identify two different types of pollution. In relation to each type of pollution state the possible causes and the effects on the environment. (20)
(d) Name and describe any one government initiative that has helped to reduce pollution and promote a greener environment. (9)
(2004, OL, Section B, 4a)

3 (a) Describe four in-store techniques that supermarkets use to encourage consumer spending. (20)
(b) Name three research methods used to gather information on the consumer. Explain how consumer research benefits (a) the retailer and (b) the consumer. (19)
(c) Name and outline the role of any one voluntary agency concerned with consumer protection (11)
(2005, HL, Section B, 4a)

4 In relation to the environment explain and give an example of each of the following:
(a) renewable resource
(b) non-renewable resource. (6)
(2004, HL, Section A, 12)

5 List three functions of the Office of Consumer Affairs. (6)
(2006, HL, Section A, 11)

6 Give details of four consumer responsibilities. (16)
(2006, HL, Section B, 4c)

7 Name and explain two rights we have as consumers. (6)
(2006, OL, Section A, 12)

8 (a) Name one statutory organisation and one voluntary organisation that works to protect the consumer AND (b) Complete the following sentence:
A guarantee is a contract between the _____ and the _____. (6)
(2007, OL, Section A, 9)

Exam Hints

Look at question 3 above from the exam paper 2005, HL, Section B. Here you will see how different topics can be asked in the one question.

CHAPTER 12

Key Points

Consumer Choices
- Factors influencing consumers: Income, personal preferences, merchandising, word of mouth, sales people, advertising, packaging and labelling

The Purchasing Process
- Classification of retail outlets: Supermarkets, voluntary supermarkets, hypermarkets, independent shops, department stores, chain stores, discount stores
- Retail psychology: Product placement, shelf position, store layout, in-store stimuli, merchandising
- Change in Irish shopping pattern: Shopping centres, 24-hour shopping, Internet shopping, environmentally friendly, available time, retail parks
- Consumer research: Field and desk research

Consumer Rights and Responsibilities
- Consumer rights: Choice, information, value for money, safety, redress
- Consumer responsibilities: To inform themselves, follow instructions, complain, use resources responsibly, to be aware of quality and value

Consumer Responsibility towards the Environment
- Environmental management: Aims, results of mismanagement
- Sustainable development: Reduce, reuse, recycle
- Renewable resources: Hydropower, biomass, solar power, wind power, geothermal
- Non-renewable resources: Coal, gas, oil
- Pollution caused by: Air, water, noise

Consumer Protection
- Sale of Goods and Supply of Services Act 1980: Goods must be of merchantable quality, fit for purpose
- Consumer Information Act 1978: Protects against false or misleading advertisements
- Electronic Commerce Act 2000: Protects when shopping online
- Statutory consumer protection agencies: National Consumer Agency, Ombudsman, European Consumer Centre, Comhairle, NSAI, Financial Regulator
- Voluntary consumer protection agencies: Consumers' Association of Ireland, Advertising Standards Authority of Ireland
- Small Claims Court: Consumer claims below €2,000, no solicitor needed

13: Social Studies

●●● Learning Objectives

In this chapter you will learn about:
1. Sociological Concepts
2. The Family
3. Historical Development of the Family in Ireland (1900–present day)
4. Family Functions
5. Marriage
6. The Family – a Caring Unit
7. Family Law

Sociological Concepts

Exam Hints

This Social Studies section is part of the core sections and is questioned in Section B of the exam paper. A lot of the points listed below have been abbreviated, so make sure you are able to expand on the points in the exam. An objective viewpoint is needed when answering the questions. Try to avoid giving your own opinion and stick with factual information. When you are answering this type of question, format your answer in one point form, as it will help you give a more accurate and less subjective answer, which will help you to receive a better mark.

Table 13.1 Sociological terms	
Culture	• The way of life of a society incorporating language, music, folklore, knowledge, roles, customs and skills passed on through generations
Society	• Society is defined as a group of people who share a similar lifestyle
Social groups	• Smaller groups of people within society who share a common purpose There are two main groups: 1 Primary social group: Small groups, e.g. consisting of family and friends 2 Secondary social group: Larger and less personal groups, e.g. school and workplace
Kinship	• A link within a group of people based on blood relations
Norms	• The normal expected patterns of behaviour within society, e.g. it is expected that all children are educated
Values	• The principles and beliefs held by society which indicate what is right and what is wrong
Mores	• The norms, values and customs that society identifies as important, e.g. honesty and fidelity

Role	• The expected part played by a person in a particular position within society, e.g. Gardaí or doctors are expected to behave in a way which is appropriate to their profession and position within society
Socio-economic grouping	• Social groups within society are often defined according to their wealth or income • In Ireland society is commonly classified as lower, middle and upper class
Social mobility	• The ability to move from one socio-economic group to another • Education and income are often the main means by which people move up or down these groupings
Socialisation	• The lifelong process of learning how to fit into society and what is acceptable behaviour • Primary socialisation takes place within the family • Secondary socialisation is learned outside the family, e.g. in school and at work
Social institutions	• Organised social arrangements which are found in many societies, e.g. marriage or family
Social change	• Changes which occur within society due to major developments, e.g. technological advancement, wars

The Family

The family is identified as a social institution, i.e. an organised social arrangement, whose fundamental function is the production and rearing of children. Our society is made up of many different types of families. Families exist in all societies throughout the world.

Modern family structure

The main types of family in Ireland today are:

1 Nuclear family
This type of family consists of parents and their children.

Characteristics
- It is small in size.
- It is mobile, which allows the family to move from place to place if employment necessitates it.
- Both parents are often wage earners (dual income families).
- Decisions are made democratically as the nuclear family is independent and not reliant on other family members.
- It is egalitarian with equal roles for men and women regarding child-minding, cleaning, etc.
- It can be isolated in a crisis if extended family members are living far apart.
- It is concluded on the death of a spouse or a divorce creating a one-parent family.

2 Extended family

This type of family incorporates grandparents, parents, children, uncles, aunts and cousins, all living in close proximity to each other and willing to help each other.

Characteristics
- It is large in size and family members are interdependent.
- It is often found in agricultural areas where farming provides the basis for economic support, although this has decreased in recent years.
- It is immobile due to the large number of people involved.
- It is long lasting as children generally settle in close proximity to where they were reared, maintaining the concept of the extended family.
- Support is provided in times of crisis, e.g. at the death of a spouse, by other family members.
- Although equality has improved amongst the sexes it could still contain segregated roles within the family. This is passed on from generation to generation.

3 Single/lone parent families

This family consists of one parent and his/her child(ren). It is created through choice, divorce, separation, desertion or the death of a spouse.

Characteristics
- It often consists of a female and her child(ren).
- A number of problems exist for many single parent families:
  - Poverty due to increased cost of living
  - Dependence on state benefits
  - Financial difficulties as increased costs of childcare prevent many single parents from returning to work
  - Emotional difficulties, e.g. depression, isolation and stress
  - Uncertainties in carrying out the role of both parents

4 Blended family

This type of family is created when two adults from separate relationships/marriages and their children form a new unit.

Characteristics
- Changes in family size when two families are joined together.
- Difficulties with discipline between step-parents and children; clear lines need to be introduced to prevent conflict arising.
- Some similar characteristics to the nuclear family (see above).

Social, economic and technological changes affecting family structure

Social changes
1. The increase in the number of separations and divorces in Ireland has enlarged the number of one-parent and blended families.

2. The introduction of contraception and family planning has resulted in a decrease in the number of children in a family.
3. Ireland is a more secular society and religion no longer has the influence on life choices that it once had.
4. Ireland has become multi-denominational with a greater acceptance of other spiritual beliefs.
5. Education is seen as vital and educational achievement is required and acknowledged in the workplace.
6. The vast majority of children complete primary school and some form of post-primary education.
7. The decline in segregated roles within the family now results in stay-at-home husbands who mind the children and do housework while their wife is the main wage earner.
8. Women have greater choice in education and the workplace. Equal pay has increased the number of women choosing to work outside the home.

Economic changes

1. An increase in the cost of living has brought about smaller family sizes.
2. There has been a decline in the dependence on agriculture as the main source of income, while production and service industries have increased drastically in recent years.
3. The reduction in unemployment has decreased the financial burden on the state.
4. The state provides financial benefits and support for single-parent families.
5. The increased cost of living and housing has resulted in both parents working outside the home. Childcare creates another financial burden on the family.
6. The economic boom has increased the cost of housing, making it more difficult for young couples to purchase their first home.

Technological changes

1. The development of appliances in the home, e.g. washing machines, save time and labour.
2. Household appliances are also contributing to the reduction in segregated roles within the family.
3. Communication technologies such as the Internet and the telephone make it easier for people to work from home and also to carry out household tasks, e.g. grocery shopping, banking and bill payment.
4. Advances in computer technology also aid parents working from home.
5. Television and films have highlighted the different expectations from other societies and cultures.

Historical Development of the Family in Ireland (1900–present day)

- In the early 1900s the traditional family in Ireland was large, economically deprived and often lived in poverty.
- Towards the end of the twentieth century this had reversed with smaller, economically sufficient families emerging.
- Three distinct periods can be identified during this transition:

	Table 13.2 Pre-industrialisation (1900–1960)
1900	1 The extended family was the most common family structure.
	2 Families were large as children were seen as an economic asset and were working from an early age
	3 The work available was unskilled and badly paid. Agriculture provided a huge proportion of employment
	4 Most marriages were arranged and were of economical benefit rather than romantic. A lot of males married later in life, if at all
	5 Child mortality (death) rates were very high and often due to poor standards of living and hygiene
	6 Women did not work outside the home. They were responsible for all tasks within the home as well as child rearing. The husband was the breadwinner which resulted in strictly segregated conjugal roles
	7 Religion played a crucial part within Irish family life
1946	8 The rural electrification scheme supplied electricity to homes which allowed electric cookers, fridges, etc. to be used, thereby reducing the workload for the mother
	9 Farming also became less labour intensive. However, this had a negative effect on the economy and created unemployment and emigration
1950	10 The general standard of living improved, women's health and education were better and the child mortality rate decreased

CHAPTER 13

Table 13.3 Post-industrialisation (1960–1990)		
1960	1	There was a decline in the rural extended family and the urban mobile nuclear family emerged
	2	Couples married younger and after 1970 both parents could work outside the home. However, it was still the norm at this time that the man was the main wage earner and the wife the homemaker
	3	Couples married for romantic love rather than economic reasons
	4	Wages increased which allowed a better standard of living
	5	Children were no longer required for their economic benefit but were nurtured and educated
1980	6	The average family size decreased due to the availability of contraception
	7	Education of all children became crucial to ensuring financial success later in life

Table 13.4 Modern family (1990–present day)
1 The advances in technology have had a huge impact on household chores, the workplace, family size and education
2 There was a further reduction in family size down to 1.4 children per family due to the wide availability of contraception and family choices
3 The number of dual income families increased
4 All families enjoy a higher standard of living and greater choice
5 The demand for childcare facilities has increased which has contributed to the stress experienced by working parents
6 The family structure has changed with the introduction of divorce in 1996. There are four basic types of family: (a) nuclear family (b) extended family (c) single/lone-parent family (d) blended family
7 The state supports family functions by providing education, financial assistance and protection for families

Family Functions

The family (in whatever form) is identified as the primary place of preparation of children for an independent adult life. The state provides assistance for some of these functions.

Table 13.5 The functions of the family

Physical	
(a) Reproduction	• Survival of the human species, observe sexual behaviour in society
(b) Nurturing	• The physical needs of the child, e.g. food, clothes and shelter are provided for life
(c) Protection	• A safe environment for the young, elderly, sick or physically and mentally disabled to live
Emotional	• The emotional needs of the child, e.g. for love and security, are met
Economic	• One or both parents may work to provide money for the needs of the family
Socialisation	• Socialisation strives to ensure that children's behaviour is acceptable within society and teach children about society's values, norms and customs
Education	• The family is identified as the primary source of education for a child

State intervention in family functions

The state can intervene in a number of family functions to ensure that they are being met.

Table 13.6 State intervention in family functions

Function	State intervention
Physical	Children's allowance every month, the provision of Community Mothers programmes
Emotional	Parenting courses and support for lone and young parents through Community Development Resource Centres
Economic	Social welfare system provides unemployment benefit, old age pension, disability allowance, back to school allowances, social and affordable housing, medical cards and public health services
Socialisation	Preschool, primary and post-primary schools
Education	The state provides full-time education for all from the age of 5–18 years old

Marriage

Marriage is a legal contract between two people. It acknowledges rights and responsibilities, which incorporate living together, child rearing and fidelity, for each person in the union.

Types of marriages

There are many different types of marriage around the world. This variety can be attributed to a number of facts with religious beliefs being the dominant factor. There are two basic types of marriage determined by the number of partners allowed in the marriage:

1. **Monogamy:** The most common type of marriage in Christian communities, a person has one husband or wife. This legally binding contract exists until the death or divorce of a spouse.

2. **Polygamy:** More than one partner at any one time. This marital arrangement is accepted in many cultures around the world, e.g. in Egypt and in Asia and among African tribes.
   (a) Polygyny involves a man having two or more wives at the same time.
   (b) Polyandry involves a woman having more than one husband.

Requirements for a legally binding marriage in Ireland
- Partners must be of the opposite sex.
- The marriage must be voluntary with both parties agreeing to the union.
- Both partners must be free to marry.
- Both partners must be over 18 years of age. Partners under 18 years of age need special permission from the courts.
- Partners must not be closely related by blood or marriage.
- Three months' written notice must be given to the registrar of the district where the marriage will take place. (In order to marry in a Catholic church a similar notice must be given to the parish priest.)
- The wedding must take place in a registered building, e.g. in a registry office, church or mosque, and in the presence of a priest, minister or registrar.
- After the wedding ceremony the couple and two witnesses must sign the register.

Rights and responsibilities of the married couple
The partners in a marriage have the following rights and responsibilities:
- They have a right to each other's company.
- The couple are expected to be faithful and loyal to each other.
- Couples are entitled to have sexual relations with each other to consummate the marriage. Non-consummated marriages can be annulled.
- Each spouse has the responsibility to provide financial support for their partner and their children under the Maintenance of Spouse and Children's Act 1976.
- Joint guardianship exists of any children born within the marriage. The parents have a legal duty to provide food, care, shelter and moral and social education for the child.
- This responsibility should be shared between husband and wife.
- The inheritance of a spouse is provided for in the Succession Act 1965.

Marriage preparation

As marriage is one of the most important stages in a person's life it is vital that the person prepares for it. A marriage is much more than the wedding day, and preparation for this significant stage can be received at home, in school and through a pre-marital course.

The couples have the option to address these issues as individuals, as a couple and in groups. These courses are facilitated by marriage counsellors, doctors, lawyers, priests and home economists.

Home
- The home provides the first experience of marriage.
- Parents become role models of how a husband and wife relationship functions.
- A content relationship provides a positive role model for what forms the basis of a happy marriage.
- In an unhappy relationship, the negative role model may lead to marital relations difficulties later in life.
- Developing positive relationships involve communication, honesty, trustworthiness and love.

School
- The introduction of social, personal and health education incorporating RSE (relationship and sexuality education) in all post-primary schools gives students the opportunity to discuss various aspects of forming and maintaining relationships and marriage.
- RE and home economics also offer a similar option.

Pre-marriage courses
Pre-marriage courses provide couples intending to marry with information regarding the expectations and reality of marriage. The courses are provided by:
- ACCORD (Catholic Marriage Counselling Service)
- Marriage and Relationship Counselling Service (non-denominational)
- Other independent groups

The areas discussed include:
- Relationships
- Family planning
- Child rearing
- Financial responsibility
- Legality of marriage
- Buying a home
- Problems such as alcoholism, gambling and abuse

Marital breakdown

Legal and social changes have had an impact on marriages and the marital breakdown procedure in Ireland.

1 Legal changes
- Due to recent changes it is easier now to obtain a divorce.
- Grounds for divorce have been widened to incorporate a greater variety of reasons for marital breakdown.
- Legal aid is provided for those who may not have the financial means to obtain a divorce.

2 Social changes
- The nuclear family is more vulnerable with less input from the extended family.
- An increasing number of women work outside the home and are therefore financially independent and unwilling to stay in an unhappy marriage.
- State benefits for lone parents allow spouses to leave unhappy unions.
- Women's attitudes have changed. They expect to be treated equally and to have a choice regarding family size, jobs, etc. within the marriage.
- Life expectancy has increased and people remain married for much longer, therefore increasing the risk of experiencing problems.
- Family problems such as alcoholism, gambling or violence can all contribute to an unhappy marriage.
- Teenage marriages have a greater risk of ending in separation.
- People who have divorced once are more likely to do so again.

Marriage counselling

Difficulties in marriage can be addressed by marriage counselling. Marriage counselling is offered by ACCORD (Catholic Marriage Counselling Service), Marriage and Relationship Counselling Services (non-denominational) and independent groups.
- Couples experiencing difficulties in their marriage may decide to get marriage counselling before deciding to separate.
- Counselling can only be successful if both parties attend the sessions and are serious about preventing separation.
- A trained counsellor provides a neutral environment for the couple to discuss their feelings and problems with the intention of trying to find a solution.
- In certain situations, e.g. if sexual problems are being experienced, more specialised counselling may be required and the counsellor would recommend an appropriate service.

If the couple decide to separate there are a number of options available to them depending on their circumstances: legal nullity, Church nullity, mediation agreement, judicial separation, divorce.

Legal nullity

The concept of nullity refers to a marriage that never existed.

A marriage is void when one of the following situations prior to or on the day of the marriage existed:
1. Either spouse was already married on the day of marriage (bigamy).
2. The marriage was not consummated due to homosexuality or impotence.
3. A legal requirement was not met, e.g. the marriage was not performed in a registered building.
4. One of the partners was forced into marriage (lack of consent).
5. One of the partners was under the influence of alcohol or drugs at the time of the marriage.
6. The partners were unable to form normal marital relationships due to psychiatric problems.

Church nullity

- Church nullity is granted by the Catholic Church.
- In order for either spouse to be able to remarry legally, a state annulment is also required.

Family mediation

The Family Mediation Service is provided for couples who have agreed to separate or divorce. This service is funded by the Department of Social and Family Affairs and was established in 1986. It is provided free of charge in a number of centres around the country. It helps the couple to negotiate their own agreement regarding:
1. Custody arrangements and the parenting of children
2. Finances
3. Any issues concerning the family home and property

Separation

Couples who separate are not entitled to remarry. There are two types of separation:
1. Legal separation
2. Judicial separation

1 Legal separation

- Legal separation can be arranged through mediation if all parties agree on the separation terms.
- Mediation can avoid court proceedings which are an expensive process. The terms of separation are documented in the Deed of Separation.
- A solicitor is necessary to draw up the Deed of Separation document.

2 Judicial separation

Judicial separation is necessary when a couple cannot agree on the terms of the separation.
- The Judicial Separation Act 1989 (amended by the Family Law Act 1995) sets out the grounds for this separation.

- **Grounds for separation are:**
1. One of the parties has committed adultery.
2. A spouse has been deserted by the other spouse for 1 year or more.
3. Due to unreasonable behaviour, e.g. alcoholism or abuse, the other spouse could not be expected to share a house.
4. A normal marital relationship has not existed for at least 1 year prior to the application.
5. The couple have not lived together for 1 year (agreed separation) or 3 years (lack of consent).

> **Points to Note**
> A Deed of Separation is a written legal agreement between a couple which highlights their future rights and obligations to each other and their children.

Divorce

Divorce was introduced in Ireland in 1996. It is governed by the Family Law (Divorce) Act 1996 which sets out the following conditions necessary for the issuing of a divorce:
- The couple have lived apart for a period of 4 years out of the previous 5 years.
- There is no realistic possibility of reconciliation. Sufficient provision has been made for the spouse, children and any other dependant relatives.
- The divorce hearing is held in the Family Circuit Court.
- The court will provide direction on, maintenance, custody and access, property division, pension adjustment order.
- The Legal Aid Board will provide solicitors, barristers and financial assistance for individuals whose annual income is less than €12,697 per annum.

The Family – a Caring Unit

Roles

Role conflict
- Each social setting will change some aspect of a teenager's behaviour, e.g. he/she behaves differently in school than when he/she is out with friends.
- A role conflict arises when the requirements of some of these roles overlap, or when the expectations of a number of individuals are to be met at the same time, e.g. parents may expect the teenager to study on week nights, while his/her trainer expects him/her to attend training, and friends want to go to the cinema.
- This role conflict can create a stressful situation as the teenager often wants to meet all expectations.

> **Points to Note**
> A role is the part played by a person in a particular social setting, influenced by his/her expectations of what is appropriate.

Family roles

One of the most important differences between the traditional family and the modern family is the change in men's and women's roles. Each person within a family has a specific role to play.

A parent's role
- A parent's role changes over time and becomes less defined as the child becomes an adult.
- The primary role is to provide for the physical, emotional and social development of the child.
- Parents should be loving and caring towards their children and nurture them.
- Today both parents are involved in child rearing, which is very different to previous generations where it was the sole responsibility of the mother.
- Parents are the role models from whom children learn most of their early social skills.
- The parents' cultural values, attitudes, religious beliefs and intolerances are passed on to their children. These beliefs become more apparent when a child spends time with others.
- Parents need to discipline their children's behaviour so that they learn to behave in an acceptable manner within society.
- Discipline is successful when parents communicate and explain why a punishment is given.
- Physical punishment contradicts the other roles of a parent and imparts an acceptance of violence to the child.

A child's role
- The fundamental role that is expected of children is to behave in a certain way, which is generally taught at home.
- The role of children has changed over time.
- The patriarchal and authoritarian upbringing of the eighteenth and nineteenth centuries has been exchanged for a relaxed and open upbringing.
- Parents now communicate with their children and explain rules and discipline.
- Parents praise and encourage their children, which helps develop positive self-esteem.
- Good discipline is necessary for the child's successful integration into society.
- A child needs to learn and implement socialisation skills.
- Physical punishment is no longer acceptable, as psychology has proven that it does not change the child's behaviour through reasoning but through a response to fear.
- Consistency is vital to ensuring a child's security and happiness.

An adolescent's role
- Adolescence is the period of transition and change from child to adult.
- Role expectations for adolescents are difficult as they move away from being children but still do not have the full responsibility of adulthood.

- Peer pressure can compromise role expectations for adolescents which can create conflict in the home.
- Extra responsibility such as babysitting can be a good experience during this time in preparation for adult roles.
- Much of adolescence is spent in full-time education. The role of the student entails specific expectations, e.g. the achievement of good grades to secure a college place.
- Discipline during this period involves compromise and identifying limits.

An older person's role

- Due to technological advances the life expectancy of people has increased. Many people now live very active and healthy lives into their eighties.
- On retirement at 65 to 70 years of age an older person's role can become less defined. Planning for retirement is vital to maintain self-esteem.
- Older people provide support for other members of the family through child-minding or financial support for house purchase, weddings, etc.
- An older person's educational knowledge and wisdom can benefit younger generations.
- Older people still like to maintain their independence even if they have physical difficulties such as impaired mobility or arthritis.

The social and economical factors which contributed to the change of roles within the family are shown in the following table.

Table 13.7 Factors influencing role changes

Social factors	Economic factors
1 Large percentage of women working outside the home	1 Increased standard of living due to higher wages
2 A decline in the traditional extended family and the emergence of the egalitarian nuclear family	2 An increase in the cost of living makes it necessary that both parents work
3 Sharing of child rearing and household tasks between parents	3 Children remain financially dependent on their parents for longer due to full-time education
4 Greater involvement of grandparents in child rearing and the social development of children	4 State benefits support families and individuals who may experience financial difficulties due to the high cost of living
5 Increased life span of the older generation due to better standards of living and healthcare	5 Back to work schemes offer the unemployed the opportunity to become financially independent
6 Increased emphasis on educational achievement; children are dependent on their parents for financial support for longer	

Gender roles

Gender refers to a person being male or female and having masculine or feminine traits.
- The behaviour which is expected from men and women within society is called a gender role.
- The traditional gender roles of both sexes have changed greatly over the last few decades and this has lead to more egalitarian roles within the family.
- Gender roles have become less stereotyped.
- The stereotype of the woman staying at home to mind the children and care for the house while the husband went to work is not valid in some societies anymore, as now both genders can take up either role. However, it is still seen as the woman's role within the family.
- The acquisition of adult stereotypes occurs very early in children, possibly when children are as young as 3 years old, as some research has indicated.
- Children generally react positively towards their own gender.
- Children imitate their parents in forming gender roles, e.g. a girl would wear high heels if her mother did.
- Gender roles are established as soon as a child is born, e.g. blue is the traditional colour for a boy and pink for a girl. The types of toys children are given to play with again reinforce adult stereotypes of male and female behaviour.

Relationships within the family

A number of relationships exist within the family structure and each one will have different characteristics and needs.
1. Child/parent
2. Adolescent/parent
3. Sibling relationship
4. Child and grandparent relationship
5. Relationships with extended family

Child/parent relationship
- This relationship meets the physical, psychological, social, mental and moral requirements of the child.
- The fulfilment of all of these requirements creates a secure, emotional and healthy person capable of forming his/her own relationships.
- A child has the following physical and psychological needs: food intake, clothing, shelter, love, security, trust and praise.
- Discipline is necessary to ensure societal norms are met.
- Excessive discipline, however, can have a negative psychological effect on a child.

Rights of a child
The United Nations set out the following rights of a child. These rights have been adopted by state and voluntary organisations. A child has the right to:

- Protection from physical, emotional and sexual abuse
- An environment that provides for their physical, psychological, social and educational needs
- Free education
- Experience love, affection and understanding
- Special care, treatment and education if disabled
- Safety from discrimination, cruelty and exploitation

Adolescent/parent relationship
- Adolescence can be a time of conflict between parents and their adolescent children.
- Adolescents often believe they 'know best' and are influenced by peers.
- Demands regarding educational achievement and college places can generate undue pressure.
- The need to be treated and accepted as an adult can often conflict with the behaviour and level of responsibility of the adolescent.

Dealing with and resolving conflict between adolescents and parents
- No limits or extreme limits of behaviour for an adolescent can bring about conflict between teenagers and their parents.
- This might be the first time negotiations will be called for to resolve this conflict.
- It is vital for the psychological development of the teenager that a positive method of dealing with and resolving the conflict is used which the adolescent can also use in future relationships.

Table 13.8 How to deal with conflict

Attribute	
Communication	<ul><li>'Listening and talking' – both sides should listen before talking</li><li>This prevents rash decisions and assumptions being made</li><li>It is vital for adolescents to feel that their parents are listening</li></ul>
Compromise	<ul><li>Through talking and listening a compromise which is acceptable to both parties can often be achieved</li></ul>
Openness and honesty	<ul><li>An open and honest relationship which has been established from an early age can often prevent conflict during the period of adolescence, as adolescents will feel free and safe to discuss issues with their parents</li></ul>
'See both sides'	<ul><li>Both parties should try to understand each other's viewpoint</li><li>Generational conflict comes about when parents recall their behaviour at a similar age, but fail to take into account the social changes which have taken place since then</li></ul>

Good communication within the family
- Communication is necessary to resolve conflict and any difficulties that may arise between family members.

- Communication involves talking and listening. All members of a family should feel comfortable and safe to express their opinion and feelings.
- Respect is paramount in good communication as it ensures each person is heard.
- Socialisation of a child would be impossible without proper communication and benefits the child in forming other relationships.
- Encouragement and praise all form part of the healthy development of a child.

Independence for the older person within the family

Due to increased life expectancy older people are living much longer after retirement. During this time independence is vital for self-esteem and self-worth.

How to achieve independence:

1 **Economic considerations**
   - Private or state pensions allow financial freedom.
   - Free travel (for people over 66) allows transport within Ireland without the responsibility of driving.
   - Medical cards allow for free medical treatment for all people over 70.

2 **Physical considerations**
- The elderly can be physically less able and might require assistance for carrying out basic chores while still living at home.
- Meals on Wheels provide balanced meals.
- Home helps assist in the cleaning and maintenance of the home.
- Sheltered housing schemes, which provide more support if necessary but where independence is still maintained, are on the increase.

3 **Social considerations**
- Family and friends can visit and help out when needed.
- A community with special activities for the older community such as Christmas parties, bingo and day trips can add to independence.

Generational conflict

A disagreement between parents and children over issues, e.g. going out with friends, clothes they choose to wear, part-time work is called a generational conflict (see 'How to deal with conflict' above).

The following factors can bring about generational conflict:
- Young people often have more liberal opinions than their parents due to technological and social changes.
- Ageism/discrimination against older people produces conflict.
- Older people can be inclined to generalise the negative behaviour of young people.
- The self-esteem of older people can be reduced due to a lack of independence brought

about by physical disability. This can make them feel vulnerable and threatened around younger people.
- Conflicts should be resolved by discussing the issues with all parties involved in order to reach a compromise/solution acceptable to all concerned.
- The respect, recognition and trust of the younger generation can help to maintain an older person's self-worth and thus help prevent generational conflict.

Special physical, mental and emotional needs

The family provides support for its members with special needs. However, it is imperative that they know when to seek outside assistance and advice. Outside assistance can be obtained through:
1. Statutory means (assistance through government based organisations)
2. Voluntary means (assistance through non-state funded organisations)

Table 13.9 Special physical, mental and emotional needs

Special physical needs	Difficulties	Family response	Voluntary support	Statutory aid
• Wheelchair bound • Blind • Deaf	• Lack of mobility • Limited access to education and employment • Dependence on others	• Provide emotional support and encouragement • Adapt house to suit needs of the individual • Promote independence	• Irish Wheelchair Association • National Council for the Blind • National Association of the Deaf • Special Olympics Ireland	• National Disability Authority (NDA) • Rehab Group • Equality Authority
Special mental needs	**Difficulties**	**Family response**	**Voluntary support**	**Statutory aid**
• Mental disability (e.g. Down's syndrome)	• Lack of independence • Limited access to education and employment	• Provide emotional support • Join organisations in locality that provide support	• Down Syndrome Ireland • Special Olympics Ireland	• Health Service Executive
• Psychiatric problems	• Low self-esteem • Unemployment	• Provide emotional support • Seek advice from outside agencies	• Schizophrenia Ireland	• Psychiatric hospitals • Health Service Executive
• Eating disorders	• Low self-esteem	As above	• Bodywhys • Overeaters Anonymous	• Health Service Executive
• Addictions (e.g. drugs, alcohol, gambling)	• Unemployment • Disruption to family life • Debt	• Seek outside assistance • Provide support for children involved • Limit access to money	• Alcoholics Anonymous • Narcotics Anonymous • Alateen	

Special emotional needs	Difficulties	Family response	Voluntary support	Statutory aid
• Abuse	• Difficulty expressing emotion • Experience guilt and anxiety • Lack of trust • Difficulties forming relationships	• Provide emotional support • Arrange counselling if necessary • Join a support group	• ISPCC • Rape Crisis Centre • AMEN	• Women's Aid • Health Service Executive
• Bereavement	• Difficulty expressing emotions • Guilt (if suicide is involved) • Loneliness • Isolation	• Provide emotional support • Join a support group to get advice • Visit the person	• Bereaved by Suicide Foundation	
• Autism	• Inability to express emotion • Difficulty forming relationships • Disruptive behaviour • Irrational behaviour	• Provide mental stimulation • Emotional support • Join support agencies to help understand difficulties	• Irish Society for Autism • Cork Association for Autism • The HOPE Project	• Health Service Executive

Family Law

The following acts cover family law:
1. The Family Home Protection Act 1976
2. The Family Law (Maintenance of Spouse and Children's) Act 1976
3. The Domestic Violence Act 1996 (The Family Law Act 1976 Section 22; Barring Orders)
4. The Family Law (Divorce) Act 1996
5. The Judicial Separation Act 1989
6. The Child Care Act 1991, 1997

The Family Home Protection Act 1976

- This act prevents one spouse from selling, mortgaging or transferring ownership of the family home without prior consent of the other spouse.
- This applies irrespective of in whose name the house is registered.
- Most family homes are in joint ownership.

The Family Law (Maintenance of Spouse and Children's) Act 1976

- This act entitles a dependent spouse and/or children to claim financial support (maintenance) from the other spouse.
- For a child to be deemed dependent, he/she has to be:
  – Under 18 years of age or
  – Under 23 years of age and in full-time education or
  – A child with a disability
- Maintenance is usually applied for following a divorce or separation. It can be claimed even if both parties are sharing a house.

The Domestic Violence Act 1996

- The Domestic Violence Act permits a spouse/cohabiting partner to apply for a safety, barring or protection order against the other spouse or partner.
- This act is intended for the protection and safety of a person who is threatened with physical, mental or sexual abuse in their home.
- If any of the court orders, e.g. Safety, Barring or Protection Order, is breeched the individual can be fined or imprisoned.

The Child Care Act 1991, 1997

- This states that the welfare of the child is of utmost importance and that the best welfare of the child is to be brought up with his/her family.
- It considers the requests of the child, taking into consideration their age and comprehension.
- A child may be removed from his/her home if the Gardaí feel that the child is at risk.
- An Emergency Care Order allows the Health Service Executive (HSE) to get custody of a child for up to 8 days.
- A Supervision Order can be granted where it is deemed necessary to monitor the child.

Making a will

A will is a legally binding document setting out the wishes of a person regarding his/her belongings and possessions once the person has died.

The estate includes the money, property and other possessions of the deceased.

The importance of making a will

- The existence of a will ensures that a person's wishes regarding his/her estate are complied with after death.
- An executor (person to carry out the will) guarantees that the wishes of the deceased are respected and that his/her affairs are in order.

- Parents can appoint guardians and trustees who look after the education and maintenance of their children in the event that both parents should die at the same time.
- If a person dies without leaving a will, their estate will be distributed according to the Succession Act 1965.

Procedure for making a will

Step 1: Make a list of everything that is to be included in the will and their location.

Step 2: List the people you wish to benefit from your will and include contact details.

Step 3: Employ a solicitor to receive advice regarding legal formalities and taxation issues.

Step 4: Appoint an executor (person who will ensure all requests regarding the will are being met). A minimum of two executors is normally recommended.

Step 5: Divide the estate by allocating certain possessions to named individuals or organisations.

Step 6: Funeral arrangements can also be incorporated in the will if somebody has specific requirements.

Step 7: To make a will legal it must be signed by the person making the will and a witness.

Step 8: Keep the will in a safe place, e.g. with a solicitor or a bank.

Capital acquisitions tax

- Capital acquisitions tax is an inheritance or gift tax.
- It has to be paid if the estate exceeds a certain value. The tax-free limit depends on the degree of relation between the deceased and the inheritor.

Exam Hints

Do not forget to look up Section B, Question 5 from the 2007 and 2008 papers.

Questions

1. According to the Irish Constitution (Article 41) the State recognises the family as the natural, primary and fundamental unit group of society. (The Irish Constitution)
   (a) Identify and describe three types of modern family structures in today's society. (18)
   (b) Discuss the effects of (i) social changes and (ii) economic changes on modern family structures. (24)
   (c) Set out the conditions required for granting a divorce under the Family Law (Divorce) Act 1996. (8)
   (2006, HL, Section B, 5)

2. As society changes so too does the structure of the modern family.
   (a) In spite of the changes in structure, family functions remain constant. Identify and describe three important functions of the family. (24)
   (b) Explain how any one function of the family has been supplemented (helped out) by other social institutions or organisations. (10)
   (c) Discuss how gender issues have affected the roles of family members in recent times. (16)
   (2006, OL, Section B, 4)

3. Ireland is changing, more than a quarter of the population is aged 50 or over and almost one in 12 people is 70 or over. (*The Irish Times*, 23 April 2005).
   (a) Discuss three reasons why people are living longer. (18)
   (b) Give an account of the advantages and the disadvantages of grandparents living with a family member who has young children. (20)
   (c) Outline the procedure for making a will. (12)
   (2006, OL, Section B, 5)

4. (a) Outline four rights of children within the family. (12)
   (b) Discuss how the state assists the family in the rearing of children. (18)
   (c) Analyse how (i) social factors and (ii) economic factors affect parenting roles within the family unit. (20)
   (2005, HL, Section B, 5)

5. (a) Outline four conditions that are necessary to make a marriage legally valid in Ireland. (16)
   (b) Identify and give an account of the options that are available to couples that are experiencing difficulties in their marriage. (24)
   (c) Explain how marriage customs can vary between different cultures. (10)
   (2005, OL, Section B, 5)

6. (a) Describe four functions of the family in modern society. (16)
   (b) Explain how the role of older people within the family has changed as a result of social and economic factors. (12)
   (c) Outline the historical development of the family in Ireland from the beginning of the twentieth century to the present day. (16)
   (d) State how the family is protected by the Family Home Protection Act 1976. (6)
   (2004, HL, Section B, 5)

7. (a) Explain how parents provide for (i) the physical and (ii) the psychological needs of young children. (12)
   (b) Outline how relationships with family members change during adolescence. (12)
   (c) Suggest how conflict between adolescents and parents can be dealt with. (10)
   (d) Discuss the importance of good communication within the family. (16)
   (2004, OL, Section B, 5)

Key Points

Marriage
- The legal union between two people of the opposite sex
- Types of marriages: Monogamy; polygamy – polyandry, polygyny
- Arranged marriages: The reasons why it is still used today
- Requirements of a legal binding marriage in Ireland: partners of opposite sex, marriage is voluntary, partners free to marry, over 18 years of age, not closely related, 3 months, written notice given, marriage takes place in a registered building
- Rights and responsibilities of a married couple: To each other's company, conjugal relations
- Marriage preparation: Home, school and pre-marriage courses
- Marital breakdown: Legal and social changes
- Marriage counselling: ACCORD, Marriage and Relationship Counselling Services
- Options available to a couple who separate: Legal nullity, Church nullity, mediation agreement, judicial separation, divorce

The Family – a Caring Unit
- Roles and responsibilities of family members
- Role conflict: Different roles a person has to play
- Family roles: Parents' role, child's role, adolescent role, older person's role
- Social and economic factors affecting the changing role of family members: Women working outside the home, increase in nuclear family, grandparents involved in childcare, importance of educational achievement, state benefits to support families, back to work schemes
- Gender roles: How this has changed within the family structure
- Different relationships within the family: Child/parent relationships, adolescent and parent relationships
- Physical needs of a child: Food, clothing and shelter
- Psychological needs of the child: Love, security, trust and praise
- The rights of a child: United Nations Charter
- Resolving conflict: Communication, compromise, openness and honesty, see both sides
- Independence for the older person: Economic, physical and social considerations
- Generational conflict: Differences between younger and older generations
- Special physical needs: Wheelchair bound, blind, deaf
- Special mental needs: Mental disability, psychiatric problems, eating disorders, addictions
- Emotional needs: Abuse, bereavement, autism
- Statutory and voluntary assistance

Family Law
- The Family Home Protection Act 1976
- The Family Law (Maintenance of Spouse and Children's) Act 1976
- The Domestic Violence Act 1996
- The Family Law (Divorce) Act 1996
- The Judicial Separation Act 1989
- The Child Care Act 1991, 1997
- Making a will

14: Elective 1 – Home Design and Management

●●● Learning Objectives

In this chapter you will learn about:
1. Housing Styles
2. House Building and Design
3. Interior Design
4. The Energy Efficient Home
5. Systems and Services in the Home: Electricity and Water
6. Heating
7. Lighting

Exam Hints

This section is examined in Section C, question 1, of your exam paper. You must answer Section A and then either part B or C. This section is worth 80 marks.

Housing Styles

Nineteenth century

Table 14.1 Early nineteenth century (1800–1850)	
Rural housing style	**Urban housing style**
Poor labourer • Single-storey thatched cottage • Thatched roof of hay, reeds or straw • Two rooms (kitchen and bedroom) • Small windows (if any) • Half-door to allow light in and keep animals out • Thick stone walls • Open turf fire **Wealthy farmer** • Two-storey house • Up to five rooms including a parlour • Slate roof **Wealthy landowner** • Large estate house • Servant quarters • Many rooms • Very few of this type of house were built	• Terraced or two-storey houses • Shop owners live over the shop • In cities poor people live in tenements in large Georgian houses • Georgian houses terraced and three- or four-storeys high • Large rooms with high ceilings, decorative cornicing and features, basements • Constructed from stone and lime plastered • Entrance door a focal point • Tenement housing divided into single rooms, rented out to poor families • Most families could only afford one room

Table 14.2 Late nineteenth century (1850–1900)	
Rural housing style	**Urban housing style**
• Two-storey stone buildings • Slate roof	• Greater variety of building materials available due to improved transportation • Gothic and Tudor style buildings for the wealthy were popular • Gothic buildings characterised by pointed windows, high pitched roofs, bay windows and brick moulding • Tudor buildings had high pitched roofs and wooden framing with plastered panels • Terraced houses had small gardens and were cramped

Early twentieth century (1900-1950)

Rural housing style
- Rural electrification scheme in 1946 improved standards of housing in rural areas.
- Very few large houses were built.
- Housing grants were introduced after WWII and this began to change the style of the country cottage. The thatched roof was replaced with slate and new rooms were added to the house.
- Other people built new single-storey and two-storey houses and used the cottage as an outhouse or storehouse.

Urban housing style
- Beginning of detached and semi-detached housing on the outskirts of towns and cities, less terraced houses being built.
- In city centres, dwellings had mostly two storeys due to cost and shortage of land.
- Many urban dwellers lived in three-storey flats with shared sanitary conditions.
- Beginning of local authority housing schemes.
- New building materials were often cheaper than previous materials.
- Brick and plastered walls were popular.
- For roofing, tiles were introduced as a cheaper alternative to slates.

Late twentieth century (1950-2000)

Urban housing style
- Development of the tower block, e.g. high-rise buildings in Ballymun, Dublin.
- Increase in both public and private housing estates.
- Smaller houses (three to four bedrooms) with smaller gardens becoming the norm.
- Variety of new building designs such as bungalows and dormer bungalows.
- Emergence of mock Tudor and Georgian houses in the 1980s and 1990s.

- New building materials, e.g. plastic, fibreglass.
- Land, especially in urban areas, becoming more expensive.
- Landed is now zoned by local authorities as residential, commercial or industrial.

Twenty-first century (2000–)

- Land has become scarcer and prices are at a premium.
- High-density housing in most urban areas.
- Increase in the number of apartments being built.
- Houses are even more compact with smaller living space and gardens.
- Housing estates are larger and need to provide amenities such as shops.
- Social and affordable housing schemes are replacing large local authority housing estates.
- House extensions, such as attic conversions, are becoming increasingly popular.
- Planning permissions for individual houses are strict and applications must follow a set list of criteria.
- New materials and designs include timber-framed houses, coloured render.
- A large percentage of people are investing in second properties both in Ireland and abroad as holiday homes.

Choice of housing style

Factors which influence the choice of housing styles include:
1. Social and cultural factors
2. Economic factors
3. Environmental factors

Social and cultural factors

1. **Personal preferences:** People's likes and dislikes influence the location and the type of house.
2. **Location:** Often a reason for people to move house, e.g. close to transport links, schools, work and other amenities.
3. **Size:** The stage of the family life, e.g. age and number of children determines how much space is required.
4. **Special requirements:** For example, for the elderly or persons with a disability.
5. **Availability:** Demands on housing in large towns and cities can limit the properties for sale.

Economic factors

1. **Income:** If income is insufficient to obtain a mortgage, renting a property may be the only alternative.
2. **Building materials:** The type and cost impacts on the overall price of the house.
3. **Fees/costs:** Fees for solicitors, architects, land surveyors, engineers, stamp duty, furniture and decoration.

4 **Skilled tradesmen:** Need to be available to carry out the work.
5 **Investment potential:** Important to ensure the value of the property increases in case it is sold at a future date.

Environmental factors
1 **Building law and regulations:** All houses must comply, e.g. they need planning permission.
2 **Energy efficiency:** Consider choice of construction materials, heating and water systems.
3 **Amenities and green space:** A house's surroundings may influence its position.
4 **Position of the house:** Whether it is north or south facing can affect the temperature in the house and hence the use of fuel.

Table 14.3 Individual housing requirements	
Group	**Requirements**
A family	• Requirements depend on the size and age of the family • A family needs living space, bedroom space, enclosed play area, outdoor entertaining area, storage, study facility for teenage children • Garage or shed, space for expansion at a later date • Location: Close to work, schools, shops
Single person	• A single person requires less space than a family, but still needs adequate living and sleeping space • An apartment or flat near work • Young, single people often prefer an urban lifestyle
Elderly	• The housing requirements of the elderly change when they become immobile • Single-storey dwellings are more suited to the elderly • The elderly need: A downstairs shower/bathroom with non-slip surfaces, handrail and specially adapted taps • Good lighting and an efficient reliable heating system • Adapted equipment to ensure safety • A monitored alarm system to provide safety and security • A small garden or patio area with little or no maintenance
Disabled	Housing requirements differ depending on the particular disability, e.g. people with a mobility problem need: • A single-storey dwelling with no steps, wide doorways • A specially adapted bathroom with a shower with rail • Kitchen units and light switches at an appropriate level • A monitored alarm system • The hearing impaired need an adapted doorbell and phone
Homeless	• Homeless people have no access to either permanent or temporary accommodation • The needs of the homeless are basically the same as everyone else's. They need consistent accommodation, e.g. in a hostel • Privacy, bathroom facilities, secure storage, access to kitchen and clothes washing facilities • Voluntary organisations: Simon Community, Focus Ireland and Threshold • Local authorities provide flats, hostels, and bed and breakfast accommodation

Evaluation of housing provision in Ireland

An evaluation of housing in Ireland needs to consider the following factors:
1 Distribution of housing
2 Highest ownership in Europe at 82 per cent
3 High rents encourage people to purchase their own homes
4 Decreased house prices has lead to an over supply of houses in Ireland
5 Increase in apartments and townhouses being built
6 Most houses belong to private sector
7 65 per cent of people live in urban areas, 30 per cent of population live in Dublin

Quality of accommodation

- The Building Regulations Act 1991 and the Home Bond Guarantee Scheme have resulted in better quality houses.
- Accommodation in the private sector consists of detached and semi-detached houses, bungalows, dormer bungalows, apartments and townhouses.
- Home owners look after the maintenance of their properties.
- Local authority accommodation consists of two-, three- or four-bedroom semi-detached or terraced houses, apartments, hostels and bed and breakfast accommodation.
- Rented accommodation is protected and monitored by the Housing Regulations 1996.

Table 14.4 Comparative costs of buying and renting	
Renting a house	**Buying a house**
Initial costs	**Initial costs**
• Deposit: Usually one month's rent in advance	• Deposit: Usually 10% of purchase price
• Lending agency fees: Applies if an agency finds the accommodation for you	• Legal fees: 1–2% of purchase price; Land Registry fees, searches
	• Lending agency fees, application fee, survey fee, searches, indemnity bond
Continuous costs	• Stamp duty depending on cost of house
• Rent payment: Weekly or monthly	
• Household bills: Electricity, telephone, heating	**Continuous costs**
• Insurance for contents	• Mortgage repayments
• Maintenance charges: Apply for certain areas	• Mortgage protection policy/life assurance
	• Home insurance: Contents and building
	• Maintenance and service charges
	• Household bills
	• Furniture and furnishings

Adequacy of housing provision
- Ireland has an oversupply of houses at the moment.
- House prices in Ireland have dropped significantly since 2007, in certain parts of the country the house prices have reduced to the 2004 level.
- The elderly, the disabled and the homeless account for over 10 per cent of the overall waiting list.
- The increase in refugees and asylum seekers has also increased the demand for suitable housing in this sector.

Social housing provision

The main providers of social housing are local authorities, voluntary housing organisations and co-operative housing associations.

1 Voluntary housing organisations
- Voluntary housing organisations provide rental accommodation for the elderly, disabled or people on a low income.
- They are approved by the Department of the Environment, Heritage and Local Government and receive assistance from them.
- They are non-profit-making organisations.
- The developments are based on the needs of the local people.
- Capital Assistance Scheme provides accommodation in one- or two-bedroom units for people with special housing needs.
- Rental Subsidy Scheme provides rental accommodation for families on low incomes.

The Housing Finance Agency was established by the Housing Finance Agency Act 1981 to provide funding for local authority housing.

2 Co-operative housing associations
- Co-operative housing associations are non-profit-making associations. They build affordable housing and share the costs, e.g. home ownership building co-ops; co-ownership housing co-operatives.

Provision of local amenities and services

Many local services and amenities are provided by the Department of the Environment, Heritage and Local Government, e.g. schools, transport links, infrastructure, street lighting. The amenities provided depend on the number of people living in the area.

House Building and Design

Choice of location

The factors which determine the choice of site include:
- Amenities: Proximity of the site to schools, work and water.
- Urban or rural setting: Urban sites are more expensive.
- Site orientation: Well-drained, free from any danger of flooding, easy access to water, sewage and roads. A slightly sloping or elevated site with good drainage and a south facing aspect provides the finest site.
- Planning permission: Local development plans.
- Building regulations: The requirements of the Planning Office must be adhered to.
- Budget: The cost of the site and budget available.

Choice of house style

The following factors affect which type of house can be built:
1 Budget: Influences the size and type of house, e.g. bungalow.
2 Planning restrictions: Planning authorities have a set of guidelines to follow.
3 Personal preferences: The likes and dislikes of the individual.
4 Site and location: The particular house style must fit in with the local environment.
5 House layout: The orientation of the site will influence where rooms are positioned to maximise exposure to light.

Planning requirements

- Planning permission is required for any development of land or property unless it is exempted. Each planning authority will have a list of exemptions.
- Planning permission is granted by your local county council, borough council, city council or town council.

Types of planning permission
1 Outline planning permission: This is sought to find out if land may be developed.
2 Full planning permission: The application must be submitted to the local planning authority along with the necessary documentation and house plans.

In order to obtain planning permission:
- Notice of planning application and the proposed site must be placed in a local newspaper.
- Within two weeks of notice, the application must be lodged with the local planning authority accompanied by the relevant fee.
- The local planning authority acknowledges receiving the application.
- The application is placed on the planning register for public inspection.
- Within 5 weeks an objection to the proposed development can be lodged.

- Within 8 weeks the planning authority informs the applicant if planning permission has been granted.
- If no objections are lodged full planning permission may be granted within 8–12 weeks.
- Conditions may be attached regarding the proposed development when full planning permission is granted.
- If planning permission is refused the applicant can appeal the decision to An Bord Pleanála.

Bylaw approval
Bylaw approval may be required for some internal renovations, extensions and outbuildings to ensure their safety and the health and welfare of those using it.

Retention
If a development or extension has been built without planning permission it is necessary to apply for its retention.

Professional services for designing and building a house

The following professional services are required for designing and building a house.

1 The architect
- Provides information and advice on the site purchase, location and house orientation.
- Designs plans to suit the individual's requirements, makes the planning application.

2 The engineer
- Provides advice on the structure of the house.
- Sorts out problems which arise during construction.
- May also oversee the whole project.

3 The surveyor
- Carries out a site survey and provides the survey report to the lending institution.
- Identifies possible future problems such as flooding and offers solutions.

4 The builder
- Is generally responsible for site preparation, construction and finishing the exterior.
- Subcontractors may be employed to carry out more specialised jobs such as plumbing.

5 The solicitor
- Is required to arrange the legal aspect of buying and selling a house.
- Offers advice on building and planning regulations, title deeds and land registry. All lending agencies require that a house purchaser applying for a mortgage has a solicitor.

6 Book of house plans
- Contains information regarding house layout, site orientation and materials.
- The plans can be ordered from the company and can be modified to suit the individual requirements of the person.

House design

The following factors influence house design.

1 Aesthetics
- The internal and external design of a house should be aesthetically pleasing.
- The exterior design should complement the surrounding environment.
- The internal layout of the rooms should be balanced and well planned to ensure maximum use of space.
- The aspect of the house should influence the positioning of windows.
- Specific details of the house should be considered, e.g. high pitched roof, stone fronted, bay windows.

2 Environmental concerns and energy efficiency
- The use of ecologically friendly materials such as wood and natural stone.
- Incorporating sufficient insulation in cavity walls, roofs, doors.
- Landscaping the garden and planting trees can protect the house from the climate and make the area surrounding the house aesthetically pleasing.
- Using a renewable energy source such as solar power in a house can reduce heating bills.
- Features in the house design which improve energy efficiency: Double-glazed windows; insulation in walls, roof and doors; zoned heating system; use of a lagging jacket; use of thermostats, timers and energy efficient appliances.
- **Building Energy Rating (BER):** Under the Energy Performance in Buildings Directive applied throughout the EU, all buildings need a BER certificate. It provides a scale of comparison for buyers and tenants showing the energy demand and performance of a building. In Ireland this is being implemented gradually (2007–2009).

3 Family requirements
When planning the design of a house the size and needs of the family should be taken into consideration. The design of the house should also provide for:
- Any future needs of the family such as a teenager study area.
- Extensions such as an attic conversion, and a garage at a later date.
- The purpose of each room and how it may need to be multi-functional to facilitate the requirements of the family, e.g. bedroom/study.
- Specific design requirements for disabled or elderly people, e.g. a bungalow.

4 Ergonomics
- Ergonomics is the science of the relationhip between people and their environment. A house which incorporates ergonomic principles allows free movement within the building.

- Ergonomics demands a certain amount of space in the house in order for work to be carried out efficiently and for people to live safely.
- The work triangle in the kitchen is an example of ergonomics in the home.
- There is also a certain amount of space necessary to allow access to toilets or to be able to open doors.

5 Cost

Table 14.5 Initial and maintenance costs	
Initial costs	**Maintenance costs**
• Land • Solicitor's, surveyor's, architect's fees • Builder (construction, roofing, plumbing) • Decorating and painting • Fittings (kitchen, wardrobes) • Furniture and furnishings (curtains, blinds) • Appliances • Landscaping	• Mortgage • Mortgage protection payments • Buildings and contents insurance • Household bills (e.g. heating, electricity) • Repairs • Painting and decorating • Garden • Replacement of furniture and furnishings

6 Technological developments
- Major advances in technology have introduced new materials in house construction and allowed the use of centralised systems.
- New technology includes: Easy to clean, stain resistant materials; intelligent appliances; thermostatic controls; monitored security systems; integrated sound and lighting systems.

Regulations of house building standards

Building Regulations Act 1991
- These regulations stipulate the building standards which must be followed to ensure the safety of a building and the health of the people who will live in it.
- The act specifies standards regarding ventilation, heating, lighting, insulation, sewage and construction.
- The local authority is responsible for the implementation of these standards.

National House Building Guarantee Scheme
Home Bond
- This scheme is operated with the National House Building Guarantee Scheme and the Department of the Environment, Heritage and Local Government.
- A builder pays a registration fee for each house built.
- Home Bond inspects the building. If everything is in order a certificate is issued.
- It protects the consumer against any major structural faults which may arise in the next 10 years.

- If the builder went out of business and did not finish the building, the deposit would be returned to the house purchaser.
- Most mortgage lenders require a home bond guarantee.

Floor Area Compliance Certificate (FACC)
- This certificate was introduced under the Building Controls Act 1990.
- The purchaser must obtain the FACC from the builder/developer in order to be exempt from stamp duty.
- It must be within a specified floor area 38–125 sq. metres.

> **Points to Note**
> **Gaeltacht Area House Grant**
> This grant is provided for building a house in a Gaeltacht area provided certain conditions are met. Areas in seven counties and some islands qualify for this grant.

Interior Design

- Elements of design = colour, pattern, texture
- Principles of design = balance, emphasis, proportion and rhythm

Colour

The way colour is used in a home provides warmth, individuality and character. Colour can:
- Enlarge a room and darken or lighten a room.
- Hide unattractive features and emphasise decorative features.
- Create ambience in a room.

Table 14.6 Types of colour

1 Primary colours	3 Tertiary colours	5 Tints
2 Secondary colours	4 Shades	6 Tone

Colour schemes
1. **Neutral:** Based around various shades of white or cream.
2. **Harmonious:** Based on colours which are next to each other on the colour wheel, e.g. red and yellow.
3. **Contrasting:** Based on colours which are opposite each other on the colour wheel, e.g. red and green.
4. **Monochromatic:** Consists of different tones of the same colour, e.g. black, grey and white.

> **Points to Note**
> Colours can be classified as:
> **Cool:** Blue, green
> **Warm:** Orange, red, yellow
> **Neutral:** White, shades of cream, colours which have no immediate strong impact
> **Pastel:** Delicate pale shades of blue, green, yellow and pink

Pattern

Pattern is a decorative design which is found on textile surfaces, e.g. fabric, carpets, and wallpaper. Pattern can be small or large bold print.

How to use pattern in the home
- Small patterns work best in small rooms, whereas large, bold patterns suit big rooms.
- Too much pattern can dominate a room and create a cluttered effect, making the room appear smaller.
- Combining patterns which have a similar design or colour can create continuity in a room.
- Types of pattern: Floral, checks, stripes vertical or horizontal, geometric, abstract.

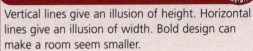

Points to Note

Vertical lines give an illusion of height. Horizontal lines give an illusion of width. Bold design can make a room seem smaller.

Texture

Texture refers to the feel or touch of an object. Texture can be rough, smooth, soft, warm or cool.

How to use texture in the home
- Different textures in a room provide variety and create interest.
- Bathrooms and kitchens often have only smooth surfaces for hygiene reasons.
- A sitting room can have both rough and smooth textures, e.g. carpet and glass table.
- Texture can also influence how we perceive colour, e.g. shiny or smooth surfaces reflect light and noise, whereas matt surfaces absorb light and sound.

Balance, emphasis, proportion and rhythm are the principles of design. By adhering to the following principles an aesthetically pleasing room can be created.

Table 14.7 Principles of design	
Principle	**Application**
Balance	• Occurs when colour, pattern, texture and furniture are in harmony • Elements complement each other; there is no overpowering feature
Emphasis	• To draw attention to a feature of interest in a room, e.g. mirror or fireplace • Colour and lighting can be used for emphasis. Emphasis adds variety and interest to a room
Proportion	• Relates to how pieces of furniture interact in size with each other and with the room • The objects in a room should be in proportion to the room size or other objects in the room
Rhythm	• To repeat a design feature, e.g. a colour, pattern or texture in a room • Rhythm creates a sense of unity and harmony

Factors influencing interior design

1 **Aesthetics and comfort:** To create an aesthetically pleasing room, colours, patterns and textures have to be incorporated in the design.
   - When deciding on a room design, it is imperative to consider the function of the room and the comfort of the individuals using it.
2 **Ergonomics:** Studies the relationship between people and their work environment.
   - The layout of a room should allow ease of access and movement for the comfort of all.
3 **Family size and circumstances:** The size and stage of the family influence the use of colour, texture and space in the home.
4 **Special needs:** Disabled and elderly people have specific requirements, e.g. wider doorways for easy access, downstairs toilet and shower room, kitchen units and light switches at an appropriate level.
5 **Cost:** The budget influences the interior design of a house.
6 **Environmental awareness:** Consider interior design from an ecological perspective.

When you design a room interior consider:
- How the function and layout of the room influence the type of furnishings.
- The aspect of the room, e.g. north or south facing.
- Heating, lighting and ventilation and the use of renewable sources of energy.
- Size and stage of the family, e.g. amount of storage space.
- Safety and hygiene, e.g. materials used in kitchen and bathroom.

How to draw a floor plan

- A floor plan is a drawing of a room or a house showing the specific dimensions, the positioning of lights, furniture and doors.

Flooring and floor covering

Flooring
There are two main types of flooring (i) solid floors and (ii) suspended floors.
1 **Solid floors:** Essentially made of concrete and usually found on the ground floor of new build homes.
2 **Suspended floors:** Usually found on the first floor of a house. They are made of joists of woods covered with tongue-and-groove wooden planks.

Floor coverings
Floor coverings are placed on top of solid or suspended floors.

Table 14.8 Classification of floor coverings

Hard coverings	Soft coverings
Ceramic tiles, slate, stone, wood, vinyl, cork	Carpets, rugs, natural fibres

Table 14.9 Criteria for selecting floor coverings	
Function	A room's function dictates which type is suitable
Budget	The amount of money available
Quality	The floor's quality depends on the fibres used
Traffic flow	The amount of wear and tear an area gets
Durability	How long the floor covering lasts
Insulation	Soft floors provide better insulation
Safety and hygiene	It needs to be non-slip for certain areas; bathrooms and kitchens require it to be easy to clean, hygienic and non-slip
Decor	The floor should complement the decor of the room
Properties	The various properties of each floor covering, e.g. soft or hard, warm or cold, need to be taken into consideration

- Properties of floor coverings, e.g. soft, hard, warm, cold, textured, absorbent, noisy, durable, low or high maintenance. They come in different colours.

Hard floor coverings

Table 14.10 Types of floor tiles		
Type	Use	Properties
Ceramic tiles	Kitchens, bathrooms, conservatories	• Cold and hard • Glazed • Durable • Easy to maintain • Wide variety of colours • Need to be laid by specialist
Terracotta tiles	Living rooms, kitchens, sun rooms	• Unglazed • Expensive • Long lasting • Chip and crack easily • Natural colours, e.g. orange and red • Need to be laid by specialist
Stone tiles	Kitchens, halls, living rooms, sun rooms	• Easy to maintain if sealed • Durable • Expensive • Cold underfoot • Limited colour

Wooden floors

Wooden floors are durable and hygienic. There are many different types of wooden floor coverings, e.g. solid, semi-solid, laminate, block/parquet.

Type	1 Construction; 2 Properties	Use
Solid	1 Planks of solid timber are placed on batons or on concrete floor. Tongue-and-groove construction. Various thicknesses 2 Hard-wearing, hard underfoot, expensive, easy to maintain, noisy, scratch easily, may warp	• Hall • Sitting room • Dining room
Semi-solid	1 Veneer of solid wood glued on softwood board. Variety of lengths 2 Durable, easy to maintain, inexpensive, hard underfoot, noisy	• Bedroom • Sitting room • Study
Laminate	1 Different qualities of laminated floor depending on the process used 2 Easy to lay, hard-wearing, scratch resistant, some are water resistant, variety of colours and wood grains, cheap alternative to solid and semi-solid floors	• Bedroom • Playroom • Sitting room • Study
Block/parquet	1 Small individual blocks of wood which can be laid in various patterns, e.g. basket weave and herringbone pattern 2 Labour intensive, scratches easily, expensive, hard underfoot, noisy	• Hall • Dining room • Living room

Table 14.11 Types of wooden floor

Vinyl floor coverings

Vinyl, made from PVC (polyvinylchloride), is a plastic floor covering available in sheet or tile form.

- **Types of vinyl floors:** Foam-backed, slip resistant, clear PVC faced.

Properties
- Durable, easy to clean, hygienic, quiet, resilient, acid, alkali and water resistant.
- Wide variety of colours and designs; foam-backed vinyl is soft underfoot.
- Non-slip, melt when subjected to high temperatures.
  Use: Ideal in kitchen, bathroom, shower room, utility room, playroom, children's bedrooms.

Soft flooring

Carpet

Carpet is available in a wide variety of colours and patterns. The quality of the carpet depends on the fibre and the construction process. There are four main types of carpet: (i) woven carpet, e.g. Axminister, Wilton; (ii) tufted carpet; (iii) bonded carpet; (iv) carpet tiles.

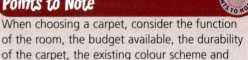

Points to Note

When choosing a carpet, consider the function of the room, the budget available, the durability of the carpet, the existing colour scheme and the maintenance required.

A wide variety of fibres are used in carpet production including natural (warm, soft, durable), synthetic (hardwearing, waterproof, easy to clean) and blended (very durable) fibres.

Table 14.12 Carpets classified according to their durability		
Durability rating	**Use**	**Features**
Medium domestic	Bedroom, study	Blended fibres, inexpensive
General domestic	Living room, sitting room	80/20 wool/nylon mix
Heavy domestic	Hall, stairs	80/20 wool/nylon mix, expensive

Natural floor coverings

Natural flooring is made from 100 per cent plant fibre, e.g. sisal, jute, coir, sea grass.

Properties
- Hard-wearing except for jute which is soft.
- Relatively inexpensive.
- Environmentally friendly.
- Complements neutral colour schemes.
- Suitable for hall, bedroom, study, living room.
- Unsuitable for rooms with high moisture content, e.g. kitchen and bathroom.

Wall finishes

Paint, wallpaper and tiles are the most popular forms of wall finishes.

Table 14.13 Criteria for selecting a wall covering	
Function of the room	• Will the room receive a lot of wear and tear? • Will it have high moisture content?
Durability	• Level of traffic flow • Number of people in the house; stage of the family
Ease of maintenance	• How can it be cleaned? • Is there a special procedure?
Cost	• How much can you afford to spend?
Decor	• Will it complement the rest of the colours and the furniture in the house?
Trends	• For example, paint effects were fashionable for a time and then were replaced by something else, e.g. metalic paints

Paint

Paint can be classified as water-based or oil/solvent-based.

Properties of paint

Paints can be cheap, durable, easy to apply, easy to maintain, available in a variety of colours and finishes.

Table 14.14 Water-based paints		
Emulsion paints	• Matt vinyl: Absorbs light, hides blemishes	• Ceiling • Bedroom • Living room
	• Silk vinyl: Washable, hard-wearing, reflects light	• Living room • Bedroom • Kitchen
Textured paint	• Contains plastic fibres which give a rough textured finish • Ideal for covering up blemishes • Hard-wearing but has limited variety of colours	• Ceiling • Dining room
Kitchen and bathroom paint	• Contains vinyl which makes it easy to maintain • Anti-fungal and anti-condensation properties • Ideal for use in high moisture areas • Durable, water resistant, easy to clean, good variety of colours, more expensive	• Bathroom • Kitchen • Utility room • Shower room
Thixotropic emulsion	• Thick non-drip emulsion ideal for ceilings • Without strong odour and quick drying • Generally one coat is enough • Limited colours as the paint cannot be mixed • Durable, easy to apply	• Ceiling

Table 14.15 Oil/solvent-based paints		
Gloss	• Hard-wearing, shiny finish, water resistant, strong odour • Unsuitable for areas with imperfections	• Anything made from wood, e.g. skirting board, doors, stairs
Satin finish	• Durable, water resistant, no undercoat required, longer drying time, strong odour • Ideal for use in high moisture areas	• Walls • Doors • Ceilings
Polyurethane strengthened	• Extremely durable, ideal for areas of hard wear and tear • Dries quickly so can be difficult to apply	• Doors • Skirting boards

Matt finish = dull appearance, absorbs light
Silk finish = shiny finish, washable
Egg shell = flat appearance, matt finish, durable

Other paint products on the market include: radiator paint, floor paint, exterior paint, bituminous paint, flame-retardant paint.

Paint effects
Paint effects such as rag rolling, sponging, stencilling and colour washing have been popular trends over the last 20 years. They have been replaced with special effect paints such as suede, metallic and blackboard.

Wallpaper

Types of wallpaper
1 **Lining paper:** Used to prepare a surface before wallpaper or paint is applied.
2 **Woodchip paper:** Similar to lining paper, ideal for covering up uneven walls, cheap and durable.
3 **Printed paper:** Machine or hand printed, design is printed or stamped (cheaper) onto the paper
4 **Washable/PVC-coated paper:** The PVC coating allows the wallpaper to be washed.
5 **Vinyl-coated paper:** A layer of vinyl is first printed with a design and then a paper backing is applied. It is durable, waterproof, strong, expensive and easy to apply.
6 **Embossed paper:** Design is pressed into the paper, creating a raised textured finish.

Wall tiles

Properties of ceramic tiles
Ceramic tiles are durable, waterproof, stain and grease resistant. Available in an assortment of designs and sizes. Good value for money; ideal for use in bathrooms and kitchens.

Table 14.16 Types of wall tiles

General purpose tiles	• Available plain or with a design
Mosaic tiles	• Small squares or circles of tiles which are difficult and time consuming to lay • Used on bathroom walls
Different shapes	• Tiles are available in rectangle, hexagonal
Patterned tiles	• The pattern, e.g. fruit, animals or flowers, is raised from the tile and provides texture
Tile panel	• A set of tiles forms a picture or design when put together. It is generally surrounded by a plain tile border.

Furniture

Furniture can be divided into three basic categories.

Table 14.17 Categories of furniture

Antique	• Furniture over 150 years old • Handmade, expensive, high quality and suitable for all rooms
Traditional	• Furniture manufactured in the last 100 years • Made of solid wood, mostly in cottage style, high quality and good value for money • Available for all rooms in the house
Contemporary	• Made from man-made materials, streamlined, can incorporate glass and metal in the design • Less expensive and widely available

Criteria for choosing furniture
- Function of the room
- Space available so furniture is in proportion to the room
- Budget and personal preferences
- Quality and craftsmanship of the furniture

The following furniture is essential to make a house habitable: bedroom furniture, dining room furniture, storage furniture, upholstered furniture.

Bedroom furniture

The main pieces of furniture in a bedroom are the bed and a wardrobe for storage. A bed consists of two main parts: base and mattress.

Points to Note

Futons, sofa beds, folding beds and water-beds are alternatives to the conventional beds.

Upholstered furniture

1 Upholstered furniture has a wooden frame with springs or padding and an outer covering of a strong durable fabric such as velvet, wool, and cotton, silk or blended fibres.
   - It is generally used for seating, e.g. for sofas and dining-room chairs.

Criteria for choosing upholstered furniture
- **Construction:** A good solid construction indicates durability.
- **Cost:** Buy the best quality you can afford.
- **Resilience:** Does the seat keep its shape after use?
- **Quality symbols:** Are there any quality symbols?
- **Outer fabric:** Should be strong, resilient, durable, easy to clean and flame resistant.

Removable covers are a convenient way of maintaining the upholstery.

Dining-room furniture
- Dining-room furniture is available in many different styles, colours and materials, e.g. wood and plastic.
- It should be sturdy, strong, easy to clean, stain resistant and the correct height.
- The table should be large enough to seat the family.
- The seating should be comfortable and provide neck and back support.

Soft furnishings

All homes will have a selection of soft furnishings, e.g. curtains, blinds, cushions, duvets, which add to the aesthetics and function of the particular room.

Curtains
The *functions* of curtains are to provide privacy and insulation, to keep light out and to add to the overall decor and ambience.

The *choice* of curtains depends on the budget, style of the room, size of the windows, and function of the room.

Curtains should be: easy to care for, stain resistant, flame resistant, colour fast, pre-shrunk, drape well, and complement the existing decor.

Blinds
Blinds are a basic window dressing which can be used with or without curtains. There is a wide selection of blinds available, e.g. roller blinds, Roman blinds, Austrian blinds, Venetian, vertical and wooden blinds.

Bed linen
Bed linen includes duvets and covers, sheets, pillowcases and pillows. Fabrics used include cotton, polycotton, silk, polyester and linen.

Materials used in the home

Wood, metal, glass, plastics and fabrics are used extensively in the home. A combination of all materials provides interest and individuality to a home.

Wood
Wood is widely used in the house, e.g. flooring, roof, doors, chopping boards. Wood can be classified as follows.

1 Hardwood (from mostly deciduous trees)
- Beech, elm, chestnut, mahogany, maple, oak, teak
  Properties: Durable, easy to maintain, expensive, susceptible to woodworm and rot, damaged by heat and moisture
  Use: Floors, furniture, doors

2 Softwood (from conifer trees)
- Pine, fir, spruce
  Properties: Softer, less durable, inexpensive, damaged by heat and moisture
  Use: All kinds of furniture, doors, floors

Table 14.18 Man-made timbers		
Type	**Properties**	**Use**
Plywood	Strong, easy to maintain, versatile, cheap	Flooring, cheaper furniture
Hardboard	Hard-wearing, dark in colour, versatile, inexpensive	DIY work, backing of furniture
Medium density fibreboard (MDF)	Durable, smooth, level, easy to work with, can be painted or laminated, cheap	Furniture, mouldings, skirting boards
Chipboard	Not long lasting, unattractive to look at, can be damaged by moisture, cheap	Flooring, laminated worktops, furniture

Metals
Metals are widely used throughout the home, especially in the kitchen. Metals can be both decorative and functional. Metals commonly used are stainless steel, aluminium, tin and copper.

Use of metals
- **Stainless steel:** Alloy made of two or more metals
  Properties: Shiny or satin finish, resistant to corrosion, easy to clean, poor conductor of heat
  Use: Cutlery, sink units, appliances, furniture trimmings
- **Aluminium**
  Properties: Malleable, lightweight, good conductor of heat, darkens and discolours easily, reacts with acid foods
  Use: Windows, appliances, saucepans, cooking foil

Glass
Glass is used throughout the home in various forms.

1 **Heat resistant glass, e.g. Pyrex**
   Properties: Hard, transparent or coloured, stain resistant, chips or cracks easily
   Uses: Ovenproof dishes, teapots, jugs

2 **Soda lime glass**
   Properties: Easy to break, transparent, unstable at high temperatures, cheap
   Uses: Jars, bottles, lightbulbs

3 **Stained glass/cut glass**
   Uses: Decorative features around the home

Plastics
Plastics are used extensively around the home. They are made from a combination of air, water, petroleum, wood, coal, natural gas and salt in the presence of heat and pressure. The two main categories of plastic are thermoplastic and thermosetting.

General properties of plastic: Tough, durable, rigid or flexible, easy to clean, hygienic, versatile, water resistant, stain resistant, resistant to chemicals and cheap.

Table 14.19 Thermoplastic and thermosetting			
Type	Properties	Examples	Uses
Thermoplastic	• Soften on heating and can be moulded and remoulded again • They harden on cooling	• Polytetrafluorethylene (PTFE)/Teflon • Polyethylene	• Non-stick finish • Kitchen utensils • Saucepans • Frying pans • Bottles • Food containers • Toys
Thermosetting	• Manufactured by pouring powder into a mould • Set after application of heat and cannot be remoulded • Produces a hard type of plastic	• Melamine formaldehyde • Phenol formaldehydes, e.g. Bakelite	• Cups • Plates • Saucers • Counter tops • Interior paddles of washing machine • Light switches • Telephones • Handles on utensils

Fabrics

Fabrics are used throughout the home and add warmth, texture, colour and pattern to a room. Fabrics are available in a wide choice of fibres, finishes and prices. Fibres are classified as natural and synthetic.
- **Natural:** Cotton, linen, wool, silk
- **Synthetic:** Viscose, polyester, nylon, acrylic

The properties of fabric are often the deciding factor in their choice of selection.

Cotton
Properties: Strong, durable, absorbent, closely woven, easy to maintain
Uses: Sheets, curtains, cushions, towels, napkins, duvet covers

Polyester
Properties: Strong, crease resistant, easy to maintain, inexpensive
Uses: Curtains, blinds, tablecloths, napkins

The Energy Efficient Home

Table 14.20 Energy supplies in the home	
Non-renewable sources	**Renewable sources**
• Electricity • Gas • Oil • Solid fuel (coal, peat, turf, wood)	• Solar energy • Wind power • Water power • Geothermal power • Biomass (bio-energy)

Non-renewable energy sources

Non-renewable forms of energy provide energy for heating and lighting in our homes and industry.

Electricity
Source: Burning fossil fuels, oil, natural gas, hydropower, wind power
Uses: Powers homes and businesses throughout Ireland
Properties: Readily available, efficient, clean, expensive
Sustainability: Electricity will not run out, but the non-renewable forms of energy, e.g. gas and oil, used to produce it will. Renewable energy sources, e.g. wind and water, need to be implemented to ensure a constant supply of electricity

Gas

Source: Occurs naturally in the seabed due to the sedimentation of decaying plant and animal life over time. The build-up of hydrocarbons from this process produces gas

Two types: 1 Natural gas supplied by An Bord Gais
2 LPG (liquid petroleum gas) supplied in bottles or tanks

Uses: Generates electricity, heats homes and water, cooking, LPG used in cars

Properties: Clean, efficient, environmentally friendly, non-renewable, unpleasant odour, danger of explosions

Sustainability: The amount of gas being consumed far outweighs what is being discovered. The gas supplies are being used up rapidly and will run out by 2050 unless new gasfields are discovered

Oil

Source: Decayed plant and animal life compressed between rock layers. Oil is found under the earth's crust as large crude oil reserves (lakes)

Uses: Heats homes and water, cooking, generates electricity, transport

Properties: Efficient with little waste but damaging to the environment

Sustainability: Consumption is greater than availability; will run out unless new oil reserves are discovered

Solid fuel – coal

Source: (Carbon) Rock formed due to the decomposition and compression of trees and other vegetation under the earth's seam millions of years ago

Uses: Heats homes and water, generates electricity, labour intensive, cheap; mining is dangerous

Sustainability: It is distributed evenly throughout the world, but it is a finite resource. There is ongoing research to try and convert coal into an oil-like substance which is economically viable. Burning coal has a hugely damaging impact on the environment due to CO_2 emissions

Solid fuel – peat/turf

Source: Formed in a similar manner to coal

Uses and properties: Heats homes, generates electricity, labour intensive, cheap, produces waste products

Sustainability: Non-renewable

Solid fuel – wood (50% carbon), e.g. fir, spruce and pine

Renewable source: Although wood is a renewable energy source often referred to as biomass, it still produces emissions which could be harmful to the environment, although generally wood is carbon neutral

Source: Trees

Uses: Heats homes, cooking, generates electricity

Sustainability: Renewable form of energy, environmentally friendly, needs good planning for utilisation as an energy source

Renewable energy sources

Solar power
Source: Sun
Uses: Heats homes and water
Sustainability: Once harnessed and utilised, it could, as a renewable energy source, infinitely supply a large proportion of the world energy requirements

Water power (hydropower)
- Hydropower harnesses fast-flowing water to turn turbines which generate electricity.
- This system is viable to operate in Ireland, but the initial costs can be very expensive.

Wind power
- Ireland is particularly suited to harness wind as a source of energy.
- Wind turbines produce electricity.
- Increased wind speeds produce more energy as the wind turbines rotate quicker.

Bio-energy
- Bio-energy is produced from biomass which is organic material, e.g. leaves, stems, wood, manure and sewage.
- Bio-fuel comes in solid (wood chips) or liquid form (rapeseed oil).

Fuel emissions
- **Carbon dioxide:** Emissions have increased due to the burning of fossil fuels. CO_2 is released into the atmosphere.
- **Methane gas:** Produced by bacteria which break down organic matter without oxygen being present, e.g. in waste dumps. Methane also leaks from gas pipes.
- **CFCs:** Used in aerosols and refrigerators.
- **Nitrous oxide:** Produced when ammonia nitrate is heated.
- **Sulfur dioxide:** Anthracite, coal and smokeless fuel, e.g. Magiglow, easy flame coal nuggets are the main contributors of SO_2 emissions.
- **Smoke/smog:** The incomplete burning of fossil fuels produces smoke. Smog is a combination of smoke and mist or fog.

Effect of emissions on the environment

Emissions cause: Acid rain, global warming/greenhouse effect, smog, respiratory problems.

Acid rain
- When fossil fuels are burnt a number of gases are produced, e.g. CO_2, SO_2.
- They combine with water vapour (rain) in the air and produce carbonic acid, sulfuric acid and nitric acid.
- These fall to the earth when it rains.
  1. Acid rain damages buildings, especially stone, metal and paintwork on many historic buildings, as well as decreasing the life of new buildings.
  2. It destroys fishlife, birds and insects as many cannot survive in acidic conditions.
  3. It damages forests and farm crops, making the land too acidic for growing crops and trees.

The greenhouse effect
- The sun heats the earth, but it is the presence of about 30 greenhouse gases which regulates the earth's temperature.
- Due to the emissions generated by human activity the overall composition of the atmosphere has changed, causing the earth to become warmer, i.e. the greenhouse effect.

The **greenhouse effect** is said to be responsible:
1. For rising temperatures
2. Rise in sea levels
3. Climatic change
4. Farming (carbon dioxide is a natural fertiliser)

How to reduce emissions
- Use cleaner fuels, e.g. natural gas.
- Remove greenhouse gases – especially CFCs.
- Use energy, e.g. electricity, more efficiently.
- Improve insulation in the home and reduce heating.
- Invest in renewable forms of energy, e.g. solar, wind.
- Invest in bacteria which do the same work as heat, e.g. smelt copper.
- Use smokeless fuel when lighting an open fire.
- Do not burn rubbish or light bonfires.

Table 14.21 Energy inefficiencies in the home and how to prevent them

Inefficiency	How to prevent inefficiencies
Electricity	
Unnecessary use of lights	• Maximise daylight in a room • Turn lights off when room is not in use. Use a timer
Bulbs	• Use low energy CFL lightbulbs
Appliances left on standby	• Always unplug appliances at the socket • Never leave appliances on standby as it uses nearly half the amount of electricity as when turned on
Energy labels on appliances	• Appliances with energy efficient labels A or B are most energy efficient
Use of oven for one dish	• When heating an oven cook a number of items to utilise the energy
Heating	
Boiler not serviced	• Have the boiler serviced annually to ensure it is working efficiently
Heating system without thermostat or timer	• Install a thermostat on the boiler and on individual heaters • Use a timer for heating rooms and water
Open fire	• Use smokeless fuel
Hot water	
No thermostat No timers	• Install a thermostat and a timer on the immersion heater
Immersion heater	• Place a lagging jacket on the water cylinder: it can reduce heat loss by up to 75%
Washing	
Baths	• A shower uses 70% less water than a bath
Running water when brushing teeth	• Turn off taps when brushing teeth
Leaking taps	• Repair any leaking taps as up to 90 litres of water can be lost per day
Washing clothes	• Use a warm rather than a hot cycle • Use a half load or eco option when washing clothes
Insulation	
Poor attic insulation	• Proper insulation in the attic will reduce heat loss by 30%
Draughts on doors and windows	• Use double-glazed windows • Use blinds and curtains to retain heat in a room

Systems and Services in the Home

Electricity

Supply of electricity in the home
- A service cable (ESB) brings electricity to the home.
- It enters the main fusebox which is housed in a special unit outside the house.
- The fusebox also contains a meter which measures the amount of electricity used in the house.
- Some times a second meter is installed which measures the use of off-peak electricity.
- From the fusebox outside the house the electricity flows into the consumer unit inside. The consumer unit is located in the kitchen, utility room or hallway. It contains miniature circuit breakers for safety.
- From the consumer unit the electricity is distributed to the rest of the house.

Circuits
- From the consumer unit a number of circuits run around the house. Each circuit has its own fuse to protect it.
- The following circuits may exist in a house: **Lighting circuit, socket circuit (upstairs and downstairs), cooker, immersion heater.**
- A radial circuit is used for an appliance such as a cooker or an electric shower as each appliance requires its own fuse.
- Each circuit only carries a certain amount of current. The circuit's fuse must correspond with that value, e.g. a lighting circuit requires a 6 amp fuse, whereas a cooker requires a 35 amp fuse.

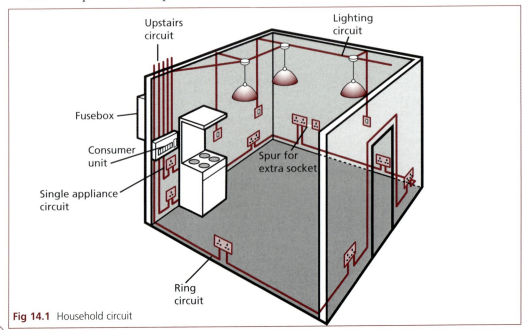

Fig 14.1 Household circuit

CHAPTER 14

- A ring circuit is the system used in all modern homes.
- A wire leads from the consumer unit all around the house and returns to the consumer unit.
- The ring loop could contain all the sockets or the light switches for the house, or one ring loop could be used for upstairs and one for downstairs.
- The ring circuit also contains an earth wire for safety.

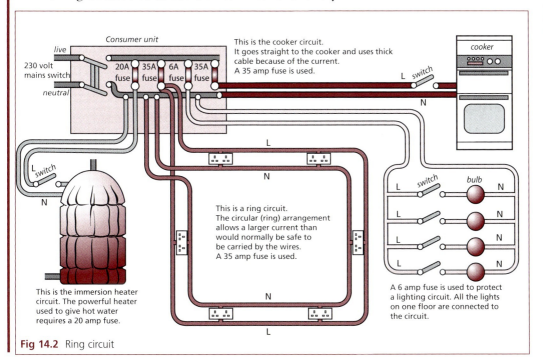

Fig 14.2 Ring circuit

Table 14.22 Definitions of electrical terms	
Term	**Explanation**
Voltage	• The amount of pressure/force necessary to drive the electric current along • In Ireland the voltage is 230
Wattage	• The rate at which appliances use electricity is measured in watts • Watts = volts x amps
Amperage	• Measures the flow of electric current • The amount of energy used by an appliance determines the amperage • Amperage = wattage ÷ voltage (wattage divided by voltage)
Kilowatt per hour (kWh)	• This is the measurement of a unit of electricity 1,000W = 1kWh

Tariffs and costing

The Electricity Supply Board (ESB) had been the main provider of domestic electricity in Ireland until February 2005.

The new companies licensed to provide electricity by the Commission for Energy Regulation include: Airtricity, Direct Independent Energy Ltd, Energia, CH Power.

Bills are issued bimonthly and contain the following information.
- **Standing charge:** €10.38 remains the same; it covers the cost of maintaining the system, meter readings and billing.
- **Unit charge:** The cost of electricity used by the household measured in units.
- **Public service obligations levy (PSO):** Introduced to cover the cost of buying electricity from generating stations using renewable forms of energy.
- **VAT:** Each bill is also subject to VAT at 13.5 per cent.

Electricity safety devices

1 Fuses
- A fuse is a safety device used in electrical appliances.
- It consists of an outer covering of porcelain or glass and a thin wire inside. This wire is thinner than the other wires in the circuit and melts quicker.
- A fuse is a deliberate weak link in the electrical circuit which melts, cutting off the electricity, if a fault occurs, e.g. if too much current passes through it.
- The size of fuse depends on the current.
- Fuses are colour coded indicating their amperage:
  Cooker = black (35 amp); water heating = blue (20 amp)

2 Miniature circuit breakers (MCB)
- MCBs are a safety device used in all consumer units instead of a fuse.
- The principle is similar to that of a fuse, but the fuse does not have to be replaced. If a fault occurs, the circuit is broken and can be turned back on with the trip switch once the problem has been identified.

3 Residual circuit device (RCD)
- RCD is an extra safety device which is fitted in all new consumer units.
- If a fault occurs in the circuit it cuts off the electric current immediately.
- This is particularly useful for electric showers or electric water heating devices.

4 Earth wires
- Earth wires in plugs and appliances are another safety device.
- If a fault develops in a live wire, the earth wire conveys the electric current to the ground and prevents electrocution.

Guidelines for the safe use of electricity
Accidents involving electricity can be avoided by paying particular attention to appliances and how they are used, the repair of faulty equipment, and never mixing water and electricity.

CHAPTER 14

Table 14.23 How to avoid accidents with electricity	
1 Never mix water and electricity	• Always dry hands before touching an electric appliance • Never bring electric appliances, e.g. heaters or radio, into the bathroom • Only use shaver sockets in the bathroom
2 Flexes and plugs	• Never overload a socket with plugs, e.g. with extension leads • Unplug all electrical appliances at night except fridge and freezer • Replace frayed or damaged flexes, broken plugs or sockets • Do not wrap flexes around appliances, e.g. around hair dryer
3 Kitchen	• Avoid using extensions cables or adapters • Never trail a flex near the hob or the sink • Unplug all appliances before cleaning them
4 Bedroom	• Never use a damaged electric blanket. • Do not place wet or damp clothes on an electric heater • Avoid using electric fires in the bedroom if possible

Water

- Water used for human consumption should be clean, bacteria free, odourless and colourless.
- The local authorities are responsible for ensuring that water used by humans is safe.

Water treatment

- Water is stored in reservoirs until it is needed by the local community.
- It must be purified to make it safe for human consumption.
- It goes through a series of treatments (see Table 14.24) before it is pumped into a final covered reservoir for storage.

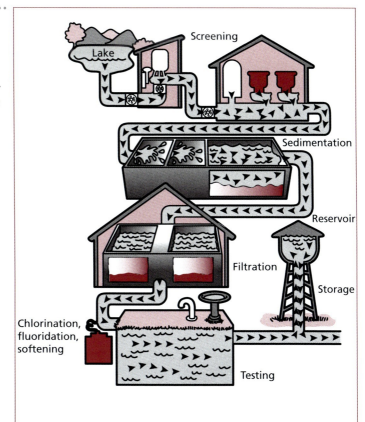

Fig 14.3 Water treatment

Table 14.24 Types of water treatment	
Screening	This removes large floating debris from the water
Sedimentation	Chemicals are added to the water which attach themselves to dirt which then sinks to the base of the tank
Filtration	Filter beds of sand and gravel are used to remove any suspended matter in the water
Chlorination	Chlorine is added to kill any bacteria
Fluoridation	Fluorine is added to protect teeth
Softening	Chlorine of lime is added in hard water areas to help soften the water
Testing	The water is tested for quality and pureness, it is then stored in a high storage reservoir until it is pumped to the community

How does water reach your home?

- Treated water is stored in covered high storage reservoirs.
- A mains pipe brings the water to the area for which it is intended.
- A service pipe connects the mains pipe with the household.
- In the house this service pipe is generally connected to the kitchen sink.
- There a stopcock allows the water supply to be turned off.
- This service pipe supplies cold water to the kitchen sink.
- Another pipe (raising mains) supplies the storage tank in the attic with cold water.
- The storage tank, which has a capacity of 230 litres, is placed in the attic so that it is high enough to create pressure to feed the system.
- A pipe leads off the storage tank to supply cold water to the bathroom taps and toilets in the rest of the house.

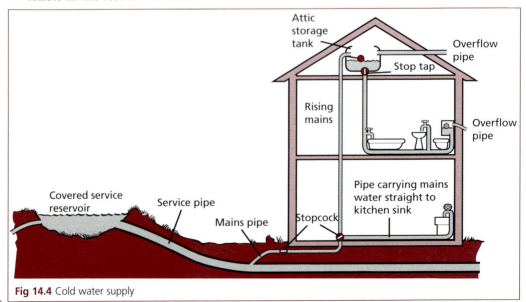

Fig 14.4 Cold water supply

Heating

Levels of thermal comfort
- The heating required in a household varies from season to season.
- The ideal temperature in a house varies from room to room; it can be controlled by timers, thermostats, and zoned heating (uses both).

- Bedroom 15°C
- Bathroom 15–20°C
- Kitchen 15–20°C
- Sitting room 17–21°C
- Hall 13–15°C

Thermostats

- Thermostats are used to control temperature.
- There are two basic types of thermostats: electric and gas thermostats.

Electric thermostats

Working principle
- A thermostat consists of a bimetallic strip made of brass and invar.
- When heat is applied the brass expands faster than the invar. The brass bends and breaks the circuit or flow of electricity.
- On cooling, the brass contracts and the connection is made again and the electricity can flow.
- A light is often used to indicate whether or not an appliance is switched on. This type of thermostat can be used, for example, for controlling the heat in a central heating boiler.
- Thermostatic radiator valves are fitted to radiators and control their heat output.
- A room thermostat is a wall-mounted device which controls the overall temperature in the house from the room it is located in.

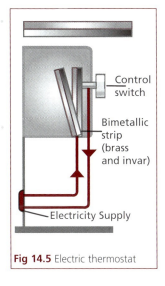

Fig 14.5 Electric thermostat

Gas thermostat

Working principle
- Gas thermostats are used to control the flow of gas to the oven or the boiler.
- An invar rod is placed inside a brass tube.
- The invar is attached to one end of the tube.
- When the temperature increases the brass expands, pulling the invar rod with it.
- A valve placed at the end of the invar rod restricts the gas flow.
- As the temperature drops the brass contracts and the gas can flow again.

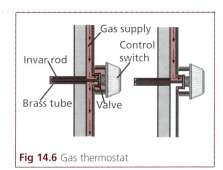

Fig 14.6 Gas thermostat

Criteria for choosing a heating system
The following criteria should be considered when choosing a heating system: Cost, size of house, convenience, energy efficiency, water heating, reliability, comfort level and safety.

Types of heating systems
1 **Full central heating:** Provides heat all over the house from one central source, e.g. a boiler. Ensures comfort and warmth in all rooms. Expensive to install but easy to operate.
2 **Partial central heating:** Heats only part of the house from a central point, usually the living area.
3 **Background heating:** Provides heat throughout the house but only at low temperatures, e.g. at 13°C.
4 **Local heating:** Individual heat source in a room, e.g. open fire, storage heater, Superser (gas radiant heater). Only provides heat in the room of the heat source.
5 **Passive solar power:** Heat is absorbed through the windows and keeps the room warm.
6 **Solar collector device:** Absorbs the heat from the sun and is used to heat the house and water.

Full central heating systems

There are two types of central heating systems:
1 **Wet central heating system:** Water is pumped through pipes to radiators in individual rooms.
2 **Dry central heating system:** Involves heating air and then using a fan to distribute it throughout the house via large ducts.

Wet central heating system (small bore central heating system)
A wet central heating system is an enclosed system where the water used in the radiators circulates continuously.
- It consists of three systems: Cold water supply, primary circulation (radiators), secondary circulation (hot water).

1 The boiler heats the cold water which flows into it from the radiators.
2 This hot water rises into the hot water cylinder and passes through a heat exchanger in the cylinder (a heat exchanger is a coiled pipe).
3 Cold water from the storage tank in the attic flows into the water cylinder at the base and circulates around the heated coil (convection currents).
4 This hot water is used to provide hot water in the taps throughout the house.
5 The hot water in the heat exchanger leaves the cylinder and heats the radiators.
6 When the water in the radiators is cold, it is pumped back to the boiler and the cycle starts again.
7 An expansion tank and pipe in the attic leads off from the primary and secondary circulation systems. This is a safety device to release pressure in the system.

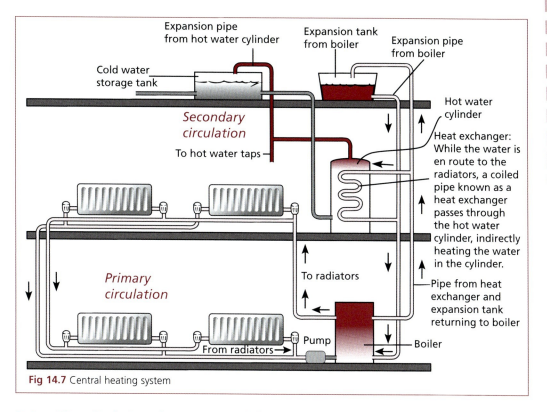

Fig 14.7 Central heating system

Scientific principles of a wet central heating system
- **Convection:** The water in the boiler and the hot water system is heated through convection currents.
- **Thermal expansion:** When the water is heated, it can flow upwards to the hot water cylinder.
- **Radiation:** Heat is radiated into the air space surrounding the radiators.

1 **Dry central heating systems:** Electric storage heaters, underfloor, ceiling heating.
2 **Electric storage heaters:** Contain heat-retaining firebricks or concrete blocks surrounded by an electric heating element.
3 **Underfloor and ceiling heating:** Elements are insulated and embedded in concrete.
4 **Ducted system:** The air is heated at a central source and blown via ducts around the house.
5 **Individual heaters:** Electric heaters, fan heaters, oil-filled heaters, convector heaters.
6 **Gas heaters:** Radiant heaters, e.g. Superser and coal-effect fires.

Insulation

Underlying principle
- Insulation prevents or slows down the loss of heat.
- Insulation should retain the heat within the house, therefore reducing the cost of heating bills.

Average heat loss
- Roof 25%
- Walls 35%
- Windows 15%
- Doors 10%
- Floors 15%

Advantages of insulation
1. It saves money.
2. It reduces the use of energy resources.
3. It acts as a noise barrier.
4. It maintains a constant comfortable temperature.

Points to Note
The Building Regulations Act 1997 (Conservation of Fuel and Energy) requires all buildings to meet minimum standards of energy efficiency.

Areas in the home that require insulation

1. **Attic:** Blanket insulation, foam insulation, loose-fill insulation, blown insulation.
2. **Storage tank and pipes:** The water storage tank in the attic is insulated apart from the base. Insulating material or split foam tubing is used on pipes to prevent freezing.
3. **Walls:** Cavity walls, internal solid walls, external solid walls.
4. **Windows and doors:** Double-glazed windows, heavy lined curtains, draught proofing, well-fitted doors and windows.
5. **Floors:** Insulation and damp-proof course, floor covering.

Ventilation

Underlying principle
Ventilation works on the principle that warm air expands and rises and cool air will rush in to take its place. The convection currents which are created allow fresh air to enter a room and stale air to be removed.

Why is ventilation needed?
- Provides a constant supply of fresh oxygen-rich air.
- Controls air temperature and removes stale air.
- Prevents condensation and helps reduce humidity levels.
- An inefficient ventilation system can lead to many medical conditions, e.g. respiratory problems, headaches and fainting.
- Lack of ventilation may cause structural damage to property over time.

Good ventilation should not cause a draught or lower the room temperature. Ensure air is changed at least once or twice an hour.

Condensation

Condensation occurs when warm air meets a cold surface, e.g. a mirror or a window, and turns into water droplets.

Points to Note
Humidity is the amount of moisture present in the air.
Warm air contains more moisture than cold air.

The effects of condensation are:
- Damage to structure, paintwork, wallpaper, wood and metal.
- Moulds on ceilings, carpets and clothes.
- Aggravation of respiratory problems.

Damp insulating materials increase heat loss from the house.

To prevent condensation
- Install a good system of ventilation and add extra ventilation in rooms with high humidity.
- Provide good insulation all over the house as this raises the internal temperature and prevents condensation.
- Have an efficient heating system.
- Use hygroscopic (moisture absorbing) materials in soft furnishings and floorings.

Forms of ventilation are:
1. **Natural:** Air brick, fireplaces, doors, windows, vents
2. **Artificial:** Cooker hoods (ducted and ductless), extractor fan, air conditioning

Artificial forms of ventilation

Extractor fan: construction
- Manufactured from aluminium or strong plastic.
- It has rotating blades, a pull cord or switch, and a motor.
- Attached to an exterior wall or window.

Working principle
1. The switch or pull cord activates the motor which causes the blades to rotate at high speeds.
2. The outside shutter opens and the stale air is drawn out.
3. Extractor fans are often found in the kitchen near the cooker, or in a bathroom or shower room.

Cooker hoods
- A cooker hood is a canopy placed over the hob or cooker in a kitchen.
- It is used to remove odours and moisture during cooking. The cooker hood can be ducted or ductless.

Working principle
1. The electrically driven fan rotates at a high speed and creates suction which draws in the stale air.
2. The air is filtered and removed from the room in the ducted hood or recirculated in the ductless cooker hood.

Ductless cooker hood
- These are generally used when there is no access to external walls.
- It consists of a metal/plastic canopy, a metal filter for grease, a charcoal filter for odours and a fan. The air is filtered and then recirculated in the room.
- The charcoal filter should be replaced and the metal filter cleaned regularly to ensure that the hood is working efficiently.

Ducted cooker hood
- A ducted cooker hood is similar in construction to the ductless cooker hood, except that it is fitted to an external wall and it contains a duct to remove the odours and moisture from the air.

Lighting

Lighting can be natural or artificial. Lighting is necessary:
- To prevent accidents in the home.
- To enable us to see what we are doing.
- To prevent eyestrain.
- To create an ambience.
- To highlight features or objects in a room.
- To form an integral part of an interior design scheme.

Types of lighting
- **Natural lighting:** Windows, doors, glass bricks
- **Artificial lighting:** Tungsten filament bulbs and halogen lights, fluorescent tubes, compact fluorescent lights (CFLs)

Artificial lights

Tungsten filament bulbs
- The bulb is made from clear, coloured or pearl glass. A filament of tungsten wire is coiled internally and surrounded by argon gas. At the base there are metal contacts.
- Electricity flows into the bulb via the contacts. It meets resistance in the filament which creates a white glow.
- Filament bulbs are inexpensive and available in a wide choice of colour and wattage.
- Can be used with a dimmer switch. Easy to install and maintain. Will last about 1,000 hours.

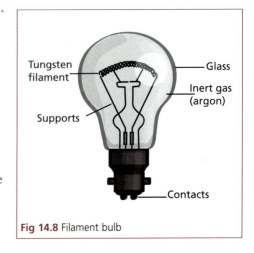

Fig 14.8 Filament bulb

Fluorescent bulbs
- Fluorescent bulbs consist of a long glass tube.
- The inside of the glass is coated with phosphor.
- There are metal contacts with electrodes at each end of the tube.
- The glass is filled with argon gas and mercury.
- The electricity flows in via the electrodes. This instigates a reaction between the argon and the phosphor lining which creates a glow.
- Fluorescent bulbs are energy efficient.
- Available in a variety of sizes from 30cm to 2.5m in length.
- Last over 8,000 hours. Lights hum and flicker when turned on.
- Contain toxic chemicals which are harmful to the environment when disposed of.

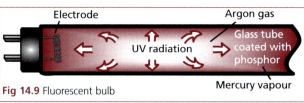

Fig 14.9 Fluorescent bulb

Compact fluorescent lights (CFL)
- Compact fluorescent lights operate in much the same way as fluorescent tubes except that they are much smaller.
- The tube is looped back on itself to reduce the overall size.
- They use 80 per cent less electricity than other bulbs.
- They are more energy efficient and reduce lighting bills.
- Initially they are more expensive to buy, but are economical in the long run.
- They operate on a low wattage (9–23 watt).
- The light is not instant; it takes a few minutes to adjust.
- Not suitable for dimmer switches.
- Aesthetically not pleasing.
- Useful for outdoor security lights.

Energy efficient lighting
- CFLs are more energy efficient. Reduce energy costs.
- Help protect the environment.
- Ideal for long periods of lighting.

Properties of light and their application
1 **Diffused light:** Scatters in all directions when it falls on a dull, non-reflective substance; this can be seen in opaque lampshades.
2 **Reflected light:** If it falls on a shiny surface it is reflected back, e.g. mirrors, tiles.
3 **Absorbed light:** Absorbed by dark and matt surfaces. It helps to create a warm, cosy ambience in a room.
4 **Refracted light:** If it passes through thick glass or a glass ridge, the glass will cause the light to bend. This is evident in glass bricks; frosted glass often used in bathrooms.
5 **Dispersed light:** If it passes through a prism it is broken into its component colours, e.g. in crystal, many colours can be identified.

Planning a lighting scheme

1 **Construction:** Incorporated into the construction of the house for wiring to be discreet.
2 **Types of lighting:** A general light, a task/direct light, an accent light.
3 **Function:** The function of the room determines which types of light are necessary.
4 **Natural light:** It is important to maximise natural light.
5 **Ambience:** A room can be enhanced by taking some of the properties of light into account and applying its principles.
6 **Safety:** Ensure that all fittings and installations are completed by a qualified professional electrician.

Table 14.25 Developments in lighting technology and contemporary light fittings

New lighting technology	Light fittings	Outside lighting
• Compact fluorescent lights • Halogen lights • Fibre optics • Low wattage lights • Touch sensitive lights • Dimmer switch	• Recessed ceiling lights • Rise-and-fall lights • Ceramic and plaster-based wall lights • Under-counter and cabinet lighting • Pelmet and window lighting • Track lighting • Up lighters and down lighters	• Sensor lights • Solar powered lights • Pool and pond lights • Step and decking lighting

Questions

Look up these questions in your exam papers 2004, HL Section C, 1b; 2005, HL Section C, 1b; 2006, HL Section C, 1a ; 2004, OL Section C, 1b; HL Section C, 1; HL & OL Section C

1 (a) Discuss how aesthetic and environmental factors influence the design of modern housing. (16)
  (b) Explain how house-building standards are regulated. Refer to at least two different methods. (14)
  (2006, HL, Section C, 1b)

2 The efficient use of energy is the responsibility of every consumer. In relation to energy use in the home give details of:
  (a) Potential energy inefficiencies and strategies for improvement. (18)
  (b) The effects of fuel emissions on the environment. (12)
  (2004, HL, Section C, 1c)

3 (a) Give an account of four factors that should be considered when choosing wall finishes for the interior of the home. (16)
  (b) Describe one type of wall finish suitable for a young child's bedroom. Give two reasons for your choice. (14)
  (2006, OL, Section C, 1c)

4 (a) Name the two main types of plastic used in the home. In relation to each list (i) its uses and (ii) its properties. (20)
  (b) Explain the underlying principle involved in double-glazing as a method of reducing heat loss through windows. (10)
  (2005, HL, Section C, 1c)

Key Points

Housing Styles
- 1800–50: Rural – small, thatch roof, stone walls. Urban – terraced, tenements, Georgian style
- 1850–1900: Rural – two-storey, slate roof. Urban – Gothic and Tudor style, different materials, terraced houses, small gardens
- 1900–50: Rural – two-storey, slate roof, electricity. Urban – housing estates, shared sanitary conditions in city, local authority housing scheme, new building materials
- 1950–2000: Urban – high-rise building, bungalows, mock Tudor and Georgian style, new building materials, land more expensive
- 2000–: Land at a premium, high-density housing, smaller and compact housing, large housing estates, amenities, social and affordable housing schemes
- Choice of housing: Social, cultural, economic and environmental factors influence housing choice
- Different housing requirements: Family, single person, the elderly, the disabled and the homeless
- Evaluation of housing provision: Distribution of housing, quality of accommodation, comparative costs of renting and buying property
- Social housing provision, provision of local amenities

House Building and Design
- Factors influencing location: Amenities, site orientation, planning permission, building regulations, budget
- Factors affecting house style: Budget, planning restrictions, personal preferences, site and location, house layout
- Planning permission: Outline and full planning permission, retention, bylaw approval, procedure of how to obtain planning permission
- Professional services: Architect, engineer, surveyor, builder, solicitor
- Factors influencing house design: Aesthetics, environmental concerns, family requirements, ergonomics, initial and maintenance costs, technological developments
- Regulations of house building standards: Building Regulations Act 1991, National House Building Guarantee Scheme

Interior Design
- Elements of design: Colour, pattern and texture
- Principles of design: Balance, proportion, rhythm, emphasis
- Planning a colour scheme: Function of the room, overall colour scheme of the house, choice of colours, aspect of the house, use of colour to highlight or hide certain features
- Factors influencing interior design: Aesthetics and comfort, ergonomics, family size and circumstances, special needs, cost, environmental factors
- Types and properties of flooring and floor covering: Solid and suspended flooring, hard, soft and natural floor covering
- Wall finishes: Paint, wallpaper, ceramic tiles
- Criteria for selecting furniture and soft furnishings: Function of room, cost, construction, quality, decor of room, personal style, space available, quality symbols
- Materials used in the home: Wood, metals, glass, plastics, fabrics

Key Points

The Energy Efficient Home
- Non-renewable sources: Electricity, gas, oil, coal, peat
- Renewable sources: Wood, solar power, hydropower, wind power, bio-energy
- Sustainability of each energy source: Use of renewable and environmentally friendly forms of energy
- Emissions: Carbon dioxide, methane, CFCs, nitrous oxides, sulfur dioxide, smog
- Acid rain: Damage to buildings, water and soil
- Global warming/greenhouse effect: Rise in temperature and in sea levels, CFCs and ozone layer
- Smog: Badly affects cities and towns
- Respiratory problems: Asthma, bronchitis
- Energy inefficiencies in the home: Use of electricity, heating, hot water, insulation
- Improving energy efficiency: CFL lights, unplug appliances, buy energy efficient appliances, have boiler serviced, use thermostat and timer, use smokeless fuel, use a lagging jacket, shower, repair leaking taps, improve insulation, double-glaze windows

Systems and Services in the Home
- Supply of electricity: Service cable to house, fusebox, meter, consumer unit indoors, ring circuit
- Electrical terms: Voltage, wattage, amperage, kilowatt per hour
- Tariffs and costing: ESB billing, standing charge, unit charge, public service levy, VAT
- Electricity safety devices: Fuses, miniature circuit breakers (MCBs), residual circuit devices (RCDs), earth wires
- Safe use of electricity: Do not mix water and electricity, ensure flexes and plugs are undamaged
- Water treatment: Screening, sedimentation, filtration, chlorination, fluoridation, softening, testing
- Cold water supply and storage: Reservoir, mains pipe, service pipe, kitchen sink, storage tank, stopcock, bathroom

Heating
- Principle of a thermostat: Bimetallic strip of brass and invar, principle of thermal expansion
- Criteria for choosing a heating system: Cost, size of house, convenience, energy efficiency, water heating, reliability, comfort level, safety
- Types of heating systems: Full and partial central heating system, background and local heating, solar heating
- Central heating systems: Wet and dry central heating systems
- Insulation in the home: Advantages, areas in the home that require insulation
- Forms of ventilation: Artificial ventilation (extractor fan, cooker hoods)

Lighting
- Types of lighting: Tungsten filament bulbs, halogen lights, fluorescent tubes, CFLs
- Properties of light: DRARD (diffused, reflected, absorbed, refracted, dispersed)
- Planning a lighting scheme: Construction, types of lights, functions, natural light, ambience, safety, aesthetics
- New developments: Light technology, light fittings, outside lights

15: Elective 3 - Social Studies

●●● Learning Objectives

In this chapter you will learn about:
1. Social Change and the Family
2. Education
3. Work
4. Reconciling Employment with Family Responsibilities
5. Leisure
6. Unemployment
7. Poverty
8. Statutory and Community Responses to Poverty and Creating Employment

Social Change and the Family

The impact of social and economic changes on the family has been considerable.

> **Exam Hints**
> This section is examined in Section C, question 3, of your exam paper. You must answer Section A and then either part B or C. This section is worth 80 marks.

1 Change in settlement patterns from rural to urban
- The urban population in Ireland has increased dramatically due to better employment opportunities, education, services and amenities, and transport links.
- Farming is less labour intensive, therefore there are fewer jobs.
- Educational opportunities are provided in urban areas such as cities and large towns.
- Many services, e.g. banking and post offices, are in limited supply in rural areas due to large numbers of young people leaving.
- Rural areas have a large elderly population, falling birth and marriage rates.
- Government initiatives to revive rural areas are the government redeployment scheme and the rural resettlement programme.

2 Reduction in working hours and increase in leisure time
- EU legislation governs the number of hours a person can work in a week.
- Overtime or shift work results in additional financial gain.
- The different work patterns offered by employers today, e.g. flexitime, shift work, part-time work and job sharing, allow people to enjoy more leisure time with friends and family.
- The restrictions on underage workers prevent the exploitation of young people in the workplace.
- Families now have more quality time together and, due to better pay, have more disposable income.

3 Improvements in the provision of social welfare and education

Social welfare
- Increased payments in social welfare have reduced the number of people living in poverty.
- The payment of child benefit, family income supplement, supplementary welfare allowance, all assist families in their day-to-day living expenses.

Education
- Education is available to everyone from the age of 4 to 18 or 19 years of age.
- The education system is free apart from the cost of books and uniforms.
- The secondary school education consists of Junior Certificate and Leaving Certificate programmes.
- The introduction of new programmes such as LCVP and LCA is intended to encourage students to remain in full-time education for longer.
- A wide variety of courses are available at third level colleges and universities.

4 Changing attitudes to marriage
- People are cohabiting first and marrying later in life.
- The Church's influence on society is diminishing.
- Divorce and separation rates are increasing.
- Marital breakdown is socially accepted.

5 Traditional roles and parenting within the family
- Traditional roles are changing due to the increased number of women working outside the home.
- Egalitarian roles, within the family, regarding finances and discipline are more common.
- Women are financially independent and better educated than before.
- It is socially acceptable for men to remain at home and look after the children.
- Maternity and paternity leave are available to parents.
- Both parents are entitled to unpaid leave.
- Corporal punishment is socially and legally unacceptable.
- Childminders have greater responsibility with regard to discipline and values.

6 Improved pay and working conditions
- Trade unions protect the rights of workers ensuring minimum wage and proper working conditions.
- The following legislation protects the rights of workers:
    - Safety, Health and Welfare at Work Act 1989, 2005
    - Employment Equality Act 1998
    - Equality Act 2004
    - The Protection of Young Persons (Employment) Act 1996
- Workers have shorter working hours and better hourly rates.

7 Increased participation of women in the workforce
- Better educational qualifications have led to better paid jobs.
- It is socially acceptable for women to work outside the family home.
- Women are having fewer children and later in life.
- There is equality of pay for the same job.
- There is more financial security for women.
- Dual income families are the norm providing more disposable income.

8 Legislation regarding equal pay and employment opportunities
- The Employment Equality Act 2004 prohibits discrimination because of gender, marital status, family status, sexual orientation, religious beliefs or membership of the Travelling community.

9 Unemployment
- The level of unemployment varies depending on the state of the economy.
- Unemployment figure in Ireland have increased significantly since 2007 with 12.2% of the population currently unemployed (ww.cso.ie)
- More affluent areas tend to have low or nil unemployment rates.
- Areas with lower socio-economic groups have a much higher percentage of unemployment.
- There has been a huge increase in the number of foreign workers in Ireland.
- Rural areas also tend to lack financial investment and can be areas of high unemployment.

Education

- Education contributes to the socialisation of young children and teenagers.
- It contributes to the physical, emotional, moral and intellectual development of the individual.
- It provides an educated and skilled workforce which contributes to the economy.

Factors that influence educational achievement
1. **Individual ability:** Inherited intellectual ability of an individual; the environment in which the individual is reared.
2. **Attitude to education:** A positive approach and appreciation of education at home results in a stimulating environment where educational achievement is encouraged and rewarded.
3. **Family size:** Large families may have limited resources to help with children's homework.
4. **Home environment:** A comfortable home with heating and lighting and adequate space for study contributes to an individual's achievement.
5. **School environment:** The school can have a huge impact on a student's performance, e.g. facilities, discipline.

6 **Peer pressure:** Positive peer pressure encourages studying and an appreciation of education and its value, while negative peer pressure has the opposite effect.

Provision of education in Ireland

- The Department of Education and Science provides education in Ireland.
- Education is compulsory from 6 to 15 years of age.

The education system in Ireland consists of the following sectors.

1 Pre-school education
- Parents have a number of options in the pre-school sector, e.g. crèche, nursery, Montessori school, day care centre, Forbairt Naíonraí Teo.
- Grants for pre-school education are available from the Department of Health and Children and the Department of Justice, Equality and Law Reform.
- Many of these grants are given to community-based initiatives in disadvantaged areas.

The Early Start Pre-School Programme
- A community-based initiative, this pre-school programme provides for 3–4 year olds in disadvantaged areas.
- It is funded, managed and evaluated by the Department of Education and Science.
- Its main aim is to provide children with a positive start in education, to prevent future school failure and to improve the overall development of students from socially disadvantaged areas.
- It is taught by primary school teachers, childcare assistants and parents.
- The curriculum consists of four main areas: Language, cognition, social and personal development.

2 Primary school education (4 to 12 years of age)
Primary school education is provided by: (a) state-funded national schools, (b) privately-owned primary schools, (c) Gaelscoileanna and (d) special needs schools.
- The Department of Education and Science provide funding for national schools and special needs schools. Privately-run primary schools are fee paying.
- While primary school education in national schools is free, the cost of books, uniforms and other equipment can be expensive.
- Primary education provides a broad, set curriculum. Subjects studied are maths, language, social, environment and scientific education (SESE), arts education (music, drama), physical education (PE) and social, personal and health education (SPHE).
- It promotes activity-based learning.
- It offers a wide choice of resources to stimulate students.
- The skills acquired by the end of primary school include reading, writing, numeracy, listening, artistic and musical.
- There is no formal exam at the end of primary school.

- The provision of special needs assistants and resource teachers helps the integration of students with physical, emotional and intellectual disabilities into mainstream education. This promotes an inclusive education system.

> **Points to Note**
> Primary schools are run by boards of management, many of whom have a religious ethos.

3 Second level/post-primary education (12 to 18 years of age)

Table 15.1 Classification of second level education

School type	Characteristics
Community and Comprehensive Schools/Colleges	• Mixed schools • Run by a board of management
Vocational schools	• Mixed schools • Managed by the Vocational Education Committee (VEC)
Secondary schools	• General single sex schools • Private secondary schools are fee paying • Based around a religious community • Managed by a board of governors

The management structure of each type of school is different but the general programmes offered are the same. They consist of:

1 Junior Certificate programme
- A three-year programme which finishes compulsory education in Ireland.
- It offers a wide variety of subjects.
- Subjects are examined by a combination of terminal written exams and practical and project work which is available at different levels; higher, ordinary, and foundation.

2 Transition year (TY)
- A programme offered in many schools throughout the country, it can be compulsory or optional.
- This programme does not lead up to an exam. Some schools offer IT exams, e.g. ECDL (European Computer Driving License).
- Transition year encourages self-awareness, self-development, teamwork and responsibility. Mini companies, drama and work experience are all part of the TY programme.

3 Leaving Certificate programme
- A two-year exam-based programme.

- Students select between five and seven subjects, which are examined at higher and ordinary level, some at foundation level. The grades gained at the Leaving Certificate exam are converted into points which are used to gain access to third level education.

4 Leaving Certificate Vocational Programme (LCVP)
- A two-year programme.
- Students study five Leaving Certificate subjects, two of which must be selected from the following vocational list: Art, accounting, agricultural science, business, construction studies, home economics and technical drawing.
- A foreign language must also be studied.
- The following three compulsory link modules must also be included: Enterprise education, preparation for work, work experience.
- LCVP is assessed by portfolio work (60%) and a written exam (40%).
- These results can be converted into points and used for third level entry.

5 Leaving Certificate Applied (LCA) programme
- A two-year programme.
- The LCA is a modular-based programme divided into four half-yearly sections:
  Year 1 = 2 modules   Year 2 = 2 modules
- The assessment is continuous with practical, oral and written exams at the end of the second year.
- Subject areas are general education, vocational education and vocational preparation.
- The course does not fulfil third level entry requirements directly but can be used to access post-Leaving Certificate courses (PLC).

6 Third level education
- Approximately 50 per cent of all students attend some form of third level college.
- However, only a small percentage of those are students from the lower socio-economic group.
- Third level institutions include universities, institutes of technology, colleges of education and private colleges, e.g. Griffith College.
- A wide range of degrees, diplomas and certificate courses are offered.

Points to Note

PLCs offer courses to school leavers and adults returning to education. They lead to certification and access to other third level institutions. PLCs are available through VECs and private colleges around the country.

Adult and second chance education
- Adult and second chance education help promote a culture of lifelong learning in Ireland.
- Adult education is provided in a number of formats around the country to suit the individual needs of adults.
- The courses can be full-time, part-time, modular, day, and evening or weekend courses.

The following bodies offer adult education:
- Universities, institutes of technology, private colleges
- Distance learning universities, e.g. Open University
- Vocational Education Committees (VECs)
- FÁS, Teagasc and Coillte
- The Vocational Training Opportunities Scheme (VTOS)
- The Adult Literacy Community Education Scheme (ALCES)

Adult education provides people with the opportunity:
- To develop basic skills of literacy and numeracy.
- To improve skills for work-based promotion.
- To gain qualifications to change careers.
- To gain a social outlet and develop hobbies and other interests.

> **Points to Note**
> The National Association of Adult Education (AONTAS) helps to promote the development of learning in adults. It provides advice and support in all areas of adult education.
> The National Adult Learning Council (NALC) is a government-based initiative established to meet the requirements of the National Anti Poverty Strategy.

Special needs education
- Special needs education provides suitable education for students with physical, emotional and intellectual disabilities, which include autism, ADHD, dyslexia, visual and hearing impairment and Down's syndrome.

Special needs education is provided by:
- Mainstream schools (both primary and secondary) with resource teachers and special needs assistants.
- Visiting teachers for the visual and hearing impaired and Down's syndrome students.
- Special classes with a low pupil/teacher ratio.
- Special schools such as COPE which provide education for students with mild to severe learning disabilities.
- Special schools for visually and hearing impaired children.
- Special schools also provide education for members of the Travelling community and teenagers in detention centres.

Equality of opportunity in education
Factors hindering equality of opportunity in education are (i) socio-economic status, (ii) gender inequality, (iii) disadvantaged areas and (iv) early school leavers. This classification is based on:
- Unemployment levels
- The lack of basic literacy and numeracy skills
- The type of housing

Contemporary initiatives for improving the accessibility of education
Government-backed initiatives aiding equality of opportunities in education for children and adults.
- Early Start project, see page 268.
- Pre-schools for Travellers: Provides pre-school education for members of the Travelling community.
- Home-School-Community Liaison Scheme: Operated by a home-school-community liaison teacher. Available in disadvantaged areas. Aims to reduce the number of early school leavers.
- Early School Leaver Initiative (8 to 15 years): Aims at ensuring students' progress from primary to post-primary education.
- Travellers' Education Needs: Provides primary education for members of the Travelling community.
- Youth Reach: Provides early school leavers with the opportunity to achieve qualifications and develop skills which help them gain employment.
- VTOS (Vocational Training and Opportunities Scheme): Offered by the VECs and open to the long-term unemployed over 21 years of age.
- Other initiatives include: Breaking the Cycle Programme, Learning Support, Junior Certificate School Programme, and Adult Literacy Programme.

Work

- Work can be categorised as: **Paid work, unpaid work** and **voluntary work**.
- It is possible that one person may be involved in all three types of work.
- **Paid work** means that there is financial gain from working.
- Paid work can be permanent, temporary, full-time, part-time or contract-based.
- **Unpaid work** means there is no financial reward for the work carried out.
- Unpaid tasks include cooking, cleaning, childminding, laundry, caring for the elderly or the disabled.
- **Voluntary work** has a higher status than unpaid work such as housework.
- It involves contributing and working within the community or charity groups, e.g. Meals on Wheels schemes or the Society of St Vincent de Paul.

Attitudes to work and work attainment

People work for financial reward, satisfaction, a sense of achievement, sense of purpose, personal identity and socialisation.

The attitudes that people develop towards work are influenced by a number of factors: Family background, parents' attitude, social grouping and educational achievement.

Job satisfaction

Job satisfaction is a very important part of employment. It can be categorised as intrinsic or extrinsic, although the majority of people have attributes of both.

Table 15.2 Job satisfaction	
Intrinsic job satisfaction	**Extrinsic job satisfaction**
• A job is experienced as fulfilling • It gives pleasure • It stimulates interest and creativity • It develops self-confidence and pride • It is challenging • High pay is not a determining factor for the job	• It is based on the bonuses associated with earning money, e.g. holidays, cars, rather than on the job itself • The job may be boring and unfulfilling but other rewards make it bearable • The status of the occupation and the ability to buy consumer goods can be motivation for some jobs

Work ethic

- A person's work ethic is his/her overall attitude to work.
- It incorporates the attitude regarding absenteeism, punctuality, honesty, commitment to work and respect for authority.
- A good work ethic can be influenced by a person's background, peer pressure and experience.
- A good work ethic is a desirable attribute in an employee.

Working conditions

- Working conditions vary from occupation to occupation but all workers should be in a safe and hygienic working environment.
- Occupations vary from manual to managerial work to service industries.
- Part-time work, job sharing, flexitime, career breaks and working from home have all contributed to significant changes to the structure of the modern workforce.
- Paid employment provides certain legal entitlements, e.g. sick pay, maternity leave, holiday pay.

Changes in work availability and work patterns

Over the last century there have been major changes both in society and in technological development which have resulted in a different work culture.
1. The effect of technological development on industry.
2. The decline in primary and secondary industries.
3. Increase in service industries.
4. Increased educational requirements to obtain employment.
5. Increased participation of women in the workforce.
6. Improved working conditions.
7. Increased flexibility in working hours.

1 The effect of technological development on industry

Technological development has brought about:
- A reduction in wage levels.
- The loss of traditional crafts or jobs.
- Less social interaction due to technological use and smaller employee numbers.
- The main element in technological development has been automation.
  - Automation refers to machinery that can now carry out the tasks which previously were done by humans
  - It is used in many industries, e.g. in food production, car manufacture, banking, house design and clothes design
  - Automation has had positive and negative effects on industry as a whole
  - It has created a need for a smaller, more skilled workforce producing consistently high-quality products

It has:
- Reduced working hours with the possibility of overtime.
- Increased leisure time.
- Reduced running costs for employers.
- Reduced or eradicated uninteresting jobs or tasks.
- Increased unemployment for unskilled workers.
- Automation provides a safer and cleaner working environment, as many dangerous or risky jobs can now be carried out by machines.

2 The decline in primary and secondary industries

Industry is divided into three main sectors:
(a) **Primary (agriculture, land-based tasks):** These industries are dependent on natural resources,(a) e.g. farming, fishing, forestry, market gardening.
(b) **Secondary (manufacturing industries):** The manufacturing sector produces products from raw materials of the primary sector, e.g. food products.
(c) **Tertiary (service industries):** The service industries provide services to the public, e.g. tourism, catering, media, transport. This area has increased drastically in recent years.

- The decline in the primary industries is attributed to a change in employment patterns.
- Primary industries are now less labour intensive due to the use of machinery.
- The decline in secondary industries is due to technological advances in the manufacture of products and the availability of cheaper raw materials in other countries, e.g. the Far East and Eastern Europe.

3 Increase in service industries

The increase in service industries is due to government grants attracting multinational companies to Ireland, e.g. in telesales. The demand for leisure and entertainment industries is growing as people have more disposable incomes.

4 Increased educational requirements to obtain employment
The increased demand for education can be attributed to the shift in the structure of industry from primary to tertiary. Most individuals now require a minimum of the Leaving Certificate exam to gain employment.

5 Increased participation of women in the workforce
A number of factors have contributed to the increased number of women in the workforce.
- It is socially acceptable; women are better educated and marry later; the increased cost of living; new flexible work patterns.
- Women occupy a large proportion of positions within the tertiary industry.
- The number of women holding top positions in some professions, e.g. in the legal profession, is very low.
- Wages for women are on average 15 per cent less per hour than men's wages.
- The lack of adequate childcare facilities and the cost are forcing many women out of the workplace.
- However, many women work in low-paid unskilled jobs.

6 Improved working conditions
The Health and Safety Authority has overall responsibility to ensure that a workplace is safe and hygienic to work in.
- The introduction of a minimum wage prevents people from being exploited by employers.
- The following legislation helps to protect employees:
  - The Safety, Health and Welfare at Work Act 2005
  - The National Minimum Wage Act 2000
  - The Parental Leave Act 1998
  - Maternity Protection (Amendment Act) 2004
  - Equality Act 2004
  - Protection of Employees (Fixed Term Work) Act 2003
  - Employment Equality Act 1998
  - The Protection of Young Persons (Employment) Act 1996

The Protection of Young Persons (Employment) Act aims to protect the employment rights of people less than 18 years of age. It also aims to protect their education by limiting the number of hours young people can work. The act sets out the maximum number of working hours and the required rest periods within a week.

The Protection of Young Persons (Employment) Act
- Young people of 14 or younger are not allowed to work during school terms.
- Outside of school terms they are not allowed to work more than 7 hours in one day or 35 hours per week.
- No more than 8 hours' work per week during the school term is allowed for 15 year olds.

Before employing a young person the employer must get evidence of his/her age, e.g. by means of his/her birth certificate, written permission from a parent or guardian, and maintain a register of the child's working hours. It is an offence to be in breach of these rules.

7 Increased flexibility in working hours
- The introduction and acceptance of flexitime, job sharing, part-time work and parental leave have provided employees with more choice regarding their employment.

The role of unpaid and voluntary work in the community

- **Unpaid work** which is home-based, e.g. caring for elderly or disabled members of the family, reduces the burden on other resources within the community such as home helps and hospitals.
- **Voluntary work** within the community generally refers to unpaid work for charities and organisations such as Trócaire or Meals on Wheels.
- It is done on a local, national or international level.
- Voluntary workers often work in disadvantaged areas with underprivileged groups, e.g. the disabled, elderly or the Travelling community.
- Voluntary groups or organisations can create an awareness of issues, e.g. environmental issues.

Table 15.3 Voluntary work	
Benefits of voluntary work for the volunteer	**Benefits of voluntary work for the community**
• Helps develop self-esteem and self-awareness • Rewarding and fulfilling activity • Provides opportunities to integrate in a community • Helps develop expertise and skills in certain areas	• Provides direct help quickly and locally • Provides a variety of services which might be lacking in state funding • Establishes a sense of community and belonging • Develops friendship and trust

Reconciling Employment with Family Responsibilities

There have been significant changes in the pattern of gender roles within the family.
1. Traditional gender roles have changed in recent years and the segregation of the roles has reduced.
2. Roles have become egalitarian with both parents taking responsibility for housework, discipline and childcare.

3 Both parents contribute financially to the home.
4 Parents are more aware of gender stereotyping in relation to home life and work and try not to reinforce beliefs from previous generations.

Impact of dual earners on family life
- Due to choice or financial needs the majority of households in Ireland have dual incomes.
- These incomes provide the family with a certain standard of living.
- Women working outside the home create positive role models for females.
- Fathers are more involved in the rearing of their children and take a bigger part in managing the home.
- Dual income families tend to have fewer children and at a later age.
- Trying to maintain a balance between work, home and individual needs can lead to role conflict and role overload in both men and women. However, women in particular may experience role conflict.
- Role overload results in reduced leisure time, increased stress and tension between spouses.
- Both parents working full- or part-time outside the home increases the need for childcare facilities.

Childcare
- Due to the number of dual career families the availability of suitable childcare facilities in Ireland has reached crisis point.
- Parents may not always be able to choose a childcare option that suits their overall needs due to the shortage of childcare facilities.
- Each family will have different requirements regarding the following criteria:

1 Environment
2 Personal preference
3 Cost
4 Age of child
5 Number of children
6 Special needs
7 Qualifications and experience

The following organisations can help people working in childcare and parents:
- Childminding Ireland
- National Childminding Association of Ireland
- National Children's Nurseries Association (NCNA)

The government has introduced the following pieces of legislation which deal with childcare:
- The National Children's Strategy 2000
- Department of Health Child Care (Pre-School Services) Regulations 1996

Evaluation of two childcare options: childminder and day care

Childminder
- A childminder cares for the child in his/her own home or in the child's home.
- A childminder can often be a relation or a neighbour.
- The childminder may not have any specific qualifications but may have experience in looking after children or is known to the child.
- If a childminder cares for more than four children he/she should be registered with the local Health Service Executive.

A childminder should:
- Have a genuine liking for children and a respect for each individual child regardless of race, gender, religion or social class.
- Have the ability to care for the social, emotional, physical and intellectual needs of the child.
    - Be free from any illness or addiction
    - Not use any illegal substance or have any previous criminal convictions
    - Not smoke around the child
    - Be trustworthy, honest and reliable
    - Have an awareness of the duty of care
    - Be able to provide a safe, clean, warm and well-ventilated environment
    - Be able to adhere to parents' wishes with regard to sleep, eating habits and discipline

Table 15.4 Advantages and disadvantages of childminders	
Advantages	**Disadvantages**
• Children become familiar with surroundings and feel secure • Childminder's home becomes an extension of the child's home • Can give more one-to-one attention and care • Tends to be more flexible with dropping-off and picking-up times • Can build up a positive relationship with the child • Less expensive due to lack of overhead costs	• Lack of training in providing for the child's needs • Lack of insurance or first aid experience • No back-up option if childminder is sick or unreliable • May be more difficult to instruct childminder, e.g. in relation to discipline or eating habits • Child may become confused if childminder's discipline differs from parents' discipline

Example of a day care centre: crèche
1. A day care centre may be the preferred option of childcare for parents, but due to high costs and limited places it may not be feasible for them to place their child in a registered day care centre.
- The primary aim of a crèche or day care centre is to provide a home from home environment in which the child is cared for.

- A crèche should meet the physical, emotional, social and intellectual needs of the child.
- A crèche should be warm, safe, secure and intellectually stimulating.

The Department of Health Child Care (Pre-School Services) Regulations 1996 specify criteria in relation to staff/child ratio, space, floor area per child, layout, equipment and designated areas.

Table 15.5 Advantages and disadvantages of day care centres

Advantages	Disadvantages
• Staff are trained and premises monitored by the Health Service Executive • May be attached to a workplace and therefore convenient • Access to a qualified nurse or first aid • Child develops social skills due to interaction and play with others • Variety of activities providing mental and physical stimulation	• Set opening and closing times • Child is more prone to infection • Very little time for individual attention • Tends to be more expensive • Children may have difficulty settling in a busy environment

Leisure

- Leisure is time spent away from work and other essential tasks.
- Leisure activities are varied and people choose a leisure activity based on their interests, physical capabilities and financial circumstances.
- Leisure activities are enjoyable and done willingly and freely.

Functions and values of leisure time
- Leisure time can contribute to the physical, emotional, intellectual and social wellbeing of a person.
- It provides relaxation and relieves stress in everyday life.
- It allows new skills to be developed.
- It encourages physical wellbeing through sporting activities.
- It can further social interaction which can benefit the individual and the community as a whole.

Influences on leisure patterns
The following factors can influence leisure patterns:
1 **Social factors:** A person's socio-economic group, disposable income or trends.
2 **Cultural factors:** A person's culture can influence their choice of leisure activities.
3 **Occupation:** A person's disposable income, the number of working hours, the type of work.

4 **Age:** Time available, young people have more time; activities change with age; middle-aged people have time and money.
5 **Gender:** Stereotyping is unacceptable in most leisure activities. Career women have less time for leisure activities compared to their male counterparts.

The role of leisure activities in personal development
1 **Physical development:** Develops muscle tone and definition, improves the level of fitness, helps control weight gain.
2 **Social development:** Encourages team-based skills, communication, new friendships, social outings.
3 **Emotional development:** Improves self-esteem and confidence, self-development, relaxation and a sense of belonging.

Evaluation of leisure facilities in your area
- Each locality or area has access to a number of leisure facilities.
- In rural areas leisure facilities are more limited compared to urban areas where most leisure activities are catered for.
- When researching the leisure facilities in your area consider the following factors.

Leisure centre evaluation
1 **Membership fee:** Is it annual or can it be paid monthly?
2 **Ongoing costs:** Do you need to buy special clothes or equipment?
3 **Facilities offered:** Is there professional advice on hand?
4 **Time required:** How much time a week do you need to spend there to get value for money?
5 **Value for money:** Do you use the facilities often enough?
6 **Emotional benefits:** Will the sport improve your self-esteem and self-confidence?
7 **Physical benefits:** Do the exercises work towards weight control and muscle tone?
8 **Social benefits:** Would you meet new people?

Unemployment

Unemployment is being 'without remunerative employment'. The employment levels in a country strongly reflect the state of the economy.

The employment rate is the number of employed persons as a proportion of the total population aged 15 to 64. Ireland is currently in a recession and the unemployment figures are 12.2% (ww.cso.ie) (2009)

There are two forms of unemployment:
1 **Short-term:** Refers to people who are unemployed for less than 6 months.
2 **Long-term:** Refers to people who are unemployed for more than 6 months.

Causes of unemployment

Unemployment can be caused by a number of factors.
1 **Seasonal factors:** Jobs in tourism, farming or fishing.
2 **Geographical factors:** Rural areas have higher unemployment figures.
3 **Technical factors:** The advance in technological development and automation.
4 **Changing requirements of industry:** Moving away from primary and secondary industries to more service-based industries.
5 **Level of demand for products and services:** Greater demand in urban areas.
6 **Residual unemployed:** People are unable to work due to physical or psychological problems.
7 **Recession:** Results in redundancies, manufacturing moving abroad.

Table 15.6 Effects of unemployment

Effects of unemployment on the individual	Effects of unemployment on the family
• Loss of earning • Loss of self-esteem and identity • Depression and dependency • Isolation • Guilt	• Financial difficulties • Loss of family home • Poverty • Tension • Education • Role model

Effects of unemployment on society
- Increase in antisocial behaviour
- Increase in poverty
- Increase in taxes
- Black economy
- Generational unemployment
- Emigration

Poverty

Poverty is being without adequate food, clothing and shelter.

Types of poverty

1 **Absolute poverty:** People who do not have enough food, clothing, warmth or shelter. They struggle to stay alive and have no viable means of rectifying the problem.
2 **Relative poverty:** Defined by the standard of living which is expected within a society. People living below this standard are living in relative poverty.
3 **Income poverty:** Defined as an income of less than 50 per cent of the average income.
4 **Consistent poverty:** The combination of income poverty and deprivation is called consistent poverty.

The poverty line
- The poverty line refers to the minimum amount of money a person would need to provide for basic needs such as food, shelter and clothing.
- The poverty line differs from one society to another.
- It is usually measured relative to the income levels in a country.

Deprivation
- Deprivation is a measure of poverty using other indicators, e.g. necessities such as a TV or a washing machine, instead of money.
- To be without these items due to shortage of money is deemed relative deprivation.

There are eight indicators used to identify deprivation in Ireland; these refer to monetary and non-monetary items.

Extent and distribution of poverty in Ireland
- During the 1960s and 1970s the number of people living below the poverty line decreased drastically.
- During the 1980s this figure increased again due to high unemployment and the downturn in the economy.
- The upturn in the economy during the 1990s led to another decrease.
- However, due to the high cost of living and housing in Ireland the number of people living below the poverty line is increasing again.
- A number of groups within Irish society are more at risk than others, e.g. women over the age of 65 are at greater risk of income poverty, and households where the main person in the house is working in the home.

The people most at risk of poverty are the elderly and disabled, the unemployed, low-paid workers, lone parents, refugees and ethic minorities, the homeless, the Travelling community, the long-term ill, large families and small rural farm holdings.

Causes of poverty
The reasons why poverty continues to be a feature of modern Western societies:
1. **Cycle of poverty:** Children brought up in poverty are more likely to repeat the cycle.
2. **Economic recession:** During periods of high unemployment and dependency on state benefits more people live on or below the poverty line.
3. **Poor education:** Lack of encouragement for educational achievement results in students leaving school early with no formal qualifications or skills.
4. **Low-paid jobs:** Lack of educational opportunities leads to unskilled low-paid employment.
5. **Family type:** Lone parents living on state benefits and large families with just one income often live in poverty.

6 **Social problems:** Alcohol, drug and gambling addictions all result in money being spent elsewhere.
7 **Increasing cost of living:** Housing costs, food bills and utility bills, e.g. electricity and heating, are all increasing and put more pressure on already limited incomes.

Cycle of poverty
- A person born to poor parents and living in poor housing conditions.
- Has a nutritionally inadequate diet based on convenience foods.
- Lacks educational encouragement at home and performs poorly in school.
- Leaves school early with no qualifications.
- Is unemployed or in low-paid inconsistent work.
- Marries or has dependent children at a young age.
- Is dependent on state benefits.
- Rears children in a poverty afflicted environment.

Cycle of deprivation in families
In the cycle of deprivation one aspect of poverty contributes to another and creates a never-ending cycle. For example, poor education leads to unemployment or poorly paid jobs, which, in turn, lead to poor education, and so on.

Cycle of deprivation in geographical areas
Poverty is a national problem. It is not confined to any particular area, although areas of high unemployment have a higher percentage than other more affluent parts.

The poverty trap
People who receive unemployment and other state benefits lose them if they return to work. If the wages they receive are less than the combined state benefits they might decide to continue living on state benefits where they receive more money. This situation is called the poverty trap.

The effects of poverty are unemployment, poor diet, lack of educational opportunity, inadequate housing, psychological problems and ill health, and family discontent.

The influence of social policy on poverty
- Ireland's type of social policy provides an adequate income to meet the needs of individuals receiving state benefit.
- The state benefits in Ireland are long term and generous compared to other Western countries, e.g. the USA.
- Housing, education, employment and healthcare all have policies which benefit the poor or the unemployed.
- Generous allowances can sometimes deter people from becoming independent of state benefits.

Statutory and Community Responses to Poverty and Creating Employment

- A statutory response is what the government and government departments are doing to deal with poverty and employment.
- A voluntary or community response is carried out by private individuals within communities and depends on corporate and individual contributions to provide its services. It is generally based locally.

Statutory responses to poverty

The government tries to help the poor and eliminate poverty with the following benefits and strategies:

1. Social welfare assistance and benefits
   - Schemes to reduce expenditure for low-income families
   - Local authority housing and schemes
2. The National Anti Poverty Strategy (NAPS)
3. Combat Poverty Agency (CPA)
4. The Community Development Programme (CDP)
5. CLÁR
6. Local Development Social Inclusion Programme
7. The PEACE Programme

Community and voluntary responses to poverty

The following organisations are voluntary and community-based:

1. Society of St Vincent de Paul (SVP)
2. Simon Community
3. Focus Ireland

Statutory responses to creating employment are Forfás, Enterprise Ireland, Industrial Development Agency (IDA), County Enterprise Boards, foreign investment, FÁS and the back to work allowance.

The IDA has recognised that Ireland's advantages for foreign investment are:
- A skilled and flexible workforce.
- The lowest corporate tax rates in the world.
- The youngest and one of the best educated populations in Europe.
- A positive political and economic environment.

Community and voluntary response to creating employment

The community and voluntary responses to unemployment include:

1 **Co-operatives:** Formed by a group pooling resources. Co-operatives are established in the agricultural sector, in fishing, construction and the financial sector, e.g. housing co-ops, credit unions.
2 **Cottage industries:** Revived in recent years by small-scale food producers manufacturing high quality food, e.g. cheese, jam and cakes. Traditional cottage industries were knitting, lace and crochet making.

Questions

1 'Volunteering is the commitment of time and energy for the benefit of society and the local community. It can empower people to fulfil their potential while contributing to social and environmental change.' (Volunteering Ireland 2004)
   (a) Differentiate between (i) voluntary work and (ii) unpaid work. (10)
   (b) With reference to the above statement, discuss:
      (i) how voluntary work empowers a person to fulfil his/her potential
      (iii) how voluntary work contributes to social and environmental change in the local community. (24)
   (c) Identify and explain the factors that affect attitudes to work. (16)
   (2005, HL, Section C, 3a)

2 There were 53,200 males and 32,400 females unemployed in the second quarter of 2005. (The Central Statistics Office 2005)
   (a) Why, in your opinion, are there more males than females unemployed in 2005? (10)
   (b) Define unemployment. (6)
   (c) Discuss the effects of unemployment on:
      (i) the individual
      (ii) the family
      (iii) society. (24)
   (d) Name and give details of one government scheme that helps create employment. (10)
   (2006, OL, Section C, 3a)

3 While Ireland has become increasingly wealthy in recent years, it still has one of the highest levels of income inequality in the EU.
   (a) Define each of the following:
      (i) relative poverty
      (ii) absolute poverty. (10)
   (b) Discuss the reasons why poverty continues to be a feature of modern society. In your answer include reference to the cycle of poverty and the influence of social policy on poverty. (24)
   (c) Give an account of two statutory initiatives aimed specifically at eliminating poverty in Ireland. (16)
   (2006, HL, Section C, 3a)

See also questions from previous exam papers: 2004, OL and HL, Section C, 3; 2005, OL and HL, Section C, 3; 2006, OL and HL, Section C, 3.

Key Points

Social Change and the Family
- Change in settlement patterns: Increase in urban population, limited job opportunities in agricultural
- Reduced working hours
- Introduction of different work patterns: Flexitime, part-time, job sharing
- Increased leisure time due to reduced working hours and more disposable income
- Improvements in education and social welfare payments
- Better social welfare payments, more people in full-time education for longer
- Changing attitudes to marriage and traditional roles within the family
- Social acceptance of divorce, separation, cohabiting couples, egalitarian roles within the family
- Improved pay and working conditions: The minimum wage
- Increased participation of women in the workforce
- Women are better educated, work outside the home and have fewer children
- Legislation regarding equal pay and employment opportunities
- Employment Equality Act 2004 helps prevent discrimination in the workforce
- Low unemployment due to economic growth, rural areas may still have high unemployment

Education
- Education aids the social, physical, emotional, moral and intellectual development of the individual, prepares the individual for the workplace
- Factors influencing educational achievement: Individual ability, attitudes to education, family size, home and school environment, peer pressure
- Education is provided by the Department of Education and Science, offers pre-school, primary, secondary, third level, special needs and adult education
- Equality of opportunity in education: Influenced by socio-economic status, gender inequality, disadvantaged areas
- Improving access to education: Early Start project, pre-school for Travellers, Home-School-Community Liaison Scheme, Early School Leaver Initiative, Traveller's Education Needs, Youth Reach, VTOS

Work
- Work includes paid, unpaid and voluntary work
- Attitudes to work and work attainment: Influences on attitudes (family background, social grouping, job satisfaction), work ethic
- Working conditions: Impact on attitude to work, workers should have a safe and hygienic environment
- People work shorter hours and receive more pay
- Change in structure of working day, e.g. job sharing, flexitime, career break
- Increase in legal entitlements, e.g. sick pay, maternity leave, holiday pay
- Increase in technology, especially for manual jobs, e.g. in farming
- Decline in primary and secondary industries, increase in tertiary industries
- Increased educational requirements, increased number of women in employment, improved working conditions, flexibility in working hours
- Benefits of voluntary work for the community and the individual: Friendship, provides services, develops self-esteem and self-confidence, gives a sense of purpose to the individual

Key Points

Reconciling Employment with Family Responsibilities
- Changes in the pattern of gender roles: Reduction in segregated roles, change in traditional roles, more egalitarian roles, dual income, less gender stereotyping
- Impact of dual earners on family life: Fathers more involved in child rearing, problem of balance between work and home life, women are more independent
- Factors influencing childcare choice: Environment, personal preferences, cost, age of child and number of children, qualifications and experience

Leisure
- Functions and values of leisure time: Contributes to wellbeing, relaxation, development of new skills, allows social interaction
- Influences on leisure patterns: Social, cultural, occupation, age, gender
- The role of leisure activities in personal development: Physical, social and emotional development

Unemployment
- Without remunerative employment; short-term and long-term unemployment
- Causes of unemployment: Seasonal, geographical, technical, changing requirements of industry, level of demand for products and services, residual workers, recession
- Effects on the individual: Loss of earning, self-esteem and identity, depression, isolation, guilt
- Effects on the family: Financial difficulties, poverty, tension, education, role model
- Effects on society: Antisocial behaviour, increase in taxes, black economy, generational unemployment, emigration

Poverty
- Poverty is being without adequate food, clothing and shelter
- Absolute poverty: Not enough food, clothing, warmth or shelter to stay alive, affects many Third World countries; homeless people in Ireland
- Relative poverty: Living below the standard of living expected within a society, varies from country to country
- The poverty line: The threshold where poverty starts
- How poverty in Ireland has changed in the past few decades
- Groups most at risk of poverty: Unemployed, women over 65, homeless, elderly, low-paid workers, lone parents, refugees and ethic minorities, Travelling community, people with disabilities, people with long-term illness, large families, small rural farm holdings
- Causes of poverty: Cycle of poverty, recession, poor education, low-paid jobs, family type, social problems, increasing cost of living
- Effects of poverty: Unemployment, poor diet, lack of educational opportunities, inadequate housing, psychological problems, ill health, family discontent
- Influence of social policy on poverty: National Anti Poverty Strategy (NAPS)

Your revision notes